UNITED STATES AND MEXICAN

# BOUNDARY SURVEY,

UNDER THE ORDER OF

LIEUT. COL. W. H. EMORY,

MAJOR FIRST CAVALRY, AND UNITED STATES COMMISSIONER.

# CACTACEÆ

## OF THE BOUNDARY,

BY

**GEORGE ENGELMANN, M. D.,**

OF ST. LOUIS.

# CACTACEÆ.

## I. MAMILLARIA, Haw. *

### Subgen. 1. EUMAMILLARIA.

Plantæ simplices seu cæspitosæ, tuberculatæ, aculeigeræ.

Tubercula plus minus teretia seu angulata, nunquam sulcata.

Areolæ floriferæ axillares, ab areolis aculeiferis penitus distinctæ, nudæ seu villosæ, nunc setosæ.

Flores ex axillis tuberculorum anni prioris antecedentiumve orti, plerumque parvi inconspicui.

Ovarium plerumque immersum: bacca versus maturitatem solum (anno secundo in plurimis) emergens, fere semper clavata, coccinea.

Semina minuta, plerumque rugulosa seu scrobiculata, rarissime verruculosa, vix lævia, fulva, fusca, seu nigra.

Most *Mamillariæ*, heretofore known and cultivated, belong to this subgenus, which is well characterized by the lateral position of the flowers.

1. M. MICROMERIS (sp. nov.): parvula, simplex, globosa; vertice depresso; tuberculis minimis verrucæformibus confertissimis; areolis solum junioribus lana laxa longa vestitis; aculeis plurimis pluriserialibus minutis ex albido cinereis, in plantis junioribus et in tuberculis inferioribus plantarum adultarum sub–20 æqualibus lineam longis radiantibus, in tuberculis floriferis (verticem plantæ adultæ versus) 30–40 stellato-porrectis, superioribus 6–8 cæteros bis terve superantibus versus apicem clavatis acutis, parte superiore demum deciduo; floribus minimis subcentralibus; sepalis petalisque 5; stigmatibus 3 stamina æquantibus; bacca elongata clavata coccinea floris rudimenta dejiciente; seminibus paucis oblique obovatis basi acutis nigris lucidis sub lente levissime verruculosis, hilo elongato ventrali.† (Tab. I and II, fig. 1–4.)

---

* I leave the character of the genus as heretofore generally circumscribed. Lemaire's genus *Anhalonium*, however, a species of which is found in our territory, in my opinion cannot be separated from *Mamillaria* so long as the generic character is founded on the organs of fructification, and not on the external shape of the plants. The expression "*Inflorescentia verticalis*," which I use in relation to the subgenera *Coryphantha* and *Anhalonium* and to the genus *Echinocactus*, although in common use, is not strictly correct: the flowers appear on the vertex of the plant, indeed, but not as the prolongation of the main axis; they are, as in all Cactaceæ, properly lateral, but produced by the young growth of the same year, while in all other Cactaceæ they spring from the growth of the preceding or former years, and, consequently, make their appearance more or less on the side of the plant, or, if on the top, only on older branches or joints.

† I look at the seed always in such a position that the radicle of the embryo points downward and the cotyledons upward, or when curved, upward and forward, or to the left. All the seeds figured in this Report are represented in this position, unless otherwise stated. We have then one *side* or *face* (produced by the always more or less distinct compression of the seed) towards the beholder, the *base* below, and the *ventral* part or edge of the seed to the left, and the *dorsal* part to the right.

The hilum is large or small, circular, oblong, oval, or elongated, mostly more or less basal, but not rarely sub-ventral or ventral; it is usually surrounded by a tumid rim, formed by the thickened testa, smoother than the other parts of the seed. The albumen, when present, or the trace of it, which is indicated by a never-wanting thickening of the endopleura, is always found, on the ventral part of the seed. The back or dorsal part of the seed is often more or less carinate, especially towards the base. The testa of the seed is pergamentaceous, yellowish, or brownish, or black; or it is hard, crustaceous, and then always black; or it is whitish and thick and bony (only in *Opuntiæ*.) The surface of the seed is smooth, often shining, or it is rugose, or pitted, or

Var. β. GREGGII: major, tuberculis globoso-ovatis paullo majoribus; aculeis rigidis 2–3-seriatis, interioribus 5–7 brevioribus robustioribus, exterioribus 15–18 paullo longioribus, omnibus radiantibus; seminibus paullo minoribus leviter verrucosis. (Tab. II, fig. 5–8.)

From El Paso to the San Pedro river, also in a single locality east of this river, in naked places on mountain-tops or sides, only on limestone, never in the porphyritic region, *C. Wright*. Var. β. was collected by the late *Dr. J. Gregg* on a mountain-ridge between Azufrora and Penos Bravos, near Saltillo, Mexico.—Small globose plants, depressed at top, simple, or very rarely (and probably only after an injury to the top of the main plant) branching; heads usually ½ to 1 inch in diameter, in largest specimens seen 15–18 lines in diameter; plants densely covered by the delicate ashy-grey spines; tubercles about ½ line long, only 1–1¼ lines distant from one another; older ones shedding the spines, and giving the base of the plant a very pretty tuberculated appearance; in the larger plants 21 or 34 spiral rows of the tubercles are the most distinct; spines not pungent, in several series, usually about one line long; on the younger tubercles of the fully-developed plant, (those I suppose which may bear flowers in their axils,) the 6–8 upper exterior spines are 2–3, or sometimes even 4 times as long as the other spines, (2–4 lines long,) thickened or clavate towards the end, with an acute point; these spines are the first to appear in the nascent tubercle, (as indeed is the case in all *Mamillariæ* where the uppermost radial spines are always developed before the others,) mixed with loose wool of almost the same length. These elongated superior spines form a small tuft in the vertex of the plant, which includes and partly hides the flowers and fruit. When they get older, apparently after the second or third year, the upper part of these long spines breaks off, leaving them of the same length as the others, but always distinguishable by their ragged end. These peculiar spines, of which I have not seen any analogy in other species, are wanting in younger plants.

The position of the flowers in this plant is rather a doubtful one. I have not seen living specimens in flower, but the structure of the tuft, the position of the berries in the dead specimens before me, and the note of Mr. Wright, "flowers central" would seem to indicate that they really appear in the new growth of the same season. In that case this species would be an anomalous small flowered and small tubercled *Coryphantha*. But I am yet inclined to consider the flowers as only *nearly central,* and borne in the axils of the last tubercles of the preceding season; all the analogies at least are in favor of our plant being a true *Mamillaria*. Flowers reduced to the simplest type of *Cactaceæ*, viz: 3–5 sepals, about 5 petals, two or three times as many stamens, and a style with 3 stigmata; diameter of flower about 3 lines; petals whitish or very light pink; fruit an elongated clavate red and somewhat juicy berry, 4–6 lines in length, without the remains of the flower on top, somewhat persistent on the plant, finally shrivelling up, obovate, grey, and hid in the tuft; so it is found in the specimens brought home. Seeds only 6–12 in each fruit, comparatively large, 0.7 line long, 0.5 in diameter, with a very large umbilicus; testa hard and brittle, though thin.

Var. *Greggii* is larger and coarser in all its parts. The specimens before me are 1–2 inches in diameter; tubercles 1–1¼ line long; exterior spines 1½–2 lines, interior stouter ones ½–1 line long. The 6–9 upper elongated spines on the younger tubercles are 3–4 lines long,

---

covered with very minute or larger warts or tubercles; these tubercles are distinct, or more or less concatenate or confluent, leaving irregular pits in their interstices. Smooth or pitted seeds I find in most *Mamillariæ* and *Echinocacti*, irregularly rugose ones in some *Echinocacti* and *Cerei*, tuberculated seeds only in *Anhalonium*, the single *Echinocactus setispinus*, and all *Echinocerei*, while the species of the other sections of *Cereus* known in our Flora generally have smooth seeds. Of the quite peculiar, large, flat, and bony seeds of *Opuntiæ*, I shall find occasion to speak hereafter.

thicker at base, very slender in the middle, and thickened again towards the very acute point. Fruit about 9 lines long; seed smaller than in the more northern form, 0.6 line in length and more distinctly tuberculated.

*Mamillaria microthele,* Muhlenpf., seems to be closely allied to our plant, but is distinguished (to judge from the descriptions) by its cespitose growth, and its distinct 1 or 2 central spines. No allusion is made in the descriptions to the remarkable vertical tuft, though the small pale rose-colored flowers are mentioned. The name, *M. micromeris,* refers to the smallness of all the parts of this species.

2. M. LASIACANTHA (sp. nov.): parvula, simplex, globosa seu ovato-globosa; tuberculis cylindricis læte viridibus; axillis nudis; areolis junioribus albido-lanatis; aculeis 40–80 pluriseriatis omnibus radiantibus maxime inaequalibus brevibus setiformibus albis rectis seu paullo recurvatis ciliato-pilosulis vel denudatis; floribus lateralibus parvis; sepalis 13 obtusis, exterioribus mucronatis; petalis 13 fere uniseriatis oblongis obtusis emarginatisve; stylo stamina brevia longe superante; stigmatibus 4–5 ovatis brevibus erectis convergentibus; bacca elongata clavata coccinea; seminibus numerosis obovato-subglobosis scrobiculatis nigricantibus, hilo basilari ovali.

Var. *α.* MINOR: caule minore ovato; aculeis paucioribus brevioribus dense pilosulis. (Tab. III.)

Var. *β.* DENUDATA: caule majore globoso; aculeis plurimis longioribus subnudis. (Tab. IV.)

About Leon spring and Camanche spring, west of the Pecos, on low limestone hills, among herbage, *C. Wright:* fl. April and May.—A pretty little species, covered with and almost entirely hidden under the innumerable soft, more or less pubescent spines. The smaller form is 9–12 lines high and 6–9 lines in diameter; tubercles in 8 or 13 spiral rows, 2 lines long and nearly 1 line in diameter; areolæ 1½ line distant from one another. Spines 40–60, 1½–2 lines long, the upper exterior ones a little longer than the rest, the innermost ones often not half as long as the others. The larger form, var. *β*, is 1–1½ inch high, and of almost the same diameter; tubercles 2½–3 lines long, in 13 or 21 spiral rows; spines 50–80 almost, or the old ones entirely naked, 1½–2½ lines long, the innermost usually much shorter. The flower is half an inch long, and, when fully open, of the same diameter; petals white, with a red streak in the centre, which at base forms a red circle around the yellow stamens; style yellowish, with 4 or 5 yellowish-green stigmata, which form together a short globose head; fresh fruit 6–10 lines long, without the remains of the flower, somewhat persistent and finally shrivelled up, greyish, obovate-clavate, deeply imbedded and hid between the tubercles; seeds 10–25 in each fruit, smaller than in the last species, and altogether different in shape and surface, about 0.5 line long, very conspicuously pitted, hard and brittle. I have named this species *M. lasiacantha* from the usually very soft pubescence of the spines. It is evidently closely allied to *M. Schiedeana,* Ehrenb.; but this is a much larger plant, with larger tubercles, very woolly axils, and its spines tipped by a silky brush. Both this and the last species belong to Prince Salm's § 3. *Polyacanthæ* ** *aculeis patentissimis adpressis.* The position of the flower, however, seems to indicate that they are widely separated from each other, though the external appearance of the plants is very much alike.

3. M. PUSILLA, DC., var. TEXANA: ovato-globosa, prolifera, cæspitosa; tuberculis teretibus versus apicem conicis, axilla longe-lanatis setosisque; aculeis pluriseriatis, extimis numerosissimis (30–50) capillaceis elongatis flexuosis vel crispatis albis, interioribus 10–12 sensim ri-

gidioribus brevioribus rectiusculis puberulis albidis, intimis 5–8 longioribus rigidis rectis pubescentibus basi bulbosis infra albidis sursum rufis fuscisve inaequalibus; florum lateralium ovario subemerso; sepalis 9–12 oblongo-linearibus obtusiusculis tenuiter fimbriatis; petalis 13–16 fere uniseriatis oblongo-linearibus obtusis vel emarginatis saepe mucronatis; stigmatibus 5 flavidis longe supra stamina exsertis; bacca elongata clavata s. subcylindrica coccinea floris rudimentis involutis coronata; seminibus plurimis obovatis scrobiculatis nigris lucidis, hilo basilari lineari. (Tab. V.)

From Eagle Pass to Santa Rosa, *Dr. Bigelow*, and, according to *Dr. Poselger*, common on the Rio Grande below: fl. March to May.—Heads 1–1½ inch in diameter, 1–2½ inches high, usually covered below with young branches, and finally densely cespitose; tubercles 3½–4½ lines long, dark-green; axillæ quite woolly, with several coarse twisted bristles mixed with the wool; exterior hair-like spines covering the whole plant as with a coarse wool, often 6–8 lines long, when straightened; interior spines slender, but stiff and pointed, 3–4 lines long, in young or weakly specimens, whitish, with dark tips, in robust ones yellow at base, brown upwards, and almost black at tip; flowers 7–10 lines long; petals dirty yellowish-white, with a reddish streak in the middle; fruit about 9 lines long; seeds 0.6 line long, hard and brittle, very similar to the seed of the last mentioned species, only a little larger and with narrow hilum.—*Mamillaria pusilla*, from the West Indies, is so near our plant that this one must necessarily be referred to it; the only difference seems to consist in the smaller number of radial spines (12–20) in *M. pusilla*, and in the greyish-green color of its tubercles.

4. M. PHELLOSPERMA (M. tetrancistra *E. partim, in Sill. Journ. Nov.* 1852): ovata seu ovato-cylindrica, simplex seu rarius e basi ramosa; tuberculis ovato-cylindricis; axillis lanatis setigeris demum nudis; aculeis radialibus numerosissimis (40–60) biseriatis, exterioribus tenuioribus brevioribus albis, interioribus robustioribus longioribus apice fuscatis, centralibus 3–4 robustioribus longioribus ex basi pallidiore atrofuscis, superioribus 2–3 rectis seu uno pluribusve hamatis, inferiore validiore sursum hamato; floribus versus plantæ apicem lateralibus; sepalis 15–17, exterioribus ovatis obtusiusculis ciliatis, interioribus oblongo-linearibus; petalis sub-12 acuminato-aristatis; stigmatibus 5; bacca obovato-clavata late umbilicata corollam marcescentem dejiciente tenui coccinea vix pulposa; seminibus magnis globosis rugosis, ad hilum massa suberosa semine ipso majore triloba fusca arilliformi auctis. (Tab. VII.)

Dry gravelly hills about the base of the mountains east of the Californian Cordilleras, near San Felipe, *Dr. Parry;* also on the lower Gila, *Dr. Le Conte, A. Schott;* on the lower Colorado, the Mojave, and east of the Colorado towards the Cactus Pass, *Dr. Bigelow.*—This interesting species was first noticed by Dr. Parry, and was described from his notes in Silliman's Journal l. c., under the name of *M. tetrancistra.* Specimens brought home since by several collectors leave no doubt that this and several other species had been confounded; and, moreover, that hardly ever all the four central spines are hooked. The original name had therefore to be altered; the one selected for it indicates the peculiar corky structure of the enlarged base of the seed.

Our species is often simple, not rarely several stems are seen coming from one base, or an older stem bears young branches at its lower part; young stems almost globose, older ones ovate, and even cylindric, 2 to 4 or 5 inches high, 1½ or 2 inches in diameter; tubercles 4–7 lines long, not so much crowded as in the allied species, in 8, or at most, 13 spiral rows. The axils of the young tubercles produce loose wool, with a few long spiny bristles, which disappear only after several years. In the smallest specimen before me I find 14–18 exterior radial spines, 4–5 lines long, and 12–16 interior ones, 5–6 lines long; in other specimens I have counted from 50–60 radial spines. The upper central spines in my specimens are mostly 5–7 lines long; sometimes I find 1 or 2 of them longer and hooked, and sometimes all 4 are said to be regularly hooked; the lower central spine is stouter and longer than the others, 6–9 lines long, with the sharp hook always turned upwards. Flower apparently about an inch long; fruit clavate or pear-shaped 6–12 lines long, and 4–6 lines in diameter, with a thin scarlet-colored integument, torulose from the protrusion of the large seeds; the withered flower falling off leaves a wide circular umbillicus; seeds large, visible through the thin pericarp, attached to conspicuous white funiculi; seed proper 0.6 or 0.7 line in diameter, with the appendage 1.2—1.5 line long. The curious spongy or corky appendage is larger than the seed itself, and buries its lower part as it were in a bluntly 3-lobed cup. Embryo almost globose, 0.6 line long, 0.5 line in diameter; cotyledons small but perfectly distinct and visible; no albumen.—Apparently near *M. ancistroides*, Lem., with 30–40 radial and 4–5 central spines, flower and fruit unknown; the radial spines are said to be homogeneous, and the axils naked.

5. M. Grahami (sp. nov.): globosa seu demum ovata, simplex seu e basi ramosa; tuberculis ovatis basi dilatatis axillis nudis; areolis orbiculatis seu ovato-orbiculatis; aculeis radialibus uniseriatis 15–30 albis saepe apice fuscatis nudis seu puberulis, summis brevioribus, lateralibus longioribus; aculeo centrali singulo robustiore longiore sursum hamato, saepe 2 rectis sursum divergentibus adjectis, omnibus e basi pallidiore fusco-atris; floribus sub vertice lateralibus rubicundis; sepalis sub-13 lineari-oblongis obtusiusculis ciliolatis; petalis sub 13 lineari-oblongis roseatis, exterioribus mucronatis, interioribus obtusis retusisve; stylo stamina brevia longe superante; stigmatibus 6–8 elongatis filiformibus suberectis; bacca ovata (viridi?) floris rudimentis coronata; seminibus oblique obovatis scrobiculatis nigris. (Tab. VI, fig. 1–8.)

Mountainous regions from El Paso, *Charles Wright*, southward and westward to the Gila, *Dr. Parry*, and Colorado, *A. Schott*, and up this latter river as far as Williams' river and Cactus Pass, *Dr. Bigelow*: fl. from June or July to August.—Stems 1–3 inches high, 1–2½ inches in diameter, simple or somewhat branching from the base, and thereby sometimes slightly cespitose; tubercles 3 lines long, and when old of a corky texture, persistent when dead and dry like those of *M. tuberculata*, disposed in 13 or 21 spiral rows. Radial spines in some smaller specimens 25–30, in larger ones often only 20–25, and in some Sonora specimens only 15–18 in number; the lateral ones are the longest, about 3–4 lines, or in the largest specimens even 5-6 lines long; lower spines shorter, upper ones the shortest and most slender. In smaller specimens only one central spine is observed, generally much longer than the radial spines, 3–9 lines long, with a wide or sometimes a narrower hook, always curved upward. In many specimens one or two upper spines are found, neither so stout nor so long as the lower hooked one, and always straight; flower 9–12 lines long, rose-colored; fruit a small oval berry, about half an inch long, apparently green when ripe; seeds among the smallest in this genus, only 0.4 or rarely 0.5 line long, slightly pitted, with a small and narrow hilum.—This pretty species has been named for *Col. J. D. Graham*, of the United States Corps of Topographical Engineers, under whose auspices many of these species were collected.

6. M. Wrightii (sp. nov.): globosa seu depresso-globosa, basi obconica, simplex; tuberculis teretibus; axillis nudis; aculeis radialibus sub-12 albidis summis 3–5 paullo robustioribus apice fuscatis, lateralibus sublongioribus, inferioribus gracilioribus; aculeis centralibus plerumque binis divergentibus uncinatis fusco-atris radiales subæquantibus; floribus lateralibus (?); sepalis exterioribus 13 triangularibus obtusiusculis fimbriatis, interioribus 8 acutis margine

petaloideis; petalis 12 lineari-lanceolatis acuminatis aristatis purpureis; bacca majuscula ovato-globosa succosa purpurascente floris rudimentis coronata; seminibus obovatis basi acutis nigris scrobiculatis, hilo subventrali parvo angusto. (Tab. VIII, fig. 1–8.)

New Mexico, near the Copper mines, *Wright*; near El Paso, *Parry*; and on the upper Pecos, east of Santa Fé, *Bigelow*.—Stems 1½–3 inches in diameter, hemispherical above, flattened or depressed in the centre, and top-shaped below; simple, as all the *Mamillariæ* of that form usually are. Tubercles 5–6 lines long; spines 4–6 lines in length, shorter in the southwestern, longer in the northeastern specimens; uppermost radial spine stouter than the others, with a brown tip, or smaller and slender, or entirely wanting; central spines usually 2 side by side, diverging laterally, or rarely one above the other; sometimes only one, or not seldom 3, the third one being below the two others; the hooks usually turned downward, or in different directions. The flowers seem to be lateral but very near the vertex, the fruit is moved more outward by the continuous growth of the plant. Flower about an inch long and fully as wide; petals and margin of inner sepals bright purple. Berry large, nearly an inch long, purplish; seed similar to that of *M. Grahami*, but much larger; and the very small and narrow hilum ventral; length of seed 0.7 line.—This species I with pleasure dedicate to my friend, *Mr. Charles Wright*, to whose indefatigable exertions botany owes so many new discoveries along the Mexican boundary line, and lately in more distant parts of the globe.

7. M. Goodrichii, Scheer: globosa seu ovata, subsimplex; vertice tomentoso; tuberculis ovatis abbreviatis; axillis junioribus lanatis setigeris demum nudatis; aculeis radialibus 11–15 (plerumque 12–13) albidis apice sphacelatis intertextis, centralibus 3–4 (in plantis junioribus subsingulis) fusco-atris, superioribus divergentibus rectis seu rarissime subuncinatis, inferiore paullo longiore robustiore sursum hamato; floribus in vertice lateralibus parvis; petalis lanceolatis acuminatis sordide flavidulis medio rubellis; stigmatibus 3 virescentibus. (Tab. VIII., fig. 9–14.)

Dry ravines near San Diego, California, *Dr. Parry;* originally brought to England from the Island of Cerro on the Californian coast.—One of the specimens of Dr. Parry, from which the above description was drawn, is 2 inches high, and 1½ inch in diameter, the other is globose and rather depressed; the tubercles are 1½–2½ lines long and of a somewhat corky texture, like those of *M. Grahami*, so that the dead ones retain their shape and do not shrivel up. The axils produce a very dense wool, and in it 5–8 stiff bristles which often reach the length of the tubercle. The radial spines are 2½–3½ lines long, the uppermost one present or wanting. The upper central spines, 2 or 3 in number, are straight, or rarely in my specimens with a tendency to form a hook; the lower central spine is the longest one, 4½–5 lines long, the narrow, or rarely wide hook is turned upward or sidewise. Flowers 6–9 lines long, 6 lines wide, dirty yellowish, the petals with red midribs.

8. M. Heyderi, Muhlenpf., of which my *M. applanata*, (Plate 9, fig. 4–14,) and *M. hemisphærica*, (Plate 9, fig. 15–17,) published in *Plantæ Lindheimerianæ*, are different forms, is common throughout the southern parts of New Mexico, and may even extend into Sonora, according to Mr. Schott's notes, unless what he has seen is a form of M. *gummifera*, (Tab. IX, fig. 18–20,) brought by Dr. Wislizenus from the mountains west of Chihuahua. The Sonora plant is stated to have 13 radial spines, the inferior ones are 6–8 lines and the superior ones 2–3 lines long, the stout central spine is of the length of the latter.

9. M. MEIACANTHA (sp. nov.): simplex, hemisphærica seu vertice depressa, basi obconica, lactiflua; tuberculis pyramidato-quadrangulatis compressis basi productis axilla nudis; areolis junioribus albido-villosis mox nudatis; aculeis paucis (5–9) rigidis rectis vel recurvatis albidis seu flavidis (demum cinereis) apice sphacelatis, inferioribus paullo longioribus, centrali singulo robusto breviore porrecto seu sursum flexo et cum cæteris radiante seu rarius nullo; floribus sordide albidis rubellisque; ovario nudo; sepalis 12–14 lanceolatis; petalis 14–16 lineari-lanceolatis acutis subintegris; stigmatibus 6–7 stamina brevia vix excedentibus flavidulis; bacca elongato-clavata incurva floris rudimenta dejiciente; seminibus minutis obovatis rugulosis fulvis. (Tab. IX., fig. 1–3.)

Throughout New Mexico, from where it was first brought home by the Missouri Volunteers in 1847; often collected since by the different explorers of the botany of those regions: fl. May and June.—Very nearly allied to the foregoing species; distinguished by the fewer more loosely arranged tubercles, which rise from a much broader base, and by the fewer, shorter and stouter spines. Plants 3–5 inches in diameter, with a broad top-shaped base, terminating in the large fleshy root; tubercles 7–9 lines long, strongly quadrangular, somewhat compressed from above, arranged in 13 spiral rows. Spines, as indicated by the name, fewer than in the allied species, 5–9, usually about 6, lowest one mostly a little longer than the lateral ones, 3–5 lines long, stout, and strongly subulate, often curved in different directions; upper spine wanting or often replaced by the stouter and a little shorter central spine, which is then turned upwards. Spines in robust specimens dirty yellowish with brown points; central one darker than the rest; in young and weakly specimens they are whitish. Flowers 12–14 lines long, somewhat urceolate; exterior petals longest, entire; interior ones a little shorter, entire or slightly denticulate; all whitish with a broad rose-colored line in the centre. The ovary does not exude the milky fluid, which the tubercles and other parts of the plant contain. Fruit ripening the second spring and summer, till then hidden between the bases of the surrounding tubercles, and for the greater part buried in the tissue of the plant; in spring the young fruit suddenly (in one or two weeks) grows to its full size, 9–12 or even 15 lines long, protruding far above the tubercles and forming an interior scarlet circle around the inner circle of rose-colored flowers. Seeds 0.5 line long subglobose-obovate, with a narrow sub-basilar hilum, yellowish brown, rugose and somewhat pitted.

10. M. SPHÆRICA, (Dietrich): e radice crassa obovata seu clavata, prolifera et demum densissime cæspitosa; tuberculis ovato-elongatis versus apicem acutatum conicis, axilla lanatis; areolis junioribus breviter tomentellis; aculeis setaceis basi bulbosis rectis seu curvatis albidis, radialibus 12—14, centrali singulo recto subulato subbreviore vix robustiore; flore subverticali magno flavo; tubo supra ovarium emersum constricto elongato; petalis sub-18 acuminatis aristatis integris; stigmatibus 8 linearibus patulis.

Hillsides on the Rio Grande near Eagle Pass, *Schott*: fl. from March throughout the season.—Dr. Poselger's specimens were collected at Corpus Christi, on the coast of Texas. Dietrich's description, taken from them, well agrees with Mr. Schott's plants and with specimens now frequently cultivated at St. Louis, from both of which the above character is drawn.—This species is remarkable on account of its exsert ovary and large flower, by which characters it closely approaches to the next subgenus; but the flowers, though apparently nearly vertical, come from last year's growth. Specimens before me are 2 inches high, 1¾ inch in diameter above, narrowed below, the old tubercles withering and leaving a short clavate scaly stem. The tubercles soon become proliferous, and the branches increase and reproduce often in such a manner as to form large and dense hemispherical masses. Tubercles 6–8 lines long; spines $3\frac{1}{2}$–$4\frac{1}{2}$ lines long; flowers $1\frac{1}{2}$–2 inches in length, and fully as widely open in bright sunshine; tube slender, funnel-shaped, remarkably constricted above the oval ovary. Fruit not seen.

### Subgen. 2. CORYPHANTHA.

Plantæ simplices seu caespitosæ, tuberculatæ, aculeigeræ.

Tubercula plus minus teretia, florifera facie superiore longitudinaliter sulcata, in stirpibus junioribus nondum floribundis sulco breviori notata, vel penitus esulcata.

Areolæ floriferæ axillares seu in tuberculo ipso supra-axillares, cum areolis aculeiferis sulco villoso plus minus profundo demum nudato subinde glandulifero junctæ, tomentosæ.

Flores ex areolis tuberculorum hornotinorum adultorum (inde laxi) seu vix evolutorum (inde congesti) oriundi, plerumque magni, speciosi.

Ovarium emersum: bacca plerumque anno primo, rarissime anno secundo, maturescens, ovata seu subglobosa, viridis seu raro coccinea, sæpissime floris rudimentis coronata.

Semina plerumque majuscula, fulva, fusca seu nigra, lævia seu scrobiculata, nunquam tuberculata.

This subgenus, characterized mainly by the vertical position of the flowers, principally comprises species from the northern border of the Cactus region, most of them, until lately, unknown, or imperfectly known, to botanists. All the *Mamillariæ* of the Upper Missouri, and most of those from Texas and New Mexico, with which I had become acquainted, have grooved tubercles and showy vertical flowers, which fact I indicated as early as 1845, in the Plantæ Lindheimerianæ, and again in 1848, in Wislizenus' Report. Dr. Poselger, who, in his travels in Texas and Mexico, had the best opportunity of studying these plants, further verified this fact, and first noted that all the top-flowering *Mamillariæ* had grooved tubercles, at least in the fully developed parts of the plant; and he justly inferred that all *Mamillariæ* with grooved tubercles (the section *Aulacothecæ*) belong here. But he went further, and removed them from *Mamillaria* to *Echinocactus*, solely on account of the vertical flowers. Now some *Mamillariæ* of this section (e. g. *M. robustispina*) do approach *Echinocactus* in the shape of their embryo, as do others (e. g. *M. macromeris*) by having an occasional sepaloid scale on the ovary; while some *Echinocacti* (e. g. *E. setispinus*, *E. horizonthalonius*) have a straight embryo with very short connate cotyledons, and others have few and somewhat fugacious sepaloid scales on the ovary, (e. g. *E. intertextus*, *E. setispinus.*) Still I think that a safe line of distinction can be drawn between them, and that *Coryphantha*, though forming a transition to *Echinocactus*, much rather belongs to *Mamillaria*. But it must be admitted that the characters distinguishing most genera of Cactaceæ are almost as difficult to define as those of the species.

11. M. NUTTALLII, β CÆSPITOSA (M. similis, *E. in Plant. Lindh.* 1845) has been collected by Mr. Wright and others in the same part of Texas where Mr. Lindheimer had originally found it, viz: from the Brazos to Austin and San Antonio; it has since also been brought from the Kansas river, but does not seem to extend into the mountains of Western Texas. (Tab. LXXIV, fig. 6–7.)

12. M. SCHEERII, Muhlenpf. β? VALIDA: magna, robusta, ovato-globosa, simplex seu ad basin parce prolifera, glaucescens; tuberculis magnis remotis patulis e basi lata subcylindricis, supra sulco profundo glandula singula paucisve munito (juniore lanato) subbilobis; axillis latis,

junioribus dense tomentoso-lanatis; areolis orbiculatis villosissimis demum nudatis; aculeis 10–20 rectis seu subinde curvatis robustis rigidis basi bulbosis albidis seu citrinis apice fuscatis, radialibus 9–16, (3–5 inferioribus lateralibusque æquilongis robustioribus compressis, 7–11 superioribus debilioribus teretioribus), centralibus 1–5 validis augulatis paulo longioribus pallidis citrinis seu rubicundis, singulo validissimo porrecto; floribus in vertice tomentosissimo laxis flavis; sepalis 16–22 lanceolatis, inferioribus ciliatis; petalis 16–20 oblongo-lanceolatis versus apicem denticulatis mucranatis; stigmatibus 6–10; bacca viridi.

Sandy ridges in the valley of the Rio Grande, from El Paso to the Cañon; also at Eagle Spring, and on prairies at the head of the Limpia, *Charles Wright:* fl. in July.—A stately plant, by far the largest of the northern *Mamillariæ;* largest specimens before me, 7 inches high, 5 inches in diameter without the spines. Tubercles loosely arranged, in the smaller specimens in 8, in the larger ones in 13 spiral rows, at base ¾–1 inch in diameter, suddenly contracted and almost cylindric, 1-1½ inch long, and 5-7 lines in diameter, spreading, ascending; tubercles on the lower part of plant shorter, more conic, and somewhat imbricated. Groove very deep, with 1-5 orbicular depressed or hemispherical warts or glands, of nearly a line diameter. Central spines 10–18 lines long, mostly yellow; lower radial about 9–15, upper 5–10 lines long, when young mostly red at base, paler in the middle, and dark purplish-black at tip, sometimes yellowish; when old, all the spines become ashy-gray with dark tip. Flowers 2 inches long, yellow, ovary 5–6 lines long. Young and small specimens have smaller tubercles, and about 6–8 radial spines 6–9 lines long, with a single straight or recurved much stouter central one, an inch long.

*M. Scheerii,* from Chihuahua, is distinguished from our plant, according to Prince Salm's description, by the shorter and fewer (8–11) radial spines, and the single "much longer, one inch long," central spine; it is globose, 3–4 inches in diameter; flowers of same size as ours, with apparently entire (?) sepals, and red-streaked yellow petals. The areolæ are described as naked, while in our plant we find the young ones very thickly covered with long wool, which disappears by age. Nevertheless, I consider ours only as a northern form of the Chihuahua species, with more numerous and stouter spines; which character very often distinguishes northern and southern varieties of one and the same species.

13. M. ROBUSTISPINA, A. Schott in litt.: robusta, simplex seu cæspitosa; tuberculis magnis patulis subteretibus sulcatis; areolis magnis orbiculatis, junioribus dense tomentosis; aculeis radialibus 12–15 robustis rigidis, inferioribus robustioribus obscurioribus rectis seu deorsum curvatis, superioribus rectis fasciculatis paullo tenuioribus; aculeo centrali singulo valido compresso deorsum recurvato, subinde altero superiore rectiore adjecto, aculeis omnibus corneis apice atratis subpollicaribus; floribus e basi tuberculorum juniorum villosissimà campanulatis luteis; tubo supra ovarium ovatum constricto tenui, intus ad basin usque filamentoso; sepalis lanceolatis, inferioribus ciliolatis; petalis numerosis; stigmatibus 9–10 patulo-erectis; bacca viridi; seminibus magnis oblique obovatis circa hilum parvum lineare centrale curvatis fuscis; cotyledonibus distinctis foliaceis. (Tab. LXXIV, fig. 8.)

On grassy prairies on the south side of the Babuquibari mountains, in Sonora, *A. Schott:* fl July.—A large plant, cespitose, perhaps from the effects of prairie fires, as Mr. Schott suggests. Tubercles nearly an inch long, and about an inch distant from one another; areolæ 3½–4 lines in diameter; spines 9–15 lines long, lower ones stouter but a little shorter than the upper ones, dark on the upper and lighter colored on the lower surface; central spines 1 or sometimes

2, stouter, but not much longer, than the others; base of lower or principal central spine nearly one line wide. Flowers, 1½–2 inches long, well characterized by the slender tube, which is contracted above the ovary, and quite similar in that respect to the flower of *M. sphærica* (see above); petals "saffron yellow"; filaments from the base of the tube, leaving no naked space above the ovary, as is the case in most species. Seeds 1.5–1.6 line long, and fully a line in diameter, the largest of any *Mamillaria* examined by me; albumen more distinct than usual in this genus; embryo curved, with somewhat foliaceous accumbent cotyledons, resembling much more the embryo of some *Echinocactus* than that of any *Mamillaria* known to me. The plant is evidently nearly allied to the foregoing, and also somewhat to the last species, but is distinguished by the very stout spines, and especially the slender and constricted tube of the flower. In *M. Scheerii* the filaments leave the lowest part of the tube free.

14. M. RECURVISPINA (sp. nov.): simplex, globosa seu depresso-globosa; tuberculis ovatis obtusis profunde sulcatis confertis subimbricatis; areolis obliquis ovatis; aculeis radialibus 12–20 basi bulbosa compressis rigidis recurvis flexuosisve albidis seu corneis apice sæpe adustis intertextis; aculeo centrali singulo (interdum secundo superiore adjecto) robustiore longiore obscuriore decurvato seu raro rectiusculo; floribus in axillis villosissimis tuberculorum juniorum subverticalibus majusculis flavicantibus extus fuscatis; sepalis lanceolatis acutis integris; petalis erosis.

Eastern parts of *Pimeria Alta*, in Sonora, especially in the Sierra del Pajarito, *A. Schott:* fl. June to August.—Heads single, mostly depressed, "4–8 inches in diameter" (a living specimen before me has only 3 inches.) Tubercles in my specimen in 13 spiral rows, 5–6 lines long, ovate, somewhat compressed from above; areolæ very oblique, ovate, 2–2½ lines long, white woolly when young. Radial spines, in my living specimen, 14–16; in a dried one, as many as 20; according to Mr. Schott's notes, 12–14. One spine is distinctly superior, and one inferior; the others are closely arranged along both sides of the areola, 4–9 lines long, upper ones often a little longer than the lower ones. Central spine 6–10 lines long, dark, mostly strongly recurved, adpressed, so that the plant can easily be handled without hurting; much like *M. compacta* from the mountains west of Chihuahua, to which it bears a strong resemblance. It seems to be fully distinguished, however, by the arrangement of the flowers, which in ours originate from the base of full-grown tubercles, and are scattered over the top of the plant, being pushed out by younger tubercles, bearing new buds; while, in the Chihuahua species, they come from the axils of young, just growing, tubercles, and are crowded on the densely woolly top. Flowers about 1½ inch long, and of the same width; petals lemon-yellow, darker, and with a brownish tinge outside along the midrib.

15. M. PECTINATA, (sp. nov.): simplex, globosa; tuberculis e basi quadrangulata conicis, inferioribus abbreviatis, summis floriferis teretibus longioribus sulcatis; areolis orbiculato-oblongis; aculeis 16–24 omnibus radiantibus plerumque subæqualibus seu summis fasciculatis longioribus, e basi bulbosa lateraliter compressa subrecurvis, pectinatis luteo-albidis demum cinereis apice sæpe sphacelatis·intertextis; floribus e vertice tomentosissimo centralibus flavis; ovario globoso; tubo brevi amplo; sepalis sub-30 acutis aristatis, exterioribus lanceolatis apice recurvis, interioribus oblanceolatis adpressis; petalis sub-30 pluriserialibus oblanceolatis seu intimis obtusis retusisve, omnibus herbaceo-aristatis; stigmatibus 9–10 linearibus luteo-albis stamina longe superantibus; bacca ovata viridi floris rudimentis coronata; seminibus elongato-obovatis compressis lævibus lucidis fuscis, hilo parvo ventrali. (Tab. XI.)

On gentle slopes of the limestone hills on the Pecos, and at Leon spring, abundant at the latter place, (*Charles Wright*): fl. in June and July.—The globose heads are 1½–2½ inches in diameter; tubercles in 13 spiral rows, lower ones 2–3 lines long, and somewhat broader at base, not grooved, or with a very short groove near the spines; upper tubercles 5–6 lines long, and grooved all the way down. Spines on lower part of plant nearly equal in length on each tubercle, 3–4½ lines long, as stiff and pointed and almost as closely and regularly set as in *Cereus pectinatus*, whence the specific name. On the flower-bearing tubercles the upper spines are elongated, mixed with a few stouter ones, and fasciculated; lower ones 5–6 lines long, and upper ones, forming a tuft about the apex of the stem, 6–9 lines long. Flower over 2 inches long, and 2¾ inches in diameter when fully open, between 11 and 12 o'clock, closing already about 1 o'clock, though exposed to the full glare of the sun. Ovary 3–4 lines long; exterior sepals reddish-green, interior ones yellow, with a darker midrib; petals of a beautiful sulphur yellow, broadest in the upper third and obtusish. Filaments reddish, short, covering the whole base of the tube, leaving no naked space. Fruit about half an inch long, ripening on the vertex, and not pushed aside by succeeding young tubercles, as it seems that no new ones are developed till the fruit is fully ripe, or probably till the succeeding spring. This is the case with several allied yellow-flowering species, but not with other red-flowering ones, hereafter to be described; in these, though the flower (or at least the flower-bud) be vertical, the succeeding rapid growth pushes them aside , and still more the berries, which finally appear quite lateral. Seed 0.9 line long, elongated, compressed, rounded at the back, quite sharp at the anterior or ventral edge, on the lower part of which, in a slight curvature, the small and narrow hilum is situated.

16. M. Echinus (sp. nov.): simplex, globosa seu subconica; vertice dense tomentoso; tuberculis in planta adulta teretibus apice conicis supra sulcatis; areolis orbiculatis; aculeis rectis seu paullo curvatis cinereo-albidis apice sæpe obscurioribus, radialibus 16–30 pectinatis, superioribus longioribus fasciculatis, centralibus 3–4 validioribus e basi bulbosa subulatis, superioribus 2–3 sursum versis et cum radialibus superioribus implicatis, inferiore validissimo subulato recto (seu rarissime paullo recurvo) porrecto; floribus verticalibus flavis; sepalis 20 lineari-lanceolatis mucronatis integris, petalis 20–30 angustis; stigmatibus sub-12 stamina longe superantibus; bacca centrali oblonga viridi floris rudimentis coronata; seminibus ut in praecedente. (Tab. X.)

On limestone hills in the region of the Pecos, *Wright*, and from Presidio del Norte to Santa Rosa, *Bigelow*: fl. in June.—A very striking plant, characterized by the unusually stout and subulate lower central spine, which together with the globular shape, gives it the appearance of some Echinite, whence the name. Specimens before me 1½–2 inches in diameter, tubercles 5–6 lines long, in 13 spiral rows. The numerous slender but very stiff whitish radical spines, laterally compressed at the thickened base, are densely interwoven and closely adpressed; lower ones about 5 lines long, lateral ones somewhat shorter, upper ones 6–8 lines long; upper interior spines stouter and rather longer than the upper radial ones, but otherwise hardly distinguishable from them; the lower central spine is also about 6 or 8 lines long, very regularly subulate from a thick base. Flowers between 1 and 2 inches long, to judge from the shriveled specimens seen, yellow; fruit over half an inch in length; seeds about 0.9 line long, entirely similar to those of the last species, to which this, perhaps, too closely approaches. All the specimens from the Pecos have very straight central spines; but some from Presidio del Norte, not otherwise different, have somewhat recurved and darker horn-colored central spines.

17. M. SCOLYMOIDES, Scheidw.; a small slender-spined form was collected by *Mr. Wright* on the Pecos, and by *Dr. Bigelow* about Santa Rosa. Tubercles compressed, incurved, imbricated; radial spines on the upper ones about 20, with 4 longer and darker incurved central ones, the upper ones bent upwards and almost mixed with the upper radial ones; lower one mostly over an inch long. This species and the two preceding may possibly be forms of De Candolle's *M. cornifera.*

18. M. CALCARATA, E. in Pl. Lindh., has been collected by *Mr. Wright* as far west as the Nueces river. His specimens have only 8 or 10 radial spines, 4–6 lines long; central spine of the same length, but stouter, often (in young specimens?) entirely wanting. *Lindheimer's* original specimens from the neighborhood of the Colorado and Guadalupe rivers, have 10–12 radial spines 8–9 lines long; central spine stouter but shorter, sometimes wanting; seeds similar to that of *M. pectinata,* but larger and very obtuse at base; 1–1, 2 lines long. (Tab. LXXIV, fig. 1.)

19. M. TUBERCULOSA (sp. nov.): ovata seu ovato-cylindrica, simplex seu ad basin ramosa; tuberculis e basi rhomboidea ovatis abbreviatis obtusis, subcompressis, profunde usque ad axillam villosissimam sulco villoso exaratis confertis imbricatis, demum nudatis suberosis persistentibus; areolis orbiculatis, novellis albo-tomentosis; aculeis exterioribus 20–30 rigidis gracilibus albidis nunc apice sphacelatis radiantibus intertextis, interioribus 5–9 robustioribus sursum cæsio-purpureis apice sphacelatis, quorum superiores longiores erecti versus caulis apicem in comam aggregati, inferior brevior robustus porrectus deflexusve; floribus in vertice densissime tomentoso centralibus pollicaribus dilute roseis; sepalis 16–18 lanceolatis arachnoideo-fimbriatis; petalis 10–13 lineari-lanceolatis aristatis subintegris; bacca ovata elongata floris rudimentis breviter convolutis coronata rubra; seminibus subgloboso-obovatis scrobiculatis fuscis, hilo ovato minuto ventrali. (Tab. X., fig. 1—6.)

From the Pecos to Leon springs, Eagle spring, and El Paso, on the higher mountains, *Wright*; especially on the rocky summits of the "Flounce mountains," below El Paso, *Bigelow*: fl. in May and June.—A very pretty and well defined species of the mountain region. Stems 2–5 inches high, 1–2 inches in diameter, often with globose branches at the base; tubercles mostly only 3 lines long, and of the same width at base, often shorter, rarely and only in very vigorous plants 4 or even 5 lines long; in 13, or on the lower part of old plants in 21, spiral rows, like the whole body of the plant, of a corky texture and substance, almost dry, and therefore not shrivelling when old, but after shedding the spines, persistent and covering the older parts of the stem as grey, corky tuberosities, whence the name. The deep, densely woolly groove, and the very woolly axilla, which loses its coating only after several years, are quite peculiar to this species. Radial spines usually 22–26, rarely less than 20, and never in the numerous specimens examined by me more than 30, very slender but stiff, usually 2–4 lines long, lower and a few upper ones 2 lines, most upper ones 3–4 lines long, uppermost rarely 5 or even 6 lines in length; lower stout central spine 3–4, upper ones 5–7, and in a few specimens even 8 or 9 lines long; those of the uppermost tubercles crowded together, erect, forming a purplish grey tuft, which surrounds and partly hides flowers and fruit. Flowers very pale purple, about one inch in diameter; berry oval, elongated, and sometimes almost cylindric, red, and by both these characters distinguished from the fruit of the allied species; remains of flower not irregularly shrivelled up as in those species, but forming a regular, conic, whitish head on the red fruit. Seeds 0.4 or 0.6 line long, unusually thick, with a very small oval, not linear, hilum.

20. M. DASYACANTHA (sp. nov.): simplex, subglobosa; tuberculis teretibus leviter usque ad basin sulcatis laxis; axillis sulcoque subvillosis mox nudatis; areolis orbiculatis novellis, albo-tomentosis; aculeis gracilibus vix spinescentibus rectis patulis, exterioribus 25–35 capillaceis albidis apice sphacelatis, interioribus 7–13 setaceis longioribus infra pallidioribus sursum purpureo-fuscis apice atratis, centrali singulo æquilongo porrecto nunc deficiente; florum parvorum centralium sepalis arachnoideo-fimbriatis; baccis verticalibus ovatis parvis; seminibus obovato-globosis angulatis scrobiculatis nigricantibus; hilo lineari subventrali. (Tab. XII, fig. 17–18.)

El Paso and Eagle springs, *Wright.*—The few specimens before me are from 1½–2½ inches high, a little less in diameter; tubercles slender, 4–5 lines long, in 13 spiral rows; grooves slightly hairy when young; axils more or less villous, soon becoming naked. Spines not strictly radiating, but loosely spreading, much more slender than in the last and the next species, often even capillary; exterior ones 3–6 or even 9 lines long; interior spines forming a circle corresponding with the interior ones, but darker, stiffer, and longer, upper ones 8–12 lines, lower ones 6–9 lines long, or in some specimens shorter and slenderer; central spine single, erect, 6–10 lines long, often wanting. The dry and shrivelled fruit, found on the tomentose vertex, was only 3½ lines long; seeds thick, sometimes triangular, with a very broad back, 0.4–0.6 line long, almost black; hilum quite different in shape and position from that of the next species, to which this is closely allied. The plant so much resembles *Echinocactus intertextus* var. *dasyacanthus* that, at first sight, it might be taken for it.

21. M. VIVIPARA, Haw. (Cactus viviparus *Nutt. Gen.*) This species is found only on the northwestern plains, along the Upper Missouri and Yellowstone rivers, and up into the Black Hills and Rocky Mountains. It is a low plant, either simple or usually profusely proliferous and cespitose, shoots always from the base of the groove on the tubercle, or the axil proper, while in *M. calcarata* they come from the upper part of the groove, just below the spines. Radial spines 12–20, stiff, white, often brown-red at the top, 3–4 lines long; central spines 4, (3 pointing upwards, and the stoutest and shortest downwards,) but sometimes less, and often more, as many even as 8, usually 4–6 lines long; flowers central, large for the size of the plant, about 1½ inch long, and even more in diameter when fully open, (which is after one o'clock, later than in most other Cactaceæ,) with thirty or more delicately fimbriate recurved sepals and 25–40 narrow acuminate purple petals, which are naked or fimbriate at base; filaments whitish or purplish, almost from the base of the tube; anthers orange; style long-exserted with 5–10 linear pale or purple stigmata, which are pointed with a short mucro. Berries becoming lateral, being pushed aside by the continuous growth from the apex of the plant, oval, ½–¾ inch long, pale green, juicy, and slightly acid, full of yellowish-brown seeds. These are 0.7–0.8 line long, obliquely obovate, somewhat concave on the compressed ventral portion about the small oblong-linear hilum, pitted; albumen more distinct than in most other *Mamillariæ;* embryo straight, linear-oblong, with very short connate cotyledons. (Tab. LXIV, fig. 3.)

The following form, from Texas, which formerly I thought I could distinguish from this northern species, seems to be connected to it by numerous intermediate forms, found in the geographically intermediate region of New Mexico:

Subspec. β. RADIOSA: ovata seu demum subcylindrica, simplex seu e basi ramosa; tuberculis teretibus laxis leviter sulcatis; aculeis radialibus numero maxime variis (12–40), superioribus longioribus robustioribus, centralibus, 3–12, quorum superiores robustiores, radialibus longiores, inferior robustus porrectus brevior; floribus in vertice demum lateralibus; sepalis 30–40 lineari-lanceolatis arachnoideo-fimbratis apice recurvis squarrosis; petalis totidem linearibus sensim acuminatis integris seu exterioribus basi fimbriatis; stigmatibus 5–10 obtusis purpureis tulis; bacca ovata floris rudimentis coronata viridi; seminibus obovatis scrobiculatis fulvis, hilo erecto parvo lineari ventrali.

Var. *α*. BOREALIS: ovata seu subglobosa, subsimplex; aculeis radialibus 12–20, centralibus 3–6 purpureo-maculatis; floribus minoribus; sepalis sub-25; petalis sub-30; seminibus minoribus ventre concavis. M. vivipara, var. *E. in Pl. Fendl. in Mem. Am. Acad.* (Tab. LXXIV, fig. 4.)

Var. *β*. NEO-MEXICANA: ovata seu ovato-cylindrica, sæpe e basi ramosa; aculeis radialibus albidis sub-30 (20–40), centralibus 6–9 (3–12) infra albidis sursum purpurascentibus apice atratis; floribus majoribus; seminibus majoribus ventre subconcavis.

Var. *γ*. TEXANA (M. radiosa, E. in Pl. Lindh.): ovato-cylindrica, subsimplex; aculeis radialibus 20–30 albidis apice adustis, centralibus 4–5 flavis seu fulvis; floribus majoribus; sepalis 40–50; petalis 30–40; stigmatibus 7–9; seminibus magnis ventre subconvexis. (Tab. LXXIV, fig. 5.)

Var. *α* has been collected in Northern New Mexico and about Santa Fé, by *Wislizenus* and *Fendler: β*, in the western parts of Texas and the southern parts of New Mexico by *Wright* and *Bigelow*; by the latter also on the upper Pecos, and in Sonora (a form with more spines than any other) by *Schott*. Var. *γ* was sent by *Lindheimer* from the Pierdenales, a tributary of the Guadalupe in western Texas: fl. in May and June.—Var. *γ* is the largest form, 2–5 inches high, with flowers 1½–2¼ inches in diameter when fully expanded, and seeds fully 1 line long. Var. *β* is an intermediate form, 1½ or 2 to 4 inches high, 1–2½ inches in diameter; tubercles 3–6 lines long; spines very variable in length and number; in smaller, younger specimens, the exterior spines are 2–4 lines, and the interior 3–6 lines long; in larger ones the former are often 3–8 lines, and the latter 5–10 lines long. Seed 0.7–0.9 line long, almost straight on the side of the hilum, or usually somewhat concave.—Var. *α*. approaches very near to *M. vivipara* of the north; the spines, however, are stouter; the flowers smaller; and the tubercles rarely proliferous; seeds as large as in the last, and of similar shape.

22. M. MACROMERIS, E. in Wisl. Rep.: simplex, seu ex sulcis tuberculorum inferiorum prolifera et demum cæspitosa, ovata seu cylindracea, læte viridis; tuberculis magnis e basi dilatata elongatis teretiusculis supra sulco (juniore villoso) ad medium ultrave usque ad areolam floriferam tomentosam supra-axillarem productò exaratis adscendentibus patulis laxis seu rarius plus minus imbricatis; aculeis gracilibus elongatis teretibus seu robustioribus sæpe angulatis compressisve rectis seu paullo curvatis, exterioribus sub-12 (10–17) patulis albidis seu junioribus subinde rubellis apice sphacelatis, inferioribus sæpe paullo brevioribus; aculeis centralibus 4 (in plantis junioribus sæpe 1–3 raro deficientibus,) longioribus robustoribus basi bulbosis plerumque nigricantibus, raro roseis fuscisve; floribus supra-axillaribus magnis e coccineo purpureis; ovario nudo seu squama una alterave sepaloidea munito; sepalis tubi 20–30 lanceolatis, inferioribus fimbriatis, superioribus integriusculis; petalis 20–25 oblongo-lanceolatis versus apicem denticulatis mucronatis; stigmatibus 7–8 supra stamina longe exsertis; bacca ovato-subglobosa nuda seu squamis paucis ciliatis instructa viridi; seminibus globoso-obovatis

lævibus fulvis, hilo oblongo-lineari ventricali; albumine parco; embryone recto; cotyledonibus minutis. (Tab. XIV–XV.)

In the valley of the Rio Grande, from Doña Ana, above El Paso, *Wislizenus*, to the cañon below that town, *Wright*, and to the mouth of the Pecos and to Eagle Pass, *Bigelow*, and lower down, mostly in loose sand, on hillocks confined by the roots of *Algarobia*: fl. July and August.—A splendid and very interesting species, 2–4 inches high; tubercles very different in size in different specimens, from 6 or 7 to 10 or 12, and sometimes even 15 lines long, generally arranged in 8 spirals. The groove is absent in the tubercles of the young plant; in the older ones it shows itself slightly, and only near the point of the tubercle, from the spine downwards; in more fully developed tubercles it becomes longer, till in the flower-bearing ones it reaches downward to the lower third, but never to the axilla; there it enlarges into the flower-bearing areola.—Radial spines 6–20 lines long, whitish or the upper ones or all rose-colored when young; central spines 1–2¼ inches long, the lowest one longer and stouter than the rest, mostly black, in some specimens paler, straight, or sometimes curved or twisted. Flower 2½–3 inches long, and of the same diameter, deep rose-color or carmine verging to purple, darker along the centre and towards the tip. Fruit 8 to 10 or 12 lines long; seeds different in size, 0.7–0.8 line long, short and thick, with a decidedly ventral hilum. Albumen distinct, more so than in most other *Mamillariæ*, but the embryo quite similar to them. The scales on the ovarium indicate an approach to *Echinocactus*, though the habit of the plant is decidedly that of a *Mamillaria*.—*M. dactylothele*, Lab. is a variety of this species.

### Subgen 3. Anhalonium.

Plantæ simplices, tuberculatæ, subinermes.

Tubercula subfoliacea, triangularia, lævia seu supra verrucoso-fissurata.

Areolæ floriferæ supra-axillares (an semper?), jubato-villosissimæ.

Flores ex areolis tuberculorum hornotinorum nascentium oriundi, in vertice congesti, mediocres.

Ovarium emersum: bacca floris rudimentis coronata, plerumque anno primo maturescens.

Semina majuscula, nigra, tuberculata.

These very curious plants, some of them looking more like some *Aloë* than like a *Cactus*, can nevertheless not be separated from *Mamillaria*. The seed is the only part of the organs of fructification which seems to offer any character, by having a hard, roughly tuberculated testa in ours as well as in another Mexican species which I had the opportunity to examine. Our species (and probably all the others) has the flower and fruit sessile upon the lower part of the tubercle; and elevated above the axil, much as in *M. macromeris;* but, unlike that plant, the lower part of the tubercle is entirely distinct from the upper one.

23. M. fissurata (sp. nov.): e radice crassa napiformi simplex, depresso-globosa seu applanata; vertice densissime villoso; tuberculis e basi applanta dilatata crassis triangularibus inermibus extus infraque lævibus seu versus marginem crenulatum rugosis, supra sulco centrali villoso lateralibusque 2 nudis profunde quadripartitis et sulcis transversalibus in tubercula irregularia angulosa numerosa multifidis; floribus e villo longo sericeo centralibus breviter tubulosis; sepalis sub-20, inferioribus lineari-lanceolatis integris carnosis albidis, superioribus spathulatis cuspidatis; petalis sub-12 spathulatis versus apicem obtusum mucronatum integriusculis seu laceris roseis; stigmatibus 5–10 erecto-patulis; baccis ovatis pallide virescentibus in lana

densa occultis; seminibus obovato-globosis tuberculatis nigris opacis, hilo basilari transverso; embryone obovato erecto. (Plate XVI.)

On hard, gravelly, limestone hills, near Fairy Springs, not far from the mouth of the Pecos, and between that river and the San Pedro, *Schott*, *Bigelow;* and higher up on the rocks of the cañon of the Rio Grande, *Parry:* fl. September and October.—The lower part of the plant is top-shaped, covered with the scale-like remains of the earlier tubercles; the upper part is hemispherical or depressed and flattened, hardly elevated above the surface of the ground, 2–4½ inches in diameter; tubercles in my specimens 6–10 lines long and a little less broad, or sometimes the upper warty part "¾ inch long and 1¼ inch wide," in 5 or 8, or rarely in 13 spiral rows. Lower part of tubercles flattened, acute at the edges, slightly carinate, more on he upper and less on the lower surface, smooth. Upper and exposed part of tubercle triangular in outline, convex, carinate and almost smooth below, convex and variously fissured and thereby verrucose above, sharp and crenate on the edges. The principal groove on the upper surface is a longitudinal one corresponding to the groove of the different species of *Coryphantha*, and like that villose; towards its base (at the base of the upper or warty part of the tubercle) it expands into the floriferous areola, upwards it ceases just under the acutish point of the tubercle without any trace of an aculeiferous areola or of spines; in the young tubercle it is coated by dense, long and straight, white or yellowish, silky wool, (about an inch long,) which from being exposed to the weather gets matted and dirty, and after several years entirely disappears. Two lateral grooves run parallel with this, and together with the many transverse fissures cut up the upper surface into numerous angular tubercles or warts. Flowers central or vertical, in the sense of the term as explained before, borne on the lower smooth part of a very young tubercle, which when bearing flower and fruit is somewhat thickened, and takes the shape and functions of a short penduncle, bearing laterally the upper part of the tubercle like a small bract. The axils even of these young tubercles are entirely naked; the long wool which covers the lower part of the flower, and entirely hides the whole fruit, being produced entirely from the areola and the central groove. Flower about an inch long and of the same diameter when fully open; ovary 3 lines long, oval; tube 4–6 lines long; 12 exterior sepals, whitish, fleshy, 8 inner ones spathulate, mucronate, with rose-colored edges 6–9 lines long, 2 lines wide; petals about 12 in a single series, 9 lines long, 2 lines wide, rose or pink-colored; stamens numerous, white with orange anthers; style white, expanding into a funnel-shaped irregularly 5–10 parted light-yellow stigma. Fruit oval, crowned with the remains of the flower, about 5 lines long, juicy. Seed 0.8 line long, strongly tuberculated, the transverse and somewhat truncate hilum basilar.

## II. ECHINOCACTUS, Link and Otto.

1. E. Scheerii, Salm: e radice tereti elongata parvus, globosus seu ovatus; costis 13 obtusis interruptis; tuberculis ovatis obtusis supra ad medium sulcatis; areolis ovato-orbiculatis junioribus albo-tomentosis; aculeis radialibus 15–18 setaceis rigidis rectis seu plerumque paullo recurvatis albidis stramineisve apice fuscatis, summo interdum elongato, centralibus 3–4 angulatis variegatis fusco-atris, superioribus rectis sursum divaricatis longioribus, inferiore porrecto hamato breviore; floribus in vertice laxis; sepalis exterioribus 13 squamiformibus, inferioribus appendiculato-auriculatis margine membranaceo laceris ciliatis, superioribus ovatis integriusculis, sepalis interioribus 8 lineari-oblongis obtusis; petalis 13 lineari-lanceolatis acutis flavo-virescentibus; stigmatibus 8 linearibus flavis; bacca virescente indistincte squa-

mata; seminibus oblique obovatis compressis minutissime tuberculatis fuscis, hilo ventrali circulari magno. (Tab. XVII.)

About Eagle Pass, on the Rio Grande, *Schott*, *Bigelow:* fl. in April.—A most elegant little species, 1½–2 inches in diameter and of the same height. Root long, terete, rather fleshy, white, about ¼ inch in diameter, such as I have not seen in any other of our *Cactaceæ*. Tubercles more distinct and less plainly arranged in ribs than in the other species of this genus; they are 4 or 5 lines high, somewhat compressed, of the same transverse diameter, and a little longer in the other direction; areola about 1½ line long, a little less broad, extending upwards into a tomentose groove, 1–2½ lines long, which terminates in the floriferous areola half-way down to the axil, as the transverse incision in the rib may be designated. This groove is much shorter or almost wanting on the tubercles, which bear no flowers. The exterior spines, with their bulbous compressed bases, are closely and regularly arranged all around the areola, and are strictly radiating; in younger plants I find 11–13, in older flower-bearing tubercles always 15–18 radial spines, 3–5 lines long, of almost equal length, or the lateral ones a little longer than the rest; the uppermost radial spine, however, is often somewhat stouter and longer, ranging rather as an upper central spine, when only 3 of these are present. The upper central spines (2 in my specimens from Eagle Pass, 3 in Salm's original plant) are stouter, somewhat compressed and angled, brown or black on the upper and whitish or mottled on the lower surface, or they are lighter throughout, with black tips; they are 8–12 lines long; the lower central spine is 2 or 3 lines shorter, black on the upper side, especially at base, and at the hooked point white on the lower surface and again on the outside of the curvature. The green flowers are about an inch long, much less in diameter even when fully open. Fruit and seed not seen by our collectors; the former is said by Dr. Poselger (who has sent me a good specimen of the plant, entirely agreeing with my specimens) to be a small green and almost naked berry; his seeds are large, about one line long, 0.8 line in diameter, with very minute and flattened tubercles, *brown* (the only *Echinocactus* with seeds of that color known to me); hilum large and circular, surrounded by a thick rim; albumen very small; embryo curved, but cotyledons small, connate, more like those of a *Mamillaria*, separating on the curvature and not at the end of the hook, as in all other hooked embryos of *Cactaceæ* known to me.

2. E. BREVIHAMATUS (sp. nov.): e radice turbinata fibrosa globoso-obovatus, atro-viridis; costis 13 compressis tuberculato-interruptis; sulcis acutis profunde incisis; tuberculis supra ad basin usque tomentoso-sulcatis; areolis orbiculatis junioribus breviter albo-tomentosis; aculeis radialibus 12 teretibus rectis albidis seu sordide flavis apice adustis, superioribus longioribus; centralibus 4 complanatis albidis apice atratis, lateralibus sursum divergentibus rectis seu paullo recurvatis aculeos radiales superantibus, summo debiliore et infimo porrecto seu deflexo deorsum hamato robustiore eos subæquantibus; floribus infundibuliformibus roseis; sepalis inferioribus (ovarii) 5–7 reniformibus scariosis ciliatis, superioribus (tubi) 8 ovato-oblongis mucronatis obtusisve; petalis 13–14 lineari-lanceolatis acutis mucronatis integris; stigmatibus 10–11 radiatis flavis stamina rubella paullo excedentibus. (Tab. XVIII, XIX.)

On the San Pedro, *Wright*, and not rare about Eagle Pass, *Bigelow:* fl. March and April.—The specimens sent by the gentlemen of the Boundary Commission were from 2 to 4 inches high, and 2–3 in diameter, of a very dark green color, and remarkable from the tuft formed on the apex by the upper central spines, in which the numerous flowers are almost entirely hidden; the lower hooked central spines stand out from the mass of the other spines, the hooks turned downward. All the specimens grew well at first, one flowered abundantly, but all soon died from an internal rot, just as all the specimens of *E. uncinatus* did, though they were treated like the other *Cactaceæ* from the same region, which are doing well. Areolæ 2 lines in diameter, 8–12 lines distant, connected with the floriferous areolæ in the axils of the tubercles by a tomentose groove of 4 or 5 lines length. Radial spines almost always 12, very rarely 1 or 2 more, 5–10 lines long, upper ones longer than the lower, and light colored, lateral ones darker when young, but difference of shade soon lost; upper central spine 8–10 lines long, lateral ones usually 14–22 lines in length, always exceeding the upper and lower one; this last one is the stoutest and broadest of all, 9–14 lines long, mostly yellowish-brown, darker on the upper, lighter on the lower surface, and with the hook brown or black; rarely 1 or 2 additional central spines are noticed. Flower 12–16 lines long, only 9 or 10 lines wide when fully open at noon; petals 7–8 lines long, 2 lines wide, pale rose colored, with a deeper colored midrib. Fruit and seed unknown.—Near the last species, distinguished by the larger size, the very different root, the smaller number of radial spines, the shortness of the upper central spine, and the red color of the flowers; other differences will no doubt be found in fruit and seed. Name from the shortness of the hook, by which the species is distinguished from most other allied forms.

3. E. UNCINATUS, Hœpf., var? WRIGHTII: glaucescens, ovatus; costis 13 compressis tuberculatis supra usque ad basin sulcatis; areolis ovato-orbiculatis, junioribus albo-lanatis; aculeis radialibus 8, inferioribus 3 brevioribus teretibus uncinatis purpureo-fuscis, cæteris 5 compressis rectis infra stramineis sursum rubellis apice fuscis, summis longioribus latioribusque, centrali singulo complanato basi angulato flexuoso elongato hamato erecto stramineo apice fusco; floribus ex areola penitus axillari ortis; sepalis inferioribus 25–30 imbricatis squamæformibus e basi longe auriculata triangularibus hyalinis, superioribus 15–25 ovato-orbiculatis cordatis acutis purpurascentibus, superioribus 18–20 lineari-oblongis obtusis purpureo-fuscis, sepalis omnibus margine membranaceo albido ciliatis; petalis 20–30 lineari-lanceolatis obtusiusculis purpureis, internis mucronatis denticulatis; stylo supra stamina numerosissima exserto stigmatibus 10 carneis suberectis; bacca ovata rubella; seminibus curvatis oblique obovatis tuberculatis hilo circulari basilari. (Tab. LXXIV, fig. 10.)

Near El Paso, and on the river below, also at Eagle springs, on stony hills and nearly to the top of the mountains, commonly in tufts of grass or hidden among low bushes, *Wright*, *Bigelow:* fl. in March and April.—Oval, 3–6 inches high, 2–3½ inches in diameter, with a long tuft of the whitish hooked central spines, which are at first difficult to distinguish from the surrounding bunches of dead grass. The adult plants have generally 3, very rarely 4 lower hooked radial spines, ¾–1¼ inch long; 5 lateral and upper radial spines 1–1½ inch long, paler and flattened; the uppermost one longer, broader, and whiter than the rest; sometimes I find 6 upper spines, when the 3 outer and more slender ones appear radial, and the 3 inner and stouter ones assume the position of 3 upper central spines; there are then 6 radial and 4 central spines. The hooked central spine is 2–4 inches long, and not annulated. Young plants have 6–7 radial and 1 central spine, all terete and purplish, with darker tips, all ½–1 inch long; in older specimens, the central spine elongates, and finally becomes flattened and whitish. Groove on the tubercles 2–3 lines long, so that the *axillary* flower is distant thus far from the spines; flower 1–1½ inch long, dark purplish-red, opening at midday in bright sunshine; filaments at least 1000, yellow below, orange at tip. Fruit ovate 8–12 lines long, pulpy red, setting off the white membranaceous sepaloid scales. Seed 0.7–0.8 line long, remarkably curved and contracted at the base; compressed, (more so in the ventral curvature,) carinate on the back, tuberculate; the small circular hilum surrounded by a very tumid, smooth, and shining rim. Albumen large; embryo hooked, with foliaceous cotyledons.

The Mexican *E. uncinatus*, of which I have seen spines and seeds collected by *Dr. Poselger* between Saltillo and San Luis Potosi, and flowers found by *Dr. Gregg*, near Parras, has 7–8 radial spines, the 3 lower ones of which are hooked, and 4 central ones, the lowest one flattened and elongated; lower sepals 36, upper ones about 14, oblanceolate, aristate, margined; petals 25, linear-lanceolate, acuminate, aristate; 8–10 stigmata; seeds 0.6–0.7 line long, very much compressed, curved, almost cochleate, smoothish and shining; circular hilum almost ventral; albumen and embryo same as in the other. (Tab. LXXIV, fig. 9.)

4. E. SETISPINUS, E. in Pl. Lindh. Many forms have been collected by the Commission; all characterized by 13 narrowly-compressed ribs, slender flexible spines, small bright-red globose fruit, and globose-obovate oblique strongly tuberculated seeds, with an almost circular basilar hilum. The heads are globose, or usually lengthened and almost cylindrical when old, but sometimes depressed; spines short or long, the central spine usually somewhat longer than the others, but in some specimens from the Rio Grande shorter, in others from Eagle Pass much longer than the others, and erect, sometimes hardly curved. Seed usually 0.6 line long; in the above-mentioned specimen from Eagle Pass 0.8 line in length. The geographical range of this species is from the Brazos south to the Rio Grande, whence *Berlandier* has sent it under the name of *Cactus bicolor*, and west to near the San Pedro.

5. E. SINUATUS, Dietr. (E. setispinus, $\gamma$. sinuatus *Poselg.*): globosus, læte viridis; costis 13 obliquis compressis acutatis interruptis; tuberculis breviter sulcatis; areolis orbiculatis, junioribus albo, seu griseo-villosis; aculeis radialibus 8–12 setiformibus flexilibus, 3 inferioribus et 3 superioribus purpureo-fuscis rectiusculis, lateralibus 2–6 tenuioribus longioribus sæpe compressis rufis seu interdum flexuosis hamatisve albidis; aculeis centralibus 4 quorum 3 superiores graciles compressi seu sub-angulati erecti plerumque recti, infimus latior compressus seu canaliculatus flexuosus elongatus stramineus basi purpurascens apice subhamatus; floribus ab areola aculeifera paullo distantibus; sepalis inferioribus 20–30 cordato-auriculatis, superioribus 15–20 lanceolatis basi auriculatis margine membranaceis; petalis 20–25 lanceolatis sulphureis; stylo longe supra stamina exserto; stigmatibus 8–12 apiculatis erecto-patulis; bacca ovata squamis 7–10 munita viridi; seminibus obovatis seu lenticularibus hilo oblongo subbasilari excisis lucidis sub lente minutissime punctatis. (Tab. LXXIV, fig. 11–14.)

On the Pecos, San Pedro, and Rio Grande rivers, *Wright*, *Schott.*—I have above given a careful description of this plant, because it is so nearly allied to the foregoing and especially to the next species, which Dr. Poselger thinks it connects. With the former it has in common only the compressed ribs and the setaceous radial spines, but is distinguished by its size, the central spines, the fruit, and especially the seed. From the next species, to which it much more closely resembles, it is distinguished by the compressed ribs, the slender radial spines, the smaller number of all parts of the flower, the small fruit, and the smaller very finely punctate seed. My specimens are 4 or 5 inches in diameter, while Dr. Poselger's were 8 inches thick; areolæ 8–10 lines apart; 3 lower spines smooth purplish-brown, lighter at top, $\frac{3}{4}$–1 inch long, lateral spines puberulent, straw-colored, 1–1$\frac{1}{2}$ inch long; central spines puberulent, 3 upper ones yellowish, generally darker at base, 1$\frac{1}{2}$–2 inches long; lower central spine much stouter and longer than all the others, and flattened or even channelled, pale-yellowish, often purplish at base, flexuous, more or less hooked, sometimes straight, 2–4 inches long. Flowers 2–3 inches long, yellow, apparently without the scarlet base of the petals, which I always find in both the allied species, externally greenish; fruit oval, 8–9 lines long, with 7–12 scales; green when ripe; seeds 0.4–0.6 line long. Dr. Poselger describes another form under the name of *E. setispinus δ. robustus*, which is said to have all four central, and often the three lower radial spines, also, more or less hooked. The seed which he has sent to me leaves no doubt in my mind that it is a form of *E. sinuatus*. In my specimens only the lateral spines sometimes are flexuous, or hooked, or almost curled.

6. E. LONGEHAMATUS, Galeotti: subglobosus seu demum ovatus, læte-viridis, costis 13–17 sæpe obliquis tuberculato-interruptis latioribus obtusis; tuberculis ovatis supra brevissime sulcatis; areolis ovatis seu suborbiculatis distantibus; aculeis junioribus demum totis cinereis; radialibus 8–12 rectis curvatis flexuosisve patulis, superioribus gracilioribus pallidioribus, infimo brevi, lateralibus longioribus subannulatis; aculeis centralibus 4 (1–4 superioribus adventitiis subinde adjectis) angulatis compressis annulatis, quorum superiores recti seu curvati seu contorti sursum versi, infimus robustior plerumque longissimus sæpe flexuosus plus minus uncinatus porrectus vel deflexus; floribus ab areola aculeifera vix sejunctis infundibuliformibus, limbo patulo; ovario ovato; sepalis scarioso-marginatis ciliatis, inferioribus 30–60 squamiformibus reniformibus, mediis 10–20 obovato-spathulatis, interioribus 15–20 demum oblongo-obovatis obtusis cuspidatis; petalis 20–30 oblanceolatis obtusis vel retusis denticulatis cuspidatis seu mucronatis sulphureis ima basi coccineis et sæpius dorso rubellis; stigmatibus 15–18 obtusis sulphureis patulis; bacca ovata squamosa viridi; seminibus globoso-obovatis hilo ovato subbasilari oblique excisis scrobiculatis lucidis. (Tab. XXI—XXIV.)

Var. *α*. CRASSISPINUS. E. flexispinus, *E. in Wisl. Rep.* non *Salm.*

Var. *β*. GRACILISPINUS: aculeis gracilioribus 16–20, exterioribus 12–14, centralibus 4–8, infimo elongato hamato. E. hamatocanthus, *Muehlenpf.*

Var. *γ*. BREVISPINUS: aculeis gracilioribus, radialibus 8–11, centralibus 4 teretibus cum infimo hamato radiales vix superantibus.

Along the middle course of the Rio Grande and near the Pecos and San Pedro rivers, on the mountains of the Limpia, and near Presidio del Norte, and southward into Mexico, but not as far west as El Paso, *Wright, Bigelow*: fl. June and July.—Heads ½ to 2 feet high, but flowering often when not more than two inches high. Ribs usually 13; areolæ roundish in younger, more elongated in older specimens, often only 6–10 lines, but in vigorous plants 1–1½ inch apart. Spines glabrous, or only the lower central one scabrous-pubescent; lateral spines whitish, all the others purplish or variegated, with paler semitransparent tips. The forms *β*. and *γ*. are those which occur in our territory; they differ in the length and number of spines, but not at all in flower and fruit. In Var. *β*. the lower and upper radial spines are 1–3 inches, the lateral ones 2–3½ inches long, upper central spines 2–5, and lower one 3–6½ inches long. Var. *γ*. is perhaps the young plant, as these plants often flower when yet quite young, and before the character of the mature plant is yet fully developed. This in a very marked degree is the case with *E. uncinatus*, var., which begins to bloom while the central spine is yet quite short and terete. Lower radial spines ½–1¼ inch, upper ones 1¼–2 inches long, lateral ones 1¼–1½ inch, and central spines all 1½–2 inches long. Flowers form a groove just above the spines, separated from the spiniferous areola by 2–5 obtuse cylindric glandular bodies which often exude a clear viscous liquid. I find them also in *E. setispinus*, *E. Emoryi*, and numerous others, and they correspond, no doubt, with the glands in the groove of *Mamillaria Scheerii* and others. They appear with the flower, and are soft and fleshy at that time; afterwards they become hardened, of the texture of the spines themselves, and are persistent. Flowers 2½–3½ inches long, externally greenish-yellow and red, internally yellow, with a red base. Fruit 1–2 inches long, coated with 25 or 40 or more scales, crowded with the remains of the flower, green and very acid, (*Bigelow*,) or insipid or sweetish when fully ripe (*Parry*;) seed larger than in the last species 0.7–0.8 line in the longest diameter, deeply and distinctly pitted under the lens.

7. E. Wislizeni, E. in Wisl. Rep. has been often collected by the different gentlemen attached to the commission between Doña Ana and El Paso, and probably on the upper Gila, but not eastward. Small specimens show only 13 ribs; full-grown ones usually have 21 or even as many as 24 ribs; areolæ from ½ to 1½ inch distant from one another; on older plants closer than on half-grown ones; 3 lower radial spines annulated; stout, 8–20 lines long; 3 upper ones somewhat slenderer, but also annulated, 1½–2 inches long; in younger specimens these latter are wanting; in old ones they move more towards the centre of the areola, and become surrounded by the upper bristly spines. Lateral bristle-spines 15–20, 1½–2¼ inches long, often twisted, spreading horizontally. All the stouter and annulated spines are red with paler semitransparent points; the weaker spines are yellowish-white. Ovary and fruit imbricately covered with 60 or 80 scales; fruit rather fleshy but not juicy, and soon hardening; seed oblique obovate 1.0–1.2 lines long; hilum small, broadly oval, subbasilar, or sometimes almost ventral; surface of the seed finely reticulated under the lens; curved foliaceous cotyledons partly buried in the large albumen. (Tab. XXV—XXVI.)

8. E. Le Contei, E. in Pacif. R. Report: This fine species, which was discovered by *Dr. Le Conte* on the lower Gila, and found again by *Dr. Bigelow* higher up on the Colorado, has been observed frequently by *Mr. Schott* in the western part of Sonora, where it flowers in August and September. The flowers, which had not been seen by any other observer, may be described thus:

Floribus plurimis subcentralibus; ovario squamis 30–50 sepaloideis reniformibus munito, sepalis tubi inferioribus 20–30 ovato-lanceolatis acutis ciliatis, superioribus 10–20 margine petaloideis obtusiusculis cuspidatis; petalis 20–30 lineari-spathulatis obtusis inciso-fimbriatis mucronatis sulphureis; tubo basi intus nudo; stylo stamina superante ad medium in stigmata sub-14 linearia fasciculata diviso. (Tab. XXVII.)

Mr. Schott's specimens were 3–4 feet high, clavate and usually only one-third as thick. Dr. Bigelow's specimens were not as slender. Flowers two inches in length, "somewhat campanulate, "petals "lemon-yellow," with a brownish tint along the midrib; tube naked for about one line above the base of the style.

9. E. Emoryi, E. in Emory's Rep., 1848: grandis, ovatus, glaucescens; costis 13–21 rectis obliquisve obtusis tuberculatis; areolis ovatis junioribus dense sordideque tomentosis; aculeis 8–9 subæqualibus robustis subangulatis annulatis paulo recurvis rubellis demum fuscis apice sub pellucido corneis, radialibus 7 seu interdum adjecto (aculeo tenuiore summo) 8, lateralibus sublongioribus, centrali singulo recurvo seu subhamato paullo robustiore; floribus magnis purpureo-variegatis; sepalis ovarii 25 reniformibus ciliolatis, superioribus spathulatis lanceolatis

acutis; petalis sub-25 lanceolatis acuminatis versus apicem fimbriato-fissis; stylo stamina vix superante profunde 18–20-partito. (Tab. XXVIII.)

On the Gila, *Emory;* the lower Colorado, *Bigelow*; and in Sonora, at Punta de Agua, Sierra del Pajarito, Sierra de la Union and Sierra de Sonoyta, *Schott*: fl. in August and September.—Largest plants 30–36 inches high and 18–24 inches in diameter, with 20 or more ribs, smaller ones a foot in diameter, and globose, only 13-ribbed. Ribs strongly tuberculated, tubercles quite distinct, especially on the younger plants, and rounded, on old plants more confluent; areolæ 6–10 lines long, 1½–2 inches apart, oval, separated from the contiguous but smaller floral areola by 2–5 terete obtuse finally ligneous glands. Radial spines mostly 1–2 inches long, in a very large specimen from Guaymas, on the Gulf of California, procured by Dr. Bigelow, and now in the Congressional Garden in Washington, nearly 3 inches long; the 4 upper lateral spines are the longest and stoutest; the lower ones, and, if present, the uppermost radial spine, (in the specimen from Guaymas sometimes two), are shorter and slenderer than the others. Flowers aggregated near the vertex, about 3 inches long, dark brown purple outside; petals red, with yellowish margins; filaments rising from the thick and fleshy upper part of the short tube, leaving its lower part naked, extremely numerous; style thick, as long as the longer (exterior) stamina, divided to the middle into 18 or 20 filiform stigmata. Fruit and seed as yet unknown.

10. E. VIRIDESCENS, Nutt.: globosus seu depressus, simplex seu e basi ramosus; vertice depresso tomentoso; costis 13–21 compressis vix tuberculatis; areolis orbiculato-ovatis junioribus tomentosis; aculeis compressis annulatis plus minus curvatis e virescente rubellis, radialibus 9–13 (18–20, ex (*Parry*) infimo robusto breviore deorsum curvato, centralibus 4 robustioribus 4-angulatis compressis cruciatis, inferiore latiore longiore mimus curvato; floribus subverticalibus e flavo virescentibus; ovario globoso squamis sepaloideis 25–40 semilunatis reniformibusve denticulatis imbricatis stipato; sepalis tubi 25–30 ovatis oblongisve obtusis; petalis 20 oblongis obtusis eroso-denticulatis; stylo usque ad medium in stigmata 12–15 linearia erecta albida diviso; bacca ovata seu subglobosa squamata virescente floris rudimentis coronata; seminibus oblique obovatis dorso carinatis minutissime scrobiculatis, hilo orbiculato parvo subventrali. (Tab. XXIX.)

San Diego, California, on dry hills and ridges *Nuttall, Parry;* on the sea-beach, *Schott*. According to Nuttall this species is about 1 foot high, and has 9 or 10 inches diameter. Dr. Parry found them usually flat, 4 or 5 inches high (above ground) and 6–7 inches in diameter. They are usually simple, but sometimes, "only when wounded or burned over by fires," they branch from the base, forming in favorable situations quite a pile of prickly balls. In a young specimen brought home by Dr. Parry, about 2 inches in diameter, with 8 ribs, I find only 9 radial slightly recurved spines; the lowest and most curved one 4–6 lines long; the 2 upper ones 6–8 lines, and the 6 lateral ones 8–9 lines long; the 4 central spines are much stouter, more distinctly angular, compressed, and annulated, 10–16 lines long, the uppermost one more curved, the lowest one almost straight. Schott, in his notes made on the spot, states the number of radial spines to be 13, much shorter than the central spines; Parry describes the radial spines of the adult plant as 18–20, not more than 6–9 lines long, while the longest central spine is about 18 lines long. Flowers disposed in a circle around the vertex, greenish, 1½ inch long, 1¼ in diameter; tube inside naked at base; stamina short; style about one inch long, more deeply divided than in other species. Fruit 8–10 lines long, of the shape and taste of a gooseberry;

bluish-green in Parry's specimens, with 25–30, in Schott's with 35–40 scales; seed 0.8 lines long, very minutely but distinctly pitted.

11. E. CYLINDRACEUS, E. in Sillim. Journn., 1852, sub *E. viridescente:* ovatus seu ovato-cylindricus, simplex seu plerumque e basi ramosus; vertice breviter tomentello; costis 21 seu pluribus rectis seu obliquis obtuse tuberculatis; areolis ovatis; aculeis robustis compressis annulatis plus minus curvatis flexuosisve rubellis apice corneis, radialibus 12 sæpe cum aculeis gracilioribus sub–5 summæ areolæ insertis, lateralibus tenuioribus, infimo robusto breviori decurvato-hamato; aculeis centralibus 4 robustissimis 4–angulatis compressis cruciatis, superiore latiore sursum suberecto, inferiore deorsum curvato; flore flavo; bacca subglobosa carnosa pallide virescente sepalis semilunatis fimbriatis stipata, floris rudimentis coronata. (Tab. XXX.)

Rocky ravines near San Felipe, on the eastern slope of the California nmountains, in latitude 33°, *Dr. Parry;* also seen by *Dr. Le Conte.* Young plants globose, older ones ovate and cylindric; the former have 13 ribs, the latter from 20 to 27; the largest specimens seen were 3 feet high and a foot in diameter. They often branch out at base, which by Dr. Parry is ascribed to the action of fire, crippling the original stem. Ribs somewhat interruptedly tuberculated; tubercles flattened horizontally. In the youngest specimens are found already 7 radial and 4 central spines, the lower radial spine much the stoutest and quite curved, the 3 upper central spines almost radiating, the lower one erect, all stout, and 1–1½ inch long. In older specimens (the one before me is globose, 4 inches in diameter, with 13 ribs) the areolæ are 6–8 lines long, 3½–4 lines wide; the radial spines (together with the 3–5 slender additional ones on the upper edge of the areola) 12–18; the lowest one is stout and much hooked, and the shortest of all; the others are from 1½–2 inches long; the 4 central spines are 1–1½ line broad, and about 2 inches long; in the most fully developed bunches of spines the 3 upper radial spines are pushed into the inner circle, so that then the number of centrals appear to be 7. The upper central spine is the broadest one, almost straight and erect; the lower one has mostly a strong downward curve. The fruit is described by Dr. Parry as a green, juicy berry, about an inch in diameter, in the axils of the uppermost spines, with yellow remains of the corolla; seed black, "intermediate in size between that of *E. viridescens* and *E. Wislizeni.*" I was inclined to consider this plant as a form of *E. viridescens*, but Dr. Parry, who has seen numerous specimens of it, is satisfied that it is quite a distinct species. It is characterized by the cylindrical growth, more obtuse ribs, more numerous, longer, and more curved spines, of which the upper, not the lower one, is the largest and broadest. It is quite remarkable that we have three so similar species on both sides of the Californian mountains as the two just mentioned and *E. polycephalus;* the western one globose, the two eastern ones cylindrical and many-headed; these entirely dissimilar in flower and fruit, and one of the eastern and the western one so much alike. It is an interesting observation that similar but quite distinct species occur on both sides of the mountains, not only in this genus, but also in *Mamillaria* and *Opuntia;* and that no species crosses that mountain range.

12. E. POLYCEPHALUS, Engelm. and Bigelow, in Pacific Railroad Report, found by *Mr. Schott* on the Gila and lower Colorado. He notes the cæspitose growth, and the heads 5–8 inches in diameter, 10–15 inches long, with 10–15 ribs. *Dr. Bigelow's* specimens from the Mojave river were much larger, but the fruit sent by Mr. Schott leaves no doubt about their identity.

13. E. PARRYI (sp. nov.): simplex, globosus seu depressus; costis 13 acutis tuberculato-interruptis, sæpe obliquis; areolis orbiculatis, seu areola florifera contigua minore addita, ovatis albo-

tomentosis; aculeis omnibus robustis angulatis plus minus compressis albidis, radialibus 8–11 rectis seu paullo curvatis, superioribus debilioribus, lateralibus robustioribus, infimo deficiente; aculeis centralibus 4 validioribus, 3 rectiusculis sursum versis, infimo valido longiore curvato deflexo; bacca sicca oblonga squamis aristatis spinescentibus tomentoque denso albo vestita floris rudimentis coronata. (Tab. XXXII, fig. 6–7.)

Desert region southwest of El Paso towards Lake Guzman, over an area of 60 or 80 miles in extent, found by *Parry* with old fruit in January, and by *Wright* and *Bigelow* without flower or fruit in April.—I have before me only a few bunches of spines; the other data are all obtained from Dr. Parry's notes. The plant is 8 or 12 inches high by 10 or 15 inches in diameter, always simple; the ribs interrupted; upper tubercles less distinct, flattened sidewise, lower older ones transverse and very distinct grooves between the ribs about an inch deep; areolæ of the spines ½ inch in diameter, orbicular, or with the closely adjoining floriferous areola oval, about ¾ inch long. Radial spines in my specimen 8 or 9, "often as many as 11;" lower ones divergent; stoutest upper ones more slender. Central spines 4, stouter and 1½–2 inches long, somewhat bulbous at base, upper and lower one, especially the last, stoutest and longest.—This species is nearly allied to the last, but even in the absence of seeds we can distinguish it by the simple globose or somewhat depressed heads, and the white spines. I have named it after *Dr. C. C. Parry*, who by his intelligent observations and copious notes about the *Cactaceæ* of the Boundary has greatly assisted me in their elucidation.

14. E. HORIZONTHALONIUS, Lemaire, var. CENTRISPINUS: glaucus, depresso-globosus (vetustus sæpius ovatus umbilicatus); costis 8 obtusissimis latissimis; sinubus superficialibus acutis; tuberculis sulco transverso inconspicuo vix distinctis; areolis orbiculatis basi truncatis prominulis, junioribus albo-lanatis; aculeis 6–8 robustis compressis annulatis recurvatis rubellis demum cinereis, radialibus 5–7, superioribus debilioribus, infimo deficiente, centrali singulo robustiore latiore deorsum flexo; floribus ex vertice densissime lanato centralibus campanulatis; ovario tuboque lana longa dense vestito; sepalis exterioribus 60–70 subulatis linearibus et lanceolato-linearibus spinoso-aristatis atropurpureis nudis ex lana copiosissima axillari vix exsertis; sepalis interioribus sub-15 obovato-lanceolatis mucronatis axilla nudis; petalis sub-36 oblongis obtusis eroso-dentatis roseo-purpureis; stylo supra stamina numerosissima flava exserto rubello; stigmatibus 6–8 brevibus erecto-patulis; bacca rubra succosa mox desiccata lana densa involuta floris rudimentis spinescentibus coronata a basi fere persistente circumscissa decidua; seminibus subglobosis rugosis minutissime tuberculatis nigris opacis, hilo transverso ventrali; embryone exalbuminoso suberecto clavato; cotyledonibus brevissimis. (Tab. XXXI, Tab. XXXII, fig. 1–5.)

Stony soil on the summit of hills, from the Pecos to El Paso, and north to Doña Ana, *Wislizenus, Wright, Bigelow, Parry*: fl. April and May, and "continuing to put out its beautiful flowers till July."—Easily distinguished by the broad obtuse ribs. The numerous specimens examined by me are all depressed, 1½–4 inches high and 2½–6 inches in diameter; but old specimens are said to be sometimes 6–8 inches high, oblong, and even cylindric; ribs in very young specimens 5, in all the flowering plants which I have seen, 8, and "sometimes 10"; in young plants the ribs are scarcely interrupted, but in older ones they are divided by more or less shallow grooves into very broad tubercles; areolæ 6–10 lines apart, covered with long wool when young; spines mostly 6–8, rarely 9, ¾–1½ inch (and usually 1 inch) long, nearly equal in length, very variable in shape and thickness, sometimes long and slender and almost terete;

in other specimens short, stout, and broad; flower $2\frac{1}{2}$ inches long, of the same diameter, open only in bright sunshine, light purple or pink; tube lighter colored; ovary very short (3 lines), globose, tips of sepals dark purple, protruding from the dense white wool which envelops the whole flower; stamens of a flower counted by Mr. Wright, 1266; berry juicy, but drying up very soon, and finally breaking off transversely, leaving the base with most of the seeds hidden in the thick wool. The seeds, even when fully ripe, look shrivelled, and are 1.2–1.5 line long; the large circular (or rather truncate and transverse) hilum is deeply immersed; embryo almost without albumen, and quite straight, with thick, very short, erect cotyledons, and a taper-pointed radicle.—Our plant seems to be a variety of *E. horizonthalonius*, which is described as having 7 straight radial spines, the lowest one a little longer than the others, and the flower pale rose-colored, with lanceolate-acuminate petals. Prince Salm's var. *β. curvispinus* seems still nearer to our plant, which has a decidedly central but no lower radial spine, just like the last and the next species; the space for the lower radial spine is covered and filled by the strongly deflexed central spine.

15. E. Texensis, Hoepf. Not observed farther west than the San Pedro and Pecos rivers. Fruit red and juicy, drying up very soon; seeds 1.2–1.4 line long, somewhat reniform, with a deep indentation including the circular hilum; testa smooth and shining, rarely (in Berlander's specimens from Matamoras, named by him *Melocactus laciniatus*,) indistinctly tuberculated; embryo curved or hooked, with the foliaceous cotyledons buried in the large albumen. (Tab. XXXIII.)

16. E. bicolor, Galeotti, var. Schottii: simplex, ovatus vel ovato-cylindricus; costis 8 obtusis tuberculatis interruptis; areolis orbiculatis; aculeis radialibus 15–17 rectis, inferioribus brevioribus teretiusculis basi bulbosis rubellis variegatis, summis 2–4 longioribus latioribus compressis albidis; aculeis centralibus 4 albidis, summo latiore longiore supra plano infra carinato recto seu paullo sursum curvato, cæteris compressis seu subteretibus brevioribus rectis; floribus magnis in vertice tomentoso subcentralibus; ovario squamis sepaloideis 10–12 reniformibus margine ciliatis imbricato, sepalis tubi 40 sensim majoribus obtusis margine pallidiore ciliatis, summis oblongis; petalis purpureis; stigmatibus 8 suberectis.

On cretaceous hills, covered with chapparal, (thorny bushes,) near Mier, on the lower Rio Grande, *Schott*: in flower in September.—Stem 4–6 inches high, 2–3 in diameter; grooves rather shallow; floral areola close to the spiniferous one, without the intervening glands which are so conspicuous in *E. longehamatus* and others, and which I find also in the Mexican forms of *E. bicolor*. The 4 upper radial spines about an inch long and flat; all the others rounded, red, paler at both ends; the lowest is the weakest and shortest one, and often somewhat curved; upper central spine 15–20 lines long; the 3 others shorter; the lower one flat above, rounded below, often reddish like the lower radial spines; flower between 2 and 3 inches long; petals bright-purple or rose-purple, gradually paler in fading; filaments springing from the whole tube down to its base. The original Mexican *E. bicolor* is distinguished by the more globose form, also by the smaller number of radial spines, (10–11,) and by the upper central spine not being carinate nor longer than the others.

17. E. intertextus, (sp. nov.): minor, ovato-globosus; costis 13 acutis interruptis subobliquis; tuberculis supra breviter tomentoso-sulcatis; areolis ovatis (in planta juniore angustioribus) approximatis; aculeis brevibus rigidis e basi albida rubellis apice fuscatis, radialibus

16–25 arcte adpressis intertextis superioribus 5–9 setaceis albidis rectis, lateralibus rigidioribus paulo longioribus infimoque robusto brevi sæpe paullo recurvatis; aculeis centralibus 4, superioribus radiales excedentibus sursum versis, inferiore brevissimo porrecto robusto; floribus parvis in vertice dense lanato congestis purpurascentibus; ovario brevissimo 5–6-squamato; sepalis tubi 20 late ovatis cuspidatis albo-marginatis; petalis 20–25 oblongis mucronatis; stylo stamina numerosissima vix superante; stigmatibus 7–8 purpureis erectis; bacca globosa sicca squamis evanescentibus subnuda basi subpersistente circumscissa; seminibus reniformibus circa hilum magnum orbiculare ventrale curvatis tenuiter verruculosis lucidis; albumine parco; embryone curvato; cotyledonibus foliaceis brevibus. (Tab. XXXIV.)

Var. $\beta$. DASYACANTHUS: ovatus seu conoideus; aculeis gracilibus longioribus e purpurascente cæsiis, radialibus 19–25 setaceis pluriserialibus, superioribus 7–9 gracilioribus brevioribus albidis fasciculatis, centralibus 4 vix robustioribus, superioribus 3 sursum versis reliquos excedentibus, inferiore porrecto paullo breviore. (Tab. XXXV, fig. 1–5.)

On stony ridges from the Limpia to El Paso, *Wright*, *Bigelow*, and westward, *Parry;* also towards Chihuahua, *Wislizenus*; var. $\beta$. common about El Paso: fl. March and April.—Stems 1–4 inches high, and a little less in diameter; areolæ 3 or 4 lines apart; upper setaceous spines pale, 2½–6 lines long, lateral spines 4–7 lines, lowest only 2–4 lines long; upper central spires 5—7 and even 9 lines, lower one 1 or rarely 2 lines long; in young plants the 13–15 radiating spines are more equal in length, and several or all of the central spines are wanting. Flowers about an inch long and wide; sepals dark purple with paler margins; petals similar, outer ones deeper, inner ones gradually lighter colored; stamens more than 650, half as long as petals. Fruit about 4 lines in diameter, tipped by the withered flower, usually with a few dry scales, with or without some wool in their axils; the base usually persistent for some time, while the upper part comes off, separating more or less regularly. Seeds nearly or quite one line long, with a very large hilum.

Var. $\beta$. has the flowers and fruit of var. $\alpha$, but is a larger plant with much longer and slenderer spines, lower central spine almost as long as the others. Spines in var. $\alpha$. appressed so that the plant resembles somewhat, and has been confounded with, *Cereus viridiflorus*. In var. $\beta$. the spines are loosely patulous, forming a tuft on the top; the whole plant is very similar to *Mam. dasyacantha;* the entire similarity of flower and fruit, and the intermediate forms of the spines, leave no doubt of both plants belonging together, though their external appearance is so very dissimilar.

## III. CEREUS, Haw.

### Subgen. 1. ECHINOCEREUS, E.*

1. C. VIRIDIFLORUS, E. in Wisl. Rep. $\beta$. CYLINDRICUS: ovatus seu plerumque cylindricus, subsimplex; costis sub-13 acutis fere interruptis; areolis confertis ovatis seu ovato-lanceolatis,

* This subgenus, which was indicated by me in the Appendix to Wislizenus' Report as a genus distinct from *Cereus*, and which Prince Salm in the latest edition of his *Hortus Dyckensis* very properly reduced to a section of that genus, is well characterized by the peculiarities of the flower and fruit pointed out in the work above mentioned. The numerous species since discovered confirm this character. The seeds, especially, are distinct from those of any other *Cactaceæ* examined by me. They are rather small, never so much as one line (between 0.4 and 0.9 line) in length, obliquely obovate or subglobose, more or less compressed, and with a circular or oblong basilar or sub-basilar hilum; testa black, hard, and brittle, always tuberculated; its tubercles large or small, equal or unequal, distinct or more or less confluent, and then leaving irregular depressions, so that the seed appears pitted or pitted and tubercled together. Embryo with little or no albumen, almost straight, or very slightly curved; the short though distinct, and even somewhat foliaceous, transverse cotyledons more or less bent, inclined to form a hook.

junioribus albo-villosis mox denudatis*; aculeis 12–18 radialibus brevibus pectinatis rigidis, adjectis plerumque supra aculeis adventitiis 2–6 brevioribus setaceis, lateralibus longioribus, inferioribus purpureis demum fuscis, superioribus plerumque albidis, rarius omnibus purpureis; aculeis centralibus nullis seu rare singulo robusto recto vel subinde curvato apice seu toto purpureo-fusco, rarissime altero graciliore superiore adjecto; floribus versus apicem lateralibus e flavo virescentibus; ovario tuboque pulvillos 25–30 (aculeolis infra 8–12, supra 3–5 albidis seu rubellis munitos) gerentibus; sepalis interioribus lineari-oblongis 10–15 virescentibus fuscatis; petalis 12–15 lineari-oblongis acutiusculis; baccis ellipticis virescentibus; seminibus parvis obovato-subglobosis tuberculatis, hilo basilari suborbiculato. (Tab. XXXVI.)

On the Limpia, and thence towards El Paso, *Wright*: fl. in May.—This is a taller form than the original species described in Wislizenus' Report, from the northern parts of New Mexico, with stouter spines and acute petals. A handsome plant, not so much on account of the inconspicuous flowers, as from the beauty of the purple and white spines, which are particularly bright when first developed in spring, and look like flowers. Stems 3–6 and sometimes even 8 inches high, 1–2 inches in diameter; spines usually 3–5 or nearly 6 lines long; central spines, if present, 6–10 lines in length, more common on the smaller northern var. *a.*, rarely present in the southern form. In a single specimen collected by *Dr. Bigelow* on the upper Pecos, I find on some of the areolæ all or most of the spines purple, and the central spine sometimes curved upwards, sometimes white, with a purple tip, or purple to the base. Flower one inch or less below the top, 1–1¼ inch long, not quite as wide even when fully open; petals 2–3 lines wide. Fruit 5–6 lines long, crowned with the withered corolla, as in all *Echinocerei;* in some rather dry fruits the corolla is quite persistent; in the more juicy ones it, as well as the spines on the fruit, are deciduous when the fruit is quite ripe. Seed 0.5–0.6 line long, tuberculated, but the tubercles somewhat confluent, very slightly in the northern form, a little more in ours, so as to show pits between the warts; seed somewhat compressed, and keeled on the back.

2. C. CHLORANTHUS (sp. nov.): cylindricus, simplex seu e basi parce ramosus; costis 13–18 subinterruptis; areolis confertis orbiculato-ovatis; aculeis 12–20 laxius radiantibus setiformibus albis, lateralibus longioribus apice sæpe purpurascentibus, adjectis supra aculeolis 5–10 brevioribus setaceis; aculeis centralibus 3–5 quorum 2 superiores breviores plerumque purpurascentes sursum divergentes, 1-3 inferiores longiores divergentes deflexique albidi; floribus in caule medio vel inferiore lateralibus virescentibus extus rufis; ovario pulvillos sub-21 (aculeolis 14–18 setaceis munitos) gerente; sepalis tubi sub-18 lineari-lanceolatis, inferioribus aculeolos axillares 3–5 gerentibus; petalis 15–18 lineari-oblongis mucronatis; filamentis styloque sulphureis; stigmatibus 8–11 viridibus adpressis; bacca subglobosa aculeolata; seminibus parvulis tuberculato-scorbiculatis. (Tab. XXXVII—XXXVIII.)

Common on stony hills and mountain sides near El Paso, *Wright, Bigelow,* : fl. April.—Stems 3–9 or 10 inches high, 1½–2 inches in diameter; areolæ 3 or 4 lines apart, not so much elongated as in the last species, and often almost orbicular; radial spines slender, patulous, not strictly radiating, pectinate or adpressed to the plant; lower lateral ones the longest, as in all these *Pectinati*, 4–5 lines long, inferior ones shorter, upper ones shortest; no

* This *tomentum* or *villus* on the young or nascent areola is so universally present, always disappearing with age, that it ceases to be a character. The differences consist only in the greater density or looseness of this tomentum, and in its color, which is almost always white, but occasionally yellowish, gray, tawny, brown, or almost black. I shall only make mention of it where it varies from the ordinary form.

central spines are present in young plants, next 1–3 appear, and well developed flower-bearing plants have always 5; the upper darker and shorter ones are about 6 lines, the lower ones 9–12 or even 15 lines long; the lowest one is the longest and regularly deflexed, so that the plant seen from above shows as many rays, formed by these spines, as there are ribs. Spines mostly white, the lower lateral and central ones often tipped with purple, upper central ones entirely purple; a specimen has been sent with all the spines almost entirely white. Flowers yellowish-green, always low down on the plant, (usually below the middle, often in the lower third) forming a circle around the stem; flowers an inch long, funnel-shaped, not fully opening even in bright sunshine. Mr. Wright, to whose careful examinations and full notes I am indebted for many data, found the stamina about 400 in number, and half as long as the petals; stigmata green, much exsert. Fruit half an inch or less in thickness, crowned with the conic remains of the flower; seed 0.5 or 0.6 line in diameter, orbicular, compressed and carinate; tubercles confluent, so as to form pits; hilum linear-oblong or oval, basilar. Name from the color of the flowers.

3. C. DASYACANTHUS, E. in Wisl. Rep.: ovatus seu subcylindricus, simplex seu e basi parce ramosus, subcæspitosus; costis 15–21 rectis seu obliquis subinterruptis; areolis confertis ovatis; aculeis 20–30 rectis rigidis patulis stellatim undique porrectis intertextis cinereis apice sæpe rubellis vel adustis, in plantis debilioribus albidis, exterioribus 16–24 quorum laterales longiores, superiores breves graciles, inferiores intermedii, interioribus 3–8 robustioribus; floribus sub vertice ipso subterminalibus magnis flavis; ovarii pulvillis 35–45 villosis aculeolos 15–18 albidos seu apice rubellos gerentibus; sepalis tubi late campanulati inferioribus 20–30 aculeoliferis, superioribus 15–20 petaloideis oblanceolatis acutis seu cuspidatis; petalis 15–25 spathulato-oblanceolatis mucronatis seu interioribus plerumque obtusis muticis; staminibus numerosissimis; stylo exserto subclavato; stigmatibus 13–18 viridibus erectis; bacca magna subglobosa aculeolata; seminibus subglobosis tuberculatis. (Tab. XXXIX, XL, et XLI, fig. 1.)

About El Paso, and down to the cañon of the Rio Grande; common on rocky hills and the edge of gravelly table-lands, where *Dr. Wislizenus* first found it in 1846, and where the gentlemen connected with the Boundary Commission have since abundantly collected it in flower and fruit, and in numerous living specimens.—The geographical range of this species seems quite limited, as it has not been sent from any other locality but the one indicated. Fl. in April and May; fr. ripe in June.—Stems 5–12 inches high, 2 or 3 or even 4 inches in diameter, densely covered by the innumerable ashy-grey or reddish spines; lower lateral spines somewhat bulbous and compressed at base, 6–7 lines long, upper ones 3–4 lines, and lower ones about 5 lines long; upper central spines shorter than the lower ones, these are the stoutest and of about the length of the lower external spines, or a little longer. Flowers large and numerous, from the upper axillæ of the past year's growth, before the growth of the same spring is much advanced, so that they appear terminal or central at first glance, as they cover the top of the plant; this is the case with many spring-flowering *Echinocerei;* others, (e. g. the last mentioned species,) produce their flowers lower down on the plant from older axillæ. Flower 3 inches or more in length, and of the same diameter, very showy, externally greenish yellow, with the centre of sepals red; petals bright yellow; stamens counted by *Mr. Wright*, over 1700, with yellowish green filaments; pistil stout; stigmata thick, erect. Flower (like those of most *Echinocerei*) open in bright sunshine only, about the middle of the day, closing in the afternoon, but reopening the next, or even the third day, unless the weather be very hot, when all the functions of the flower are performed in one day. Fruit subglobose, 1–1½ inch in diameter, green or greenish purple, when fully ripe "delicious to eat, much like a gooseberry." Seeds 0.6 line long, subglobose, very little oblique, with an oblong basilar hilum, strongly and distinctly tuberculated, like those of *C. cæspitosus;* embryo almost straight, or rather the cotyledons slightly bent forward.

4. C. CTENOIDES (sp. nov.): subsimplex, ovatus; costis 15–16 obliquis subinterruptis; areolis lanceolatis confertis; aculeis rigidis albidis demum cinereis intertextis, radialibus 14–22 pectinatis basi bulbosa lateraliter compressis arcte adpressis sæpe subrecurvis, lateralibus longioribus, summis brevissimis, centralibus 2–3 raro 4 uniseriatis abbreviatis robustis basi bulbosis; floribus versus apicem lateralibus campanulatis flavis; ovarii ovati pulvillis sub-40 aculeolos 12–16 breves setaceos albidos seu apice fuscatos gerentibus; tubi campanulati sepalis inferioribus 30 squamiformibus ad axillas setis 3–10 munitis, sepalis interioribus 12–15 lanceolatis acutis intimis obtusis, omnibus mucronatis; petalis 25–30 spathulatis obtusis retusis vel obcordatis denticulatis flavis basi angustata virescentibus; filamentis numerosissimis virescentibus brevibus; stylo albido; stigmatibus 10–12 obtusis erecto-patulis viridibus. (Tab. XLII.)

From Eagle Pass to Santa Rosa, *Bigelow*; on the Pecos, *Wright*; fl. June and July (in St. Louis).—Stems 2–4 inches high, 1½–2½ inches in diameter; aspect of plant very similar to *C. pectinatus*, to which I allude by the Greek name, of the same meaning. Areolæ about one line long, also about one line apart; spines whitish or ashy, and in some specimens with light brown tips; sometimes I find only 14–16 radial spines, (1 upper, 1 lower, and 6–7 pairs of lateral ones); the older and larger ones have 7–9 pairs of lateral spines, 1 lower one, and often 3–5 small bristly upper spines. Upper spines ½–1 line, lower one 1—2 lines, and the others 3–4 lines long. Central spines in a single longitudinal series one above the other, 1–3 lines long. Flower bright yellow, with a light green centre and dark green stigmata, open from 8 or 9 till one o'clock, 2½–3¼ inches long, 2½–3½ inches in diameter, the broad and obtuse petals forming an even uninterrupted margin all around. Ovary with 38–44 pulvilli, scales obsolete, wool short, bristles about 15 in each bunch, 2–3 lines long. Pulvilli of tube 25–35, with green fleshy sepals, the lower ones with 8–10 short, and the upper ones with 3–4 longer (5–6 lines long) bristles; petals 1½–1¾ inch long, ½ inch wide, lower part of the tube narrow, and for about 1½ line naked inside; filaments very numerous and very slender; anthers small pale yellow; stigmata rather slender, 3 lines long. Our plant looks distinct enough from *C. dasyacanthus*, which is taller, has a larger number of ribs, rounder and shorter areolæ, patulous and usually more numerous spines, and more and longer central ones, also flowers almost vertical, with stouter spines on their tube; but it may, after all, be only a form of it, just as *Echinocactus intertextus* and *E. dasyacanthus* belong together, and as *C. viridiflorus* and *C. chloranthus* may be joined; intermediate forms, however, have not yet been observed. It has already been stated that the flowerless plant so closely resembles *C. pectinatus* that it can hardly be distinguished from it except by the fewer ribs; the color of the flowers, to be sure, is very different, but, though no instance is yet known among *Cerei* where yellow and purple flowers are found in the same species, this may not be impossible, and we may possibly have to unite all these forms.

5. C. PECTINATUS, E., var.? RIGIDISSIMUS: ovato-cylindricus; costis 20–22 interruptis; areolis lineari-lanceolatis confertissimis, junioribus parce lanosis; aculeis omnibus radiantibus arcte adpressis subrecurvis e basi bulbosa subulatis acutissimis rigidissimis albidis flavidis rubellisve subpellucidis, lateralibus 12–16 longioribus robustioribus, infimo singulo vix breviore,

superioribus 3–6 setaceis brevibus fasciculatis; floribus sub vertice lateralibus; ovarii pulvillis 50–60 aculeolos 8–12 rigidos gerentibus; sepalis tubi 40 inferioribus subulatis ad axillam aculeiferis, superioribus 20 lanceolatis acuminatis; petalis sub-20 spathulatis acutiusculis incisota-dentatis purpureis; stigmatibus sub-12; bacca ovato-globosa aculeolata; seminibus tuberculatis.

In the Sierras of Pimeria Alta in Sonora, and farther west, *A. Schott*: fl. June and July.—Stems 4–8 inches high, 2 inches in diameter; areolæ 2–2½ lines long in the larger full-grown specimens, 3 or 4 within one inch of the rib; in a small specimen, with only 15 ribs, smaller areolæ and smaller and more numerous spines (30–35, only 1–1½ line long); 12 or more bunches of spines are crowded within the same space. Spines all radiating and interlocking, extremely rigid and acute, variegated, the latest ones of each season being rose-colored, and the earliest ones a pale yellowish, thus forming variegated rings around the stem. Lateral spines 3–4½ lines long, lower one 2 lines long, upper ones still shorter. Flowers near the depressed vertex, just on the outer edge of the rounded top, 2½–3 inches long, bright pink, or purple. Fruit subglobose, nearly an inch long, pulpy and edible; the fleshy part of the stem is also eaten by the inhabitants, who call this plant "Cabeza del Viejo." Seed (not quite ripe) 6 lines long, strongly tuberculated, closely resembling that of *C. cæspitosus*. I can distinguish this plant from *C. pectinatus* only by the greater rigidity and thickness of the radial, and the entire absence of the central spines. The forms allied to *C. pectinatus* are very difficult to distinguish, and it is quite probable that they may run into one another, as Dr. Poselger, who has seen thousands of them in Texas and Northern Mexico, is inclined to think. I find that *C. pectinatus* has always a distinct single inferior spine, which is only a little shorter than the lower lateral spines; while *C. cæspitosus* has generally several of the lowest spines much shorter and weaker than the lateral ones. *C. adustus*, the flower of which is not yet known, has fewer ribs, oval areolæ, and the lowest spine much as in *C. pectinatus*.

6. C. CÆSPITOSUS, E. in Pl. Lindh., which extends from the Arkansas river to Saltillo, has been found by *Mr. Wright* as far west as the Nueces and the San Pedro. The loose darkish wool and slender bristles on the extremely numerous (80–100) pulvilli of the flower-tube, and especially the position of these pulvilli,—not in the axil, but considerably above it on the sepal, just below its foliaceous tip,—distinguish this species from the nearly allied *C. pectinatus*, as well as from all other *Echinocerei* known to me. This structure of the sepals seems to imitate and explain the morphology of the tubercles in *Mamillaria*, demonstrating them not to be a branch or an axis, but the fleshy petiole of an abortive or depauperate leaf, which sometimes is indicated by an indistinct scale above the fasciculus of spines, or by the point of the tubercle of an *Anhalonium*. This species has 12–18 ribs, 20–30 radial spines, rarely with 1 or 2 central ones here and there; flower 2–3 inches in diameter; petals sometimes, though rarely, curly, as in our figure, mostly plain; stigmata 12–18; fruit 9–10 lines long, oval, generally bursting irregularly; seed 0.6–0.7 line long, obovate, oblique, sometimes almost globose, very strongly tuberculated, with an oval hilum. The name *C. cæspitosus*, which would apply much better to a number of other species of this section, was given before any of these were known; it not inaptly represents a common state of the plant when it makes 5–12 heads, but not rarely it is almost or quite simple. (Tab. XXXIII—XXXIV.)

7. C. LONGISETUS, (sp. nov.): subsimplex, ovato-cylindricus; costis 11–14 interruptis tuberculatis; areolis orbiculatis; aculeis setaceis flexilibus albis patulis radialibus 18–20 rectis basi

bulbosa compressis, superioribus tenuioribus brevioribus, inferioribus longioribus, centralibus 5–7 bulbosis, quorum superiores radialibus vix longiores, 1–3 inferiores elongati divaricati deflexi sæpe flexuosi. (Tab. XLV.)

Mountains about Santa Rosa, in Coahuila, *Bigelow.*—Stems simple, or somewhat branching at base, 2–3 inches in diameter, 6–9 inches high; ribs fewer, more distinctly tuberculated, and less compressed than in most other species, and easily distinguished thereby. and by the orbicular areolæ, from the otherwise similar-looking, pale-spined forms of *C. chloranthus.* Upper radial spines 2½–3 lines, lowest and lateral ones 6–7 lines long ; upper central spines hardly longer than these ; lower central ones always 3 in well-developed plants, 1½–2 or even 2¼ inches long. Flower and fruit of this peculiar and pretty plant as yet unknown ; the former said to be red. Name from the length and slenderness of the spines.

8. C. Rœtteri, (sp. nov.): ovato-cylindricus ; costis 10–13 interruptis ; areolis ovato-orbiculatis subconfertis ; aculeis e basi bulbosa subulatis rubellis apice obscuris demum cinereis, exterioribus 8–15 additis sæpe supra aculeis centralibus, lateralibus longioribus, infimo singulo breviore ; aculeis centralibus 2–5 robustioribus plerumque sub-brevioribus ; floribus sub vertice lateralibus magnis purpureis ; ovarii pulvillis 20–24 aculeolos 10–15 albidos fuscatosve gerentibus ; sepalis tubi inferioribus aculeoligeris sub–15 triangulari-lanceolatis, superioribus 8–10 oblanceolatis spathulatis ; petalis 8–12 spathulatis ; tubo intus basi nudo ; stigmatibus 10–12 viridibus suberectis stamina numerosissima brevia longe superantibus ; bacca subglobosa ; seminibus oblique obovatis compressis inæqualiter tuberculatis subscrobiculatisque, hilo basilari parvo oblongo. (Tab. XLI, fig.3–5.)

Sand-hills south of El Paso, *Bigelow ;* near El Paso or Frontera, *Wright :* fl. April.—A single living specimen, preserved in the Congressional Garden in Washington, is 5 inches high and 2½ in diameter, and has 12 ribs ; areolæ in this and the dried specimens are 4–6 lines apart ; lower lateral spines 5–7 or 8 lines long, lowest one a little shorter, upper ones 2–3 lines in length ; central spines usually only 4–6 lines long, rarely one or the other longer ; always stouter than the others, and with very thick and bulbous bases. Flowers 2½–3 inches long, purple, very similar to the flower of *C. Fendleri* or *C. enneacanthus ;* fruit 8–10 lines long, and rather less in diameter ; seeds 0.7 line long, strongly but irregularly tuberculated ; tubercles here and there somewhat confluent. In the arrangement of its spines this species considerably resembles *C. dasyacanthus,* and I have formerly taken it for a smaller variety of that species ; but it differs from it by the smaller number of ribs, the fewer and stouter spines, which place it almost intermediate between the *Pectinati* and the *Decalophi,* the red flower, the small fruit, and the larger and irregularly tuberculated seed. I take great pleasure to acknowledge my indebtedness to the modest and faithful artist, *Mr. Paulus Rœtter,* who has adorned this memoir by his skillful pencil, by naming this species after him.

9. C. Fendleri, E. in Pl. Fendl.: simplex, seu parce e basi ramosus, ovatus seu ovato-cylindricus, perviridis; costis 9–12 rectis seu obliquis tuberculato-interruptis ; areolis orbiculatis, junioribus dense tomentosis subconfertis; aculeis basi bulbosis, radialibus 7–10 rectis seu sæpe curvatis, inferioribus robustioribus, infimo 4-angulato albido, sequentibus 2 obscuris, cæteris albidis seu sæpius fusco-variegatis, superioribus tenuioribus pallidis, summo deficiente seu robusto elongato curvato; aculeo centrali valde bulboso teretiusculo elongato fusco-atro sursum curvato rarissime deficiente; floribus magnis purpureis subverticalibus; ovarii tubique pulvillis 25–35 aculeolos 3–12 albos sæpe adustos gerentibus; sepalis interioribus 12–15 lineari-

lanceolatis seu spathulatis acutis seu cuspidatis; petalis 16–24 oblongo-linearibus seu obovato-spathulatis acutis seu obtusis mucronatis sæpe eroso-denticulatis; stigmatibus 12–16 stamina numerosissima vix superantibus erectis; bacca ovato-globosa ex viridi purpurascente pulvillis aculeolatis 18–20 stipata; seminibus oblique obovatis curvatis paullo compressis scrobiculatis (tuberculis irregulariter confluentibus,) hilo ovato seu subcirculari basilari; embryone paullo curvato.

In various situations, among rocks or in alluvial river-bottoms from Santa Fé, *Fendler;* to the cañon of the Rio Grande below El Paso, *Wright*, *Bigelow;* and from the country fifty miles east of the Upper Pecos westward to Zuñi and the Aztec mountains, *Bigelow*, and to the Copper mines, *Thurber:* fl. May and June.—Stems single or few together, 3–8 inches high, 2–3 inches in diameter, not many together, and those usually of unequal height, not level-topped, like *C. phœniceus* and others; areolæ 4–7 lines apart; spines very variable, but always characterized by their bulbous base, by the lower ones being stouter and longer than the upper ones, partly white and dark, and by the long and dark central spine, which is always curved upwards. Radial spines mostly 7, a white and angular one below, 6–12 lines long; the two next ones hardly longer, more terete, black on the upper and usually white on the lower surface; then comes a pair of white or rarely variegated spines, scarcely shorter, above them two weaker, whiter, and shorter spines, 3–6 or 7 lines long. This is the usual form, especially in the north; often, however, two more upper spines are found, and sometimes a slender, or oftener a stout and dark-colored spine, not rarely 12–15 lines long, is placed on the upper edge of the areola, similar to, but always smaller than, the central spine. All these forms are occasionally seen on the same specimen. In some southern specimens I observe now and then a few small additional upper spines. The form which I have described in *Pl. Fendlerianæ* as *β. pauperculus*, and which *Dr. Bigelow* collected also on the Pecos, has mostly only six spines: five lower and lateral radial ones and the central one, which, more or less, assumes the place of the absent upper radial spine. This, however, is not a constant form, as transitions to the usual arrangement of spines are often seen on the same specimen. Central spine very much thickened at base, almost terete, black, often with a lighter tip, curved upwards, 1–2 inches long. Flower 2½–3½ inches long and wide, not fully open before noon, closing again after 2 o'clock; spines on the ovary 2½–4, on the upper part of the tube 4–8 lines long, distinctly bulbous at base, and often angular; petals 4–7 lines wide, acute or obtusish; stamina about 1600 in a specimen examined by *Mr. Wright*, only from the upper and wider part of the tube, the lower and narrow part 3–4 lines long, naked. Fruit 1–1¼ inches long, purplish-green, edible; seeds 0.7 line long, very oblique, irregularly pitted by the tubercles, as it were, running together in twisted lines.

10. C. ENNEACANTHUS, E. in Wisl. Rep.: ovato-cylindricus, obtusus, læte viridis, simplex seu plerumque dense cæspitosus; costis 7–10 obtusis infra dilatatis sursum compressis tuberculatis sulco transverso sæpe interruptis, sinubus profundis acutis; areolis orbiculatis remotis; aculeis rectis, radialibus 7–12 (plerumque 8) albis subpellucidis, inferioribus longioribus, centrali singulo (raro 2 superioribus tenuioribus additis) basi bulboso teretiusculo seu plerumque plus minus compresso triangulatoque albido stramineo seu obscuriore radialibus longiore; floribus subterminalibus seu lateralibus; ovarii pulvillis 25–35 in squamæ triangularis axillis villosis aculeolos 6–12 albidos seu fuscatos gerentibus; sepalis tubi inferioribus 18–20 cum aculeolis longioribus paucioribus, superioribus 10–18 oblanceolatis acutis; petalis 12–15 oblongo-obovatis erosis obtusis acutisve; stigmatibus 8–10 viridibus elongatis erectiusculis; bacca

subglobosa e purpureo virescente; seminibus minutis obovatis subobliquis tuberculatis, hilo oblongo. (Tab. XLVIII, fig. 2–4, and tab. XLIX.)

Along the Rio Grande, from El Paso, *Wright*, *Parry*, to Eagle Pass, *Schott*, *Bigelow*, and into Mexico, *Wislizenus:* fl. April and May. A widespread species, assuming many forms, sometimes approaching the next. Stems generally branching and cæspitose, 3–6 inches high, 1½–2 or 2½ inches in diameter, fresh green, in winter often reddish; even when in full growth appearing flaccid or shrivelled. Areolæ 6–10 lines apart; spines remarkably transparent, much smaller on the lower part of the plant than on the upper one, all bulbose at base, especially the central ones. Upper radial spines 3–5 lines, lateral ones 5–12 lines, lower ones 8–16 lines long, all usually less than one inch. In some specimens the radial spines are almost equal in length; in others they differ very much. Central spine extremely variable in color, size and shape; when young usually yellowish or brownish, at last ash-colored; in younger plants terete; in perfectly developed ones triangular and flattened, 8 or 10 to 15 or 20 lines long; sometimes we find one or two additional shorter and angular central spines above the principal one, diverging upwards. Flowers 2–3 inches long, and of the same and even greater width when fully open; the smallest were obtained at Eagle Pass, bright purplish-red; these have more numerous as well as slenderer and shorter spines on the ovary, and bloom earlier; the larger flowers come from El Paso and Chihuahua, from larger plants with longer spines. Berry 10 or 12 lines long, greenish or purplish, pleasant to eat; seed 0.5 line or less in the longest diameter, its tubercles very prominent and distinct.

11. C. STRAMINEUS, (sp. nov.): ovato-cylindricus, versus apicem attenuatus, læte viridis, cæspitosus densissimeque agglomeratus; costis 11–13 sursum compressis obtusis tuberculatis transverse sulcatis; areolis orbiculatis remotis; aculeis radialibus 7–10 (plerumque 8) rectis seu paullo curvatis basi bulbosis teretibus seu inferioribus subinde angulatis albis subpellucidis subæqualibus; aculeis centralibus subquaternis basi bulbosis angulatis elongatis radiales longe excedentibus sæpe flexuosis stramineis fuscatis, nascentibus sæpe roseis seu purpureis, superioribus sursum divergentibus, inferiore latiore porrecto seu paullo deflexo; floribus lateralibus grandibus; ovarii squamis 30–40 triangularibus et sepalis tubi late campanulati 20–30 inferioribus oblongis abrupte cuspidatis in axilla villosa aculeolos paucos flexuosos elongatos gerentibus; sepalis superioribus 10–15 oblongo-obovatis obtusis seu cuspidatis; petalis 15–18 late obovatis obtusis eroso-denticulatis; stigmatibus 10–13 elongatis erecto-patulis; bacca ovato-subglobosa magna purpurascente aculeolis elongatis numerosis deciduis armata; seminibus obovatis obliquis tuberculatis; hilo oblongo parvo; cotyledonibus subcurvatis. (Tab. XLVI—XLVII et tab. XLVIII, fig. 1.)

On high gravelly table-lands, and on the mountain-slopes about El Paso, extending east to the Pecos and west to the Gila, *Wright*, *Bigelow*, *Parry:* fl. June; fruit ripe in July and August.—A most remarkable plant, on account of the immense masses it forms, one plant often consisting of 100 or 200 heads in a regular hemispherical mass, which is covered and defended by the long, flexuous, straw-colored spines: those have suggested the specific name of the plant. Single heads 5–9 inches high and 2–3 inches in diameter, tapering towards the top, at base closely impacted together. Areolæ in vigorous plants ¾–1 inch apart, in older plants becoming more approximate. Radial spines ¾–1¼ inch long, on the lower part of the plant shorter. Central spines 2–3 or even 3½ inches long, straight or variously twisted, and the younger ones red or brown. Flower 3 or 4 inches in length, and spreading as wide or wider, appearing very full from the broad (8–12 lines) and numerous petals of a bright purple or deep pink color, inclining to crimson. Ovary with only few spines (2–4 lines long) on each pulvillus; the spines on the tube more numerous and about twice as long. These spines increase in number and length during the growth of the fruit, so that at maturity we find 8 or 10 in each fascicle, ½ to 1 inch in length. Fruit 1½–2 inches long, 1½ inch thick, readily shedding the spines, purple, of a delicious taste, intermediate between a strawberry and a gooseberry. The small seeds (0.5–0.7 line long) cannot be distinguished from those of the last species. The tubercles are large for the size of the seed and very distinct.

12. C. DUBIUS (sp. nov.): ovato-cylindricus, pallide viridis, cæspitosus; costis 7–9 obtusis tuberculatis; sinubus latis parum profundis; areolis orbiculatis remotis; aculeis albidis subpellucidis, radialibus 5–8 teretibus seu subangulatis, superioribus sæpe deficientibus, centralibus 1–4 bulbosis angulatis elongatis rectis seu incurvis; floribus lateralibus; ovarii pulvillis 20 in squamæ triangularis axilla parce villosa aculeolos paucos breves gerentibus; sepalis tubi inferioribus 16–20 ovato-lanceolatis cum aculeolis 1–3 longioribus; sepalis superioribus sub-10 oblongo-spathulatis obtusis; petalis sub-10 spathulatis obtusis pallide purpureis; stigmatibus 8–10; bacca subglobosa virescente-purpurea fasciculis aculeolorum 8–12 elongatorum deciduis armata; seminibus globoso-obovatis obliquis confluento-tuberculatis, hilo circulari. (Tab. L.)

Sandy bottoms of the Rio Grande, and from El Paso, *Wright*, *Bigelow*, to below Presidio, *Parry*, with *Algarobia*, *Fouquiera*, and *Larrea;* fl. June and July.—Stems 5–8 inches high, not so densely cæspitose as the last one, of a pale green color and soft flabby texture; ribs few, broad; grooves shallow; radial spines 6–12 or 15 lines long, lower ones longer than upper ones, or the upper spines very commonly entirely wanting, and replaced by the three upper central ones; central spines 1½–3 inches long, the lower one somewhat stouter and longer than the upper ones. Flower 2½ inches long, of the same diameter; petals fewer and narrower than in the last species, only 6 lines wide, paler, (rose-colored,) and mostly quite obtuse and almost entire. Ovary in this, as in the last species, remarkably small and undeveloped, while the flower is fully open; its spines few and short, growing afterwards in length and numbers more than is noticed in any other species. Ripe fruit 1–1½ inch long, with 20–24 pulvilli, on each of them 9–12 bristly spines, 4–9 lines long; fruit green or rarely purplish, insipid or pleasantly acid. Seed larger than in the two last species, 0.6–0.7 line long, subglobose-obovate, with a circular hilum; the tubercles not distinct as in the others, but confluent, and forming pits in the interstices.—These three species are very nearly allied, but are said to be easily distinguished in their wild state; the characters given above are said to be quite constant, and seem to establish them as good species.

13. C. ENGELMANNI, Parry in Sill. Journ. 1852: ovato-cylindricus, e basi parce ramosus; costis 11–13 interruptis; areolis orbiculatis subconfertis, junioribus villosis; aculeis radialibus 13 sub-angulatis albidis apice adustis rectis seu paullo curvatis, lateralibus 6 longioribus, inferioribus 3 vix brevioribus, superioribus sub-4 parvis; aculeis centralibus 4 angulatis gracilibus rectis multo longioribus, inferiore longiore albido porrecto seu deflexo, superioribus fulvis arrectis; floribus sub apice lateralibus; ovarii pulvillis sub 30 aculeolos rigidos 8–14 gerentibus; sepalis tubi inferioribus 15–20 ovato-lanceolatis ad axillam villosam aculeiferis; petalis purpureis; stigmatibus 12 erectis viridibus; bacca ovata; seminibus oblique obovatis tuberculato-foveolatis, hilo subbasilari oblongo. (Tab. LVII.)

Mountains about San Felipe, on the eastern declivity of the Californian Cordilleras, *Parry;* common in the Gila valley, especially near the Casa Blanca, above the Pimas village, *Schott*: fl. in June.—Loosely cæspitose, not more than 4 or 6 or at most 8 stems together; stems 5–10 or even 12 inches high, 2–3 inches in diameter; radial spines 3–6 lines long; central ones 1–2 inches long, upper one the shortest, lower one the longest. Flower rather low down on the plant, between 2 and 3 inches long; fruit at last naked, fleshy, 1½ inch long, an inch in diameter; seed 0.6–0.7 line long, similar to that of *C. Fendleri*, to tubercles running together, and forming irregular pits.

14. C. POLYACANTHUS, E. in Wisl. Rep.: ovato-cylindricus, plerumque ramosissimus, cæspitosus, glaucescens; costis 9–13 subcompressis obtusis interruptis; areolis suborbiculatis remotiusculis seu demum confertis; aculeis teretibus robustis rigidis rectis albidis seu e cinereo rubellis apice obscuris demum totis cinereis, exterioribus 8–12 parum bulbosis, lateralibus longioribus, centralibus 3–4 bulbosis paullo robustioribus æquilongis seu longioribus, junioribus sæpe corneo-fuscoque variegatis; floribus sub vertice lateralibus diu noctuque apertis; ovarii pulvillis 16–20 tomentosis aculeolos 6–15 variegatos gerentibus; sepalis tubi inferioribus 10–12 triangulari-lanceolatis aculeiferis, superioribus lineari-lanceolatis seu oblanceolatis spathulatisve mucronatis seu summis obtusis; petalis 18–22 spathulatis obtusis integris seu erosis chartaceis coccineis basi pallidioribus erecto-patulis; tubo intus basi nudo, staminibus brevibus; stylo exserto; stigmatibus sub-8 erectis; bacca subglobosa; seminibus majusculis irregulariter tuberculatis; hilo subbasilari parvo angusto; embryone parcissime albuminoso; cotyledonibus brevibus incurvis. (Tab. LIV–LV.)

A common plant at El Paso, *Wright, Bigelow, Parry, Thurber*, and as far south as the mountains west of Chihuahua, *Wislizenus*, on table-lands and mountains, and also on sand-ridges or stony hills: fl. March and April, fr. in June.—Heads 5–10 inches high, 2½–4 inches in diameter, pale green or glaucous; areolæ ½–1 inch apart; spines very variable; exterior ones not strictly radiating but spreading; upper ones about 6 lines; lateral and lower ones 9–12 lines long; central spines in young specimens single, in older and more perfect ones always 3–4; in some hardly longer than the radial ones, 9–12 lines long, but usually longer, and sometimes 2 or even 2½ inches long; lower central spine always longer than the others. Flowers 2–3 inches in length, spreading not quite so wide, remaining open day and night, often for 4 or 5 days, and profusely adorning the plant for 4 or 6 weeks in succession; petals rigid and somewhat concave, rounded, of a deep red or blood color; the base of the tube inside naked for 3 or 4 lines; stamens about 600; berry ¾–1¼ inch long, greenish-purple, of a pleasant gooseberry taste; seeds larger than in any other *Echinocereus* known to me, 0.8–0.9 line long, oblique; hilum small subbasilar; embryo with some albumen, (which is not common in this genus,) large, a little curved; cotyledons almost foliaceous, approaching the form observed in the cylindric *Cerei*.

15. C. PAUCISPINUS (sp. nov.): ovatus seu ovato-cylindricus, perviridis, simplex, seu parce ramosus, costis 5–7 interruptis; sulcis latis sursum acutis; areolis remotis; aculeis 3–6 seu rarius 7 robustis basi bulbosis rectis seu subrecurvis radiantibus, infimo pallidiore, cæteris rufis fuscisve, omnibus demum nigrescentibus, centrali nullo seu rarius singulo robusto subangulato atrofusco sursum verso seu porrecto; seminibus obovatis obliquis subconfluento-tuberculatis, hilo basilari elliptico. (Tab. LVI.)

From the San Pedro to the mouth of the Pecos, on rocks and gravelly limestone hills, *Wright, Bigelow*.—Stems 5–9 inches high, 2–4 inches in diameter, not cæspitose like the last species to which it seems to be allied, but either simple or with few branches from near the base; ribs few, grooves wide and shallow; areolæ 8–10 lines apart; spines few and dark colored, 9–15 lines long, upper one often shorter, and central spine when present 15–20 lines long; flower and fruit unknown; the seed sent by Mr. Wright is similar to that of *C. polyacanthus*, 0.7–0.8 line long, oblique, with slightly confluent irregular tubercles, and a large and wide hilum.—This species on the Pecos seems to take the place of the more western *C. polyacanthus*, which farther east is represented by *C. Rœmeri*, and farther west by *C. phœniceus*; from all these it is distinguished by the few ribs and the few dark spines.

16. C. Berlandieri (sp. nov.): humilis, perviridis; caule subtereti articulato-ramosissimo; tuberculis conicis distinctis 5–6-fariis; areolis parvis orbiculatis; aculeis tenuibus subsetaceis, 6–8 brevibus radiantibus albidis, 1 centrali plerumque multo longiore fuscato; floribus lateralibus magnis purpureis; ovarii puvillis sub-20 breviter albo-tomentosis aculeolos capillaceos basi bulbosos 8–10 longiores albidos et 1–2 robustiores fuscos gerentibus; sepalis tubi exterioribus 8–10 aculeoliferis, superioribus 13–16 oblongo-linearibus acuminatis seu cuspidatis; petalis 14–18 late linearibus seu lineari-oblanceolatis elongatis fere loricatis mucronatis apice denticulatis patulis demum reflexis; stigmatibus 7–10 viridibus; bacca ovata viridi subsicca; seminibus parvis obovato-subglobosis tuberculatis, hilo circulari.—(Tab. LVIII.)

On the Nueces, *Berlandier*. Frequently in cultivation under the wrong names of *C. repens* or *C. Deppii*, doubtless introduced from southern Texas: fl. May and June.—A spreading and procumbent plant, with erect branches contracted at base, and thereby articulated, 1½–6 inches long, ¾–1 inch thick, either terete with distinct spirally disposed tubercles, or the tubercles arranged in 5 or 6 ribs. Areolæ 4–6 lines apart; radial spines bristle-like, weaker than those of the next species, 4–5 lines long, sometimes a stouter and darker one at the upper end of the areola; central spine yellowish-brown, shorter on the lower part of each branch, longer towards the top, from 5–6 to 10–13 lines in length. Flower 3–4 inches long, or when fully open spreading almost 4 inches and only 2 inches in height; bristles of the tube below 2–3 lines, upwards 4–6 lines long, the tomentum white and short; petals long and narrow, 3–4 or rarely 5 lines wide, bright rose-purple; filaments short, pale rose-colored; stigmata long and suberect; berry about 9 lines long, densely covered with the elongated mottled hair-like spines; seeds 0.5 line long, strongly and distinctly tuberculated, contracted at base. Nearly allied to *C. pentalophus*, DC., which, however, is an erect plant.—Named for *Dr. J. L. Berlandier*, who made known this as well as many other plants of the lower Rio Grande.

17. C. procumbens, E. in Pl. Lindh. 1850: humilis, perviridis; caule subtereti seu 4–5 angulato articulato-ramosissimo; tuberculis distinctis spiralibus seu 4–5 fariis; areolis parvis orbiculatis; aculeis rigidis brevibus albidis apice fuscis, 4–6 radiantibus, centrali nullo seu singulo paullo longiore obscuriore; floribus sub apice ramorum lateralibus magnis; ovarii pulvillis sub 25 albido-villosis aculeolos rigidos 6–9 breves variegatos gerentibus; sepalis tubi exterioribus 12–15 aculeoliferis, superioribus sub-15 lineari-lanceolatis acuminatis; petalis 18–20 lineari-spathulatis acutis seu obtusis, integris seu plerumque eroso-dentatis patulis demum recurvis violaceis basi flavidis; stigmatibus 10–14 stamina flavicantia superantibus; bacca ovata viridi irregulariter dehiscente; seminibus parvulis lenticularibus basi hilo oblongo truncatis verruculosis. (Tab. LXIX, fig. 1-11.)

On the Rio Grande below Matamoras: fl. May and June.—Similar in habit to the last, but more slender; branches ½ to 3 or 4 inches in length, 6–8 lines in diameter; tubercles 4–5 lines apart, in 4 rows when the branches appear acutely quadrangular, or in 5 rows when they are more terete. Radial spines 1–2 lines long, central one on lower part of joint wanting, or hardly longer than the radial ones, on the upper part 2–4 lines long. Flower about 3 inches long and of same width; petals often reflexed, 4–6 lines wide. Fruit 6 or 8 lines long; seed between 0.4 and 0.5 line long, much compressed, with a narrow hilum; its tubercles very much smaller than in the last species. Our plant bears a close resemblance to the last mentioned one, but may always easily be distinguished by the characters enumerated.

18. C. TUBEROSUS, Poselger: e radice tuberosa tenuissimus, teres, lignosus, sursum sensim incrassatus, cylindricus, demum articulatus parceque ramosus, debilis, erectus seu geniculatus et reclinatus; costis 8 vix prominulis; areolis parvis confertis, junioribus parce sordide tomentosis; aculeis 9–12 radiantibus parvulis subulatis albidis rectis adpressis, inferioribus paullo longioribus, centrali singulo e basi crassa subulato longiore toto seu versus apicem fusco sursum arrecto; floris subterminalis (?) tubo brevi; pulvillis squamatis albo-lanatis aculeolatis; sepalis superioribus 8 lineari-lanceolatis; petalis 16 oblanceolatis acuminato-aristatis roseis patentibus; filamentis brevibus; stylo elongato; stigmatibus 8 viridibus; bacca subsicca villosa setosaque floris rudimentisque coronata; seminibus minutis oblique obovatis compressis tuberculato-rugosis scrobiculatis. (Tab. LXIX, fig. 12.)

On the Texan side of the Rio Grande, between Reynosa and Camargo, *Dr. Poselger;* on the Chacon hills, 3 miles below Laredo, and also near Mier, on arid rocky ridges, always among shrubs, "which support its weak and otherwise almost decumbent stem," *A. Schott.*—Tuberous root globular, ¾–1½ inch in diameter; stem 1–2 feet high; lower part ligneous, scarcely as thick as a quill; upper younger part and branches 4–8 lines in diameter; young branches few, clavate; ribs very little prominent; areolæ 1–2 lines apart; radial spines a line long or less; central spine 2–3 lines long, in weak specimens whitish, in robust ones the upper half or the entire spine brown or black, rigidly erect and appressed, generally reaching to the second areola above. The flower, which I have not myself seen, is described by Dr. Poselger in a letter as being terminal, "so that the ovary is a complete continuation of the stem." I suppose that it rises from the upper, but certainly not the recent areolæ; and that it cannot be truly terminal, i. e., a continuation of the axis, which would be in opposition to the character of the whole family. Schott also figures the plant as bearing fruit at the end of the branches. Flower over 2 inches long and of the same diameter, opening for several days, but only in bright noonday sunshine; ovary and tube covered with very woolly pulvilli in the axils of reddish scales, with 6 or 8 long white or black bristles; petals rose-colored or purple, about an inch long. Fruit covered with long wool and black and white bristles, resembling very much that of *C. cæspitosus.* Seed smaller than that of any other *Cereus* examined by me, only 0.4 line in the largest diameter, rugose from confluent tubercles which leave large pits between them. Albumen none; embryo almost straight, with distinct transverse cotyledons. Flower, fruit, and seed identify this species with the *Echinocerei,* thus furnishing another instance, if such were still needed, of the importance of the organs of fructification in the study and arrangement of the *Cactaceæ,* and of the fallacy of expecting the external shape of these plants to furnish characters for generic or subgeneric division. Without the knowledge of the flower and fruit, *C. tuberosus* would no doubt have been classed with the *Cerei articulati,* while in reality it is the slenderest *Echinocereus,* connected with the ordinary ovate or globose forms through *C. Berlandieri* and *C. procumbens.*

Subgen. 2. EUCEREUS.*

19. C. EMORYI, E. in Sill. Journ.: caule cylindrico 2–3-pedali prostrato; ramis adscendentibus seu erectis; costis 15 tuberculatis; sinubus acute incisis; areolis confertis orbiculatis, junioribus fusco-tomentosis; aculeis rectis rigidis gracilibus aciculatis e virescenti flavis numerosissimis intertextis, exterioribus 40–50 tenuissimis stellatim porrectis, centrali singulo robustiore multo longiore; floribus subterminalibus flavis; tubo breviusculo aculeolato; bacca globosa aculeatissima; seminibus magnis obovatis acute carinatis basi acutis lucidis minutissime sub lente tuberculatis, hilo ventrali angusto; cotyledonibus foliaceis hamatis incumbentibus. (Tab. LX, fig. 1–4.)

On dry hills and mountains, near the coast of California, about San Diego, growing in thick masses, and covering patches of 10 or 20 feet square, *Dr. Parry;* not north of the boundary line, *Dr. Le Conte.*—Prostrate stems 2–3 feet long; branches 6–9 inches high, 1½ inch in diameter; flowers abundant near the top of the branches, rather short, yellow, 2 or 2½ inches wide. Fruit 1½ inch in diameter, densely covered with numerous pulvilli, each bearing 20 or 25 stiff yellow spines, from 2 to 6 lines in length, 3 of them stouter and longer than the rest, often about an inch in length; some indistinct remains of the dead flower are hidden among the spines. Seed 1.2–1.4 line long, with a very prominent keel and linear hilum. The short aculeolate flower, persistent on the spinose fruit flower, would seem to refer our plant to *Echinocereus,* but the seed and embryo permit no doubt about its position. I have seen specimens of a fruit of a columnar *Cereus* from the Pacific coast near Mazatlan, sent by the late Dr. J. Gregg, which is a gigantic representative of our California fruit, and suggests the idea that on the western coast of our continent several species exist of a still unknown section of *Cereus.*—This plant, peculiar to the western termination of our boundary line, fitly bears the name of the energetic and distinguished commissioner under whose auspices the greater part of the interesting plants here described have been collected.

20. C. VARIABILIS, Pfeiff., a tall species, 3–10 feet high, is common to the east as well as west coast of tropical Ameriea, extending northward to the mouth of the Rio Grande, and up that stream towards Matamoras. Full-grown stems 3–4 angled, with few and stout spines; but young shoots with 8 ribs and numerous slender spines; flowers white, nocturnal; fruit oval, about 3 inches long, spinose, crimson externally and internally; seeds obliquely obovate, compressed, smooth, and shining, 1.5–1.7 line long; hilum subventral, narrowly oblong, linear, albumen almost none; embryo much curved; cotyledons large, foliaceous, incumbent. (Tab. LX, fig. 5–6.)

21. C. GREGGII, E. in Wisl. Rep.: e radice crassa napiformi erectus, gracilis, 2–3-pedalis; ramis paucis erectis 3–6-angulatis atro-virentibus sæpe rufescentibus; costis acutis; sulcis latis planiusculis; areolis oblongo-linearibus confertis seu subconfertis, junioribus lana e cinereo

* This section is proposed here only as a receptacle for our few *Cerei* not included in the other subgenera. It is not impossible that the greater part of the species of this genus will have to be referred here, but it is more probable that a careful examination of the flower and fruit of the numerous southern *Cerei* will necessitate the formation of several other subgenera. Not being familiar with the great majority of the species, I refrain from characterizing *Eucereus.* I will only state that the few species referred here have an elongated stem; spines on the flower-bearing and sterile part of the plant not different; tube of the flower elongated and beset with hairy or spiny pulvilli; stigmata whitish; berries usually with deciduous (or persistent?) spines; dry remains of the flower usually at length deciduous; seeds mostly smooth and shining, and the embryo hooked, with curved foliaceous cotyledons.

nigricante demum decidua vestitis; aculeis e basi bulbosa crassa abrupte subulatis acutissimis brevissimis nigricantibus, vetustis cinereis, radialibus 6–9 subrecurvis, infimis 3 tenuioribus longioribus, centralibus binis superimpositis brevibus, rarius singulo; floribus lateralibus albidis seu ochroleucis (nocturnis?); ovarii ovati pulvillis orbiculatis obscuro-villosis vix aculeolatis; tubi elongati sepalis 40–60 squamiformibus linæri-lanceolatis acuminatis, inferioribus aculeolos paucos breves, superioribus plures capillares gerentibus; sepalis interioribus 15–20 et petalis totidem lanceolatis acuminatis; stylo stamina æquante; stigmatibus sub-10 erecto-patulis albidis; bacca ovata basi contracta apice rostrata floris rudimentis siccis recurvis demum deciduis coronata pulvillis aculeoligeris mox nudatis munita coccinea pulposa; seminibus magnis oblique obovatis rugosis tenuissime tuberculatis; hilo subbasilari circulari; albumine parcissimo; embryone cotyledonibus foliaceis incumbentibus hamato.

Var. *α*. CISMONTANUS: areolis elongatis; floris tubo minus gracili aculeolis brevioribus munito; petalis latioribus. (Tab. LXIII, LXIV.)

Var. *β*. TRANSMONTANUS: areolis ovato-orbiculatis; floris tubo graciliori aculeolis longioribus tenuiter capillaceis flexuosis munito; petalis lineari-lanceolatis longe acuminatis. (Tab. LXV.)

From the San Pedro in western Texas, *Parry*, *Wright*, *Bigelow;* to the Gila, *Emory;* and Sonora, *Thurber*, *Schott;* and from the Rio Grande, south to Chihuahua, *Gregg*, *Wislizenus*, in gravelly or hard clayey soil, nowhere a common plant: fl. May and June.—Root a large fleshy, dirty-yellowish tuber, often 4–6 inches in diameter and 6–10 inches long, generally producing but one stem 2–3 feet high, with erect branches; stem thin at base, rather terete and ligneous, upwards 9–12 lines in diameter, usually 4–5, angled. The acute ribs at first sight seem crenulated, the pulvinate areolæ being separated by a slight depression, and the spines being scarcely visible without a close examination. Areolæ 1–1½ line long, in younger shoots 5–6 within one inch of the rib, in older plants about 3 areolæ in the same space. Spines remarkably short and sharp from a disproportionately thick base, only ½–1 line long; the 3 lowest spines are the longest, and run into a fine bristle-like point, often somewhat curved and not rarely crossing each other; above them 2 or usually 3 pairs of lateral spines, points of the lower ones diverging downward, and of the upper ones rather upward; central spines mostly 2, very short and thick, the lower one turned downward, the upper one upward. The spines seem to grow in size for several years, as on the older part of the stem they are twice as thick, though not any longer than the younger ones; they also become irregular, some of the smaller apparently dropping out, while the larger ones crowd into the vacant space, (see figure.) The flowers have been seen by only *Dr. Gregg* and *Mr. Thurber;* they seem to be nocturnal, as the latter gentleman collected them in the early morning hours, commencing to fade. Ovary 9–12 lines long, whole flower 6–8 inches long, about 2½ inches in diameter; bristles at base of tube 1–2 lines, or upwards 4–6 lines, and in var. *β*. 6–10 lines long; style not reaching above the large anthers; stigmata about 10, suberect. Berry ovate, 1¼–1½ inch long, an inch in diameter, slightly contracted at base, but not stiped nor even clavate, as I formerly was induced to believe, somewhat rostrate at the upper end, bright scarlet, fleshy, and edible. Seeds 1.2–1.5 line long, 1 line thick, with a large hilum; the warts of the testa are flat and very minute, but the large wrinkles are very distinct to the naked eye. The young seedling has quite short cotyledons, which finally form a thickened ring around the base of the young stem; this stem is always triangular, of a reddish-brown color, the edges showing an almost continuous line of the characteristic small and sharp spines; the root very soon swells, as our figure shows, and assumes the shape of a small carrot, almost as large as the stem itself; in old specimens the root is very much larger than the whole stem and branches together.

Subgen. 3. LEPIDOCEREUS.*

22. C. GIGANTEUS, E. in Emory's Rep. 1848: erectus, elatus, cylindricus, versus basin apicemque sensim attenuatus, simplex seu parce ramosus, candelabriformis; ramis paucis erectis caule brevioribus; vertice applanato tomentoso; costis infra sub-13 sursum 18–21 rectis, vetustis (versus caulis basin) obtusis obtusissimisque, sursum e basi lata acutatis acie obtusatis subrepandis; sinubus ad basin caulis latissimis versus apicem profundis acutis angustioribus angustissimisque; areolis prominentibus ovato-orbiculatis, junioribus albido-tomentosis; aculeis rectis basi valde bulbosis tenuiter sulcatis et subangulatis albidis seu stramineis demum cinereis; radialibus 12–16, imo summisque brevioribus, lateralibus (præcipue inferioribus) longioribus robustioribus, subinde aculeis adventitiis paucis setaceis summo areolæ margini adjectis; aculeis centralibus 6 robustis albidis basi nigris apice rubellis demum totis cinereis, 4 inferioribus cruciatis quorum infimus longissimus validissimus deflexus, 2 superioribus brevioribus lateralibus sursum divergentibus; floribus versus apicem caulis ramorumque aggregatis; ovarii ovati sepalis 30–40 squamiformibus triangulatis acutis ad axillam albido, seu fulvo-villosam aculeolum unum alterumve nigricantem deciduum gerentibus; sepalis tubi ampliati breviusculi 30–40 orbiculato-subdeltoideis mucronatis, inferioribus in axilla lanigeris, superioribus nudis; sepalis intimis 10–15 spathulatis obtusis carnosis (pallide viridibus albescentibus); petalis sub-25 obovato-spathulatis obtusis integris crispatis coriaceo-carnosis crassis (ochroleucis seu albidis); staminibus numerosissimis superiori tubi parti adnatis, inferiore nudo; stylo stamina paullo superante; stigmatibus 14–18 filiformibus fasciculatis; bacca obovata seu sæpe pyriformi squamis triangulatis carnosis parvis ad axillam lanatis munita, floris rudimentis deciduis; pericarpio duriusculo coriaceo demum valvis 3–4 irregularibus patulis reflexisve dehiscente; seminibus numerosissimis in pulpa saccharina coccinea nidulantibus oblique obovatis lævibus lucidis exalbuminosis; hilo oblongo basilari; cotyledonibus foliaceis incumbentibus hamatis. (Tab. LXI, LXII, et tab. front.)

In rocky valleys and on mountain sides, often in mere crevices of rocks, from the valley of Williams' river, lat. 35°, *Bigelow*, to Sonora, lat. 30°, *Thurber*, *Schott;* and from the middle Gila, *Emory*, down to near its mouth, *Parry*. I cannot find that it has been collected west of the Colorado, though it is probably also an inhabitant of the Californian peninsula: fl. May to July; fruit ripe in July and August. The *Suwarrow* or *Saguaro* of the natives.—Young plants, as *Dr. Bigelow* observed, are almost always found under the protecting shade of some shrub, especially of Frémont's "green-barked Acacia" (*Cercidium Floridanum*) so characteristic of the barren wilderness; and not rarely the dead stems of this plant are found near the older *Cerei.* Young plants retain their globose shape for several years; a specimen in my possession, 5 or 6 inches high, is supposed to be between 8 and 10 years old. It flowers at the height of 10 or 12 feet, but grows up to 4 or 5 times that height; stems have been measured 46 feet high, and higher ones are stated to occur, so that the first statement of *Col. Emory* is not at all improbable, viz: that this plant sometimes has been found 50–60 feet high. The stem is thickest in or a little above the

* This subgenus is proposed for the two tall western species with uniform spines, short flowers, ovary and tube with numerous scale-like imbricated sepals, fleshy petals, pale stigmata, smooth seeds, and hooked embryo. Probably *C. Chilensis*, and perhaps other species from the Pacific slope of the continent, will find their place here. A drawing of *C. Chilensis*, among the papers of the United States Exploring Expedition, represents a flower almost identical with that of *C. Thurberi*.

middle, and tapers upwards and downwards; one was found by *Dr. Bigelow* to be at one foot above the ground 13 inches, and 10 feet higher more than 23 inches, in diameter. The fleshy part of the plant is, as he notes, bitter, and not acidulous, as in most species of Cacti. The ligneous skeleton consists of thick (1–2 inches thick) and somewhat terete perpendicular bundles of fibres, corresponding in number and position to the grooves of the stem; in younger plants and on the upper part of the older ones these sticks are distinct, and sway in the wind like so many reeds, but at the lower part of the older stems they are reticulately connected with one another by ligneous tissue, the open meshes corresponding (just as in the cylindric *Opuntiæ*) with the bunches of spines or tubercles; in the oldest stems the inner cavity becomes nearly filled by the same tissue. Stems mostly simple; older ones often with a few erect branches; they are rarely much branched, but specimens have been observed where 5–9 branches sprang from the same part of the main stem; the primary branches very rarely produce secondary ones. The branches usually drop off from the skeleton of the dead stems; but in very old specimens they remain, and present a view like the one in our landscape plate opposite the title-page, which is taken from an accurate sketch made on the spot by *Mr. Mœllhausen.*—Ribs at the base of the stem few (12–15), broad, obtuse, often almost obliterated, and generally without spines; higher up the number of ribs increases to about 18–21; they are triangular with an obtusish edge, separated by deep triangular acute grooves; towards the top of the plant the young ribs are narrowly compressed, with obtusish edges and narrow grooves between them. The somewhat pulvinate areolæ are 7 lines long, nearly 6 lines in diameter, about an inch distant from one another, sometimes more closely approximate; at first they are covered with a thick yellowish or tawny tomentum. Lower and upper radial spines 6–12 lines long, sometimes a few additional shorter flexuous setaceous spines are placed above; lateral ones 12–18 lines long, the lower ones longest; the 4 lower central spines straight, or very slightly curved downwards 20–30 lines, the 2 upper central spines 15–18 lines long, diverging upwards. The stoutest spines are one line in diameter, their bulbous base fully twice as thick. In old age, and towards the base of the stem the 6 central spines fall off first, leaving the radiating ones appressed to the stem; finally these also come off, together with the whole areola. The flowers are produced in abundance near the summit of the stems and branches; the fruit is usually found 6–12 inches from the centre of the top. Specimens of flowers have been sent by *Mr. Thurber* and by *Mr. Schott;* those of the former are not over 3 inches long; the others have a longer tube, and are between 4 and 5 inches in length and 3–4 inches in diameter; the flowers are probably open day and night. Ovary 1–1⅓ inch long; lower scales of the tube triangular; upper sepals fleshy, greenish-white, ¾–1 inch long, lower ones 2, upper ones 3–4 lines wide; petals of a light cream color, 1–1½ inch long, 6–8 lines wide above, very thick and fleshy, and very much curled. Filaments light yellow, adnate to the upper half of the tube, its lower part for the length of 1 or 1½ inch naked. Stigmata over half an inch long, slender, suberect, of a greenish-yellow color. Fruit 2½–3 inches long, 1½–2 inches in diameter, oval or obovate, or often narrowed at base and almost pear-shaped, (perhaps where many are crowded together;) the remains of the flower falling off leave a broad convex scar; the color of the fruit is green, and towards the upper end reddish. The pericarp has the hardness of a green cucumber, somewhat softer towards the apex, and is about 2 lines thick; it bursts open on the plant with 3 or usually 4 valves, which are red on the inside, and when spreading horizontally, or somewhat recurved, look like a red flower. The crimson-colored sweet but rather insipid pulp has the consistency of a fresh fig; it completely separates from the rind, and, drying up from the heat of the sun, falls to the ground. The innumerable black seeds are 0.7–0.9 line long. Those brought by *Mr. Thurber*, and largely distributed in this country and in Europe, have well germinated; the cotyledons are short and acute; the seedling plant is globose, grows very slowly, and is rather delicate.

23. C. THURBERI, E. in Sillim. Journn.: caulibus erectis seu adscentibus elatioribus fasciculatis articulatis 13–14-costatis; sinubus planiusculis; areolis subremotis pulvinatis griseo- seu fulvo-tomentosis; aculeis 7–15 gracilibus rectis flexuosisve fusco-atris demum cinereis valde inæqualibus irregulariter fasciculatis; floribus infra caulis apicem lateralibus aggregatis; ovarii squamis sepaloideis 80–100 pluribusve triangularibus imbricatis axilla lanam copiosam albidam sel fulvam sæpeque aculeolos paucos nigricantes gerentibus; sepalis tubi sub-50 olivaceis, inferioribus acutiusculis, superioribus obovato-spathulatis obtusis; petalis obtusis carnosis albidis; bacca magna globosa aculeolata demum nuda olivacea intus coccinea; seminibus numerosissimis oblique obvatis dorso carinatis læviusculis (sub lente minutissime tuberculatis) lucidis exalbuminosis; hilo oblongo subbasilari, embryone cotyledonibus foliaceis curvatis incumbentibus breviter hamato. (Tab. LXXIV, fig. 15.)

In a rocky cañon near the mountain pass of Bacuachi, Sonora, *Thurber;* on all the sierras of Sonora westward of the Sierra Madre, and more common southward, *Schott;* called there *Pitahaya:* fl. June and July; fruit in July and August.—Stems 5–15 from one root, fasciculated, erect or ascending, "curved *inward,*" 10–15 feet high, articulated, lower joints 2–3, upper ones 5–6 feet long, 4–6 inches in diameter; ribs 13–14, very slightly prominent. The skeleton of this species, according to *Mr. Schott's* observations, consists of flattened bundles of wood, very loosely connected by transverse fibres, so as to form a kind of hollow tube. Areolæ pulvinate covered with brownish or ashy wool, only about three lines in diameter, 12–15 lines apart. Spines irregularly fasciculated, 7–10, according to *Mr. Schott's* notes; but 15 in the flower-bearing bunches before me. (Might not the flower-bearing spines be more numerous and perhaps more slender than the others, indicating a transition to *Pilocereus*?) Spines slender, flexible, almost setaceous, very uneqal in length, 5–18 lines long in the same bunch, partly deciduous. Flowers usually 6–12 inches below the top of the plant, about 3 inches in length; ovary very densely imbricate with sepaloid scales, which bear dirty wool and often short bristly spines in their axils; in some specimens they are wanting, in others they also invest the fruit, but are easily brushed off at maturity. Fruit 3 inches in diameter, like a large orange, of delicious taste, the crimson pulp dotted with numerous black seeds. These are 0.9–1.0 line long only, a little larger than those of the last species, which they very much resemble, and very minutely tuberculated. The seeds germinate like those of *C. giganteus,* with very short acute cotyledons, and grow up with a globose head like the *Echinocerei* while all the *Eucerei* which I have seen germinating at once grow up in a cylindric or prismatic column.

### Subgen. 4. PILOCEREUS.*

24. C. SCHOTTII, (sp. nov.): caulibus suberectis elatioribus fasciculatis articulatis 4–7-(plerumque 5-) costatis flavo-viridibus; areolis in caulibus sterilibus remotis aculeos radiales

---

* *Cereus Schottii,* described in the text (evidently a *Pilocereus,* as that genus has been established by Lemaire) leaves no doubt in my mind about the propriety and necessity of a reunion of the "*Old man Cactus*" and its allies with *Cereus.* As a subgenus, *Pilocereus* would be characterized by the difference of the sterile and the flower-bearing parts of the plant, (the latter having more numerous. longer, and thinner, often hair-like spines,) and by the smaller flowers with all the parts reduced in number The other characters ascribed to *Pilocereus* (filaments from the whole surface of the tube and even from the top of the ovary and especially the short and globose cotyledons,) are not found in our species.

4–6 robustos breves cinereos obscuros singulumque centralem breviorem obscuriorem gerentibus, in caule superiore florifero confertis lanam cinerascentem aculeosque 15–25 setiformes elongatos flexuosos angulosos rubello cinereos declinatos et quasi pendulos ferentibus; floribus in aculeorum barba pene occultis carneis; tubo gracili supra ovarium globosum 10-squamatum constricto decurvo intus basi nudo sepalis 10–12 lanceolatis instructo; petalis 10–12 oblongis obtusiusculis; stigmatibus 5–6 fasciculatis; bacca parva globosa squamosa pulposa coccinea floris rudimentis coronata; seminibus oblique obovatis carinatis lævissimis lucidis, hilo angusto subventrali; albumine parcissimo; embryone hamato cotyledonibus curvatis foliaceis incumbentibus seu subinde obliquis. (Tab. LXXIV, fig. 16.)

Sierra di Sonoyita, and southeast towards Santa Magdalena, Sonora, where it is named *Zina*, or *Sina*, or *Sinita* by the inhabitants, *Schott*: in August with flower and ripe fruit. —Stems 8–10 or more from the same base; 8–10 feet high, ascending at base, and, when full grown, always curved outward at the top, the reverse of *C. Thurberi*; often many plants together, forming thickets, and covering a large space of ground; not rarely associated with the just-mentioned species. Stems of 2–4 articulations of 4 or 5 inches diameter; lower part entirely denudated of the quite deciduous spines. Spines of the sterile joints, or young plants, 5–7, not over 3 or 4 lines long; areolæ of the flowering joints 3 lines in diameter, covered with a dirty whitish tomentum, 2–3 lines apart; spines irregularly fasciculated, 10–25 in number, and from 1 to 4 inches long, flexuous and pendulous. Flower somewhat hidden in this reddish-grey beard, and its tube evidently bent downward by it; length of flower $1\frac{1}{2}$–$1\frac{3}{4}$ inch; sepals without any wool in the axils, olivaceous; lower ones triangular, acute; upper ones lanceolate; petals dirty flesh-color; stamina comparatively few, leaving the top of the ovary and the lower part of the tube naked; stigmata 5–6, filiform, broom-shaped, exactly like those of *C. giganteus* or *C. Thurberi*. Berry scarlet, 3 or 4 lines in diameter; seeds very similar to those of *C. giganteus*, but larger, 1.0–1.2 line long; germination very much like that of the last two species; cotyledons of seedling plant acute, short, spreading; head globose, but soon somewhat elongated, while both others remain globose for a long time. *C. Schottii* is closely allied to *Pilocereus scoparius*, Poselg. from Vera Cruz. This, however, is a larger plant, 20–25 feet high, 1 foot in diameter, with 12–15 ribs on the sterile, and 20–25 on the flowering part. I have named this interesting species, the only *Pilocereus* of our Flora, after its zealous discoverer, whom I have often had occasion to mention in these pages, and who, with all his other arduous duties in the field, still found leisure and inclination to study the Botany of the boundary from the Pacific to the Gulf of Mexico.

## IV. OPUNTIA, Tourn., Mill.*

### Subgen. 1. STENOPUNTIA.

Articuli complanati. Aculei non vaginati.
Flores parvi. Petala parva, subulata, erectiuscula (aurantiaca).
Stigmata pauca (1–3), acuta.
Bacca? et Semina?

* Besides its strictly differential characters (viz: the rotate corolla and the flat bony seeds with large foliaceous cotyledons) this genus is distinguished from the other Cactaceæ by its subterete, subulate and deciduous leaves, and by its barbed spines, which I do not find in any other plant of this family. These spines render *Opuntiæ* so much more disagreeable and even dangerous than other *Cacti*; in several species (*O. fragilis*, *O. Bigelovii*, *O. frutescens* and others) the joints easily separate from the stem and adhere by their barbed spines to the skin or clothes of the passer-by, the most annoying burs. Besides these spines which are

The habit of the two species, the only ones yet known, is entirely that of the next subgenus; but the small flower (less than 1 inch in diameter) has numerous very small and narrow petals, and few and acute stigmata. *O. grandis*, the only other species known, has 2 or 3 stigmata, and *O. stenopetala* only one stigma. I must remark here, that all the ovaria I have opened contained no ovules and not even a cavity. May not the acute single style (an unique and anomalous case in this family) be in some connexion with this sterility, and may these flowers not be abortive or staminate forms?

1. O. STENOPETALA (sp. nov.): prostrata; articulis magnis crassis; pulvillis ad marginem confertissimis fusco-setulosis; aculeis sub-3 compréssis ancipitibus curvato-deflexis seu patulis, adjectis sæpe 1–3 minoribus, omnibus atrofuscis; floribus ex areolis fulvo-villosis; ovari obconici tuberculati pulvillis 30–40 confertis albido-tomentosis setosis; sepalis tubi petalisque sub-25 lineari-subulatis acuminatis aristatis aurantiacis erecto-patulis; imo tubo nudo; stylo medio globoso-ventricoso apice indiviso acuto staminibus sub-breviore. (Tab. LXVI.)

Common on the battle-field of Buena Vista, south of Saltillo, Mexico, *Dr. J. Gregg*, 1848: fl. July.—The specimens before me consist of dried segments of joints, bearing flowers; joints apparently large, perhaps 7 or 8 inches in diameter, pulvilli about 1¼ or 1½ inch apart on the surface, but much crowded towards the edges, with much dirty-white wool, short dark brown bristles, and very dark, almost black, spines, lighter at the tip. The stouter spines 1½–2 inches long, flat on the upper, rounded on the lower surface, often much curved. Floriferous pulvilli very woolly; ovary about 9 lines long, leaves (or sepals) on the tubercles deciduous, very slender, 2–2½ lines long; sepals and petals 4–6 lines long, not more than one line broad at base, very slenderly acuminate, fleshy; sepals greenish-red; petals orange. Stamens numerous, half as long as the petals; style very much inflated in the middle, and to all appearances (I have carefully examined about six flowers) with a single pointed stigma. No fruit or seed was obtained, nor is it probable that these flowers would have ripened fruit, as no ovula could be found. Cannot this curious plant be obtained living? It is interesting to find in the Mexican *O. grandis*, mentioned above, (which has long been cultivated in European gardens, but has only lately, for the first time, flowered in Prince Salm's collection,) a very similar species, confirming this subgenus; this is an erect plant, with smaller joints, two white spines on the pulvilli, and 2 or 3 acute stigmata.

---

usually, although not in every species, present, bristles are almost invariably found on each pulvillus, usually small, (less than 1 or 2 lines long, sometimes longer) and very numerous, mixed with soft wool. These bristles are extremely sharp and barbed backward, like the spines, and are loosely attached at their insertion; consequently, when touched, they come off from the plant and adhere most annoyingly to the skin or clothing. Both the *areola aculeifera* and the *areola florifera* are united in this genus into one circular or oblong *pulvillus* in the axil of the deciduous leaf. The spines occupy the lower, and the bristles the upper part of this *pulvillus;* between the bristles, and surrounded by them, and always above the spines, the young shoots or flowers originate. These bristles correspond with the bristles and wool in the axils of some *Eumamillariæ*, and with the tomentum of the floriferous areola in *Coryphantha* and *Echinocactus*, but are quite distinct, morphologically, from the spines themselves. In *Eumamillaria* the aculeiferous and floriferous areolæ are entirely separate; in *Coryphantha* they are united by a long groove; in *Echinocactus* by a short one, or are quite contiguous, although always distinct; in *Cereus* we do not observe a persistent floriferous areola; the flower, as well as the young bud, bursts the epidermis above and close to the spiniferous areola, where a kind of floriferous areola is formed and continues till soon after the fall of the fruit, when it gradually disappears. In all these plants, the floriferous areola occurs only on the fully developed part of the plant, capable of bearing flowers. But in *Opuntia* the pulvillus (which in its lower part is the spiniferous, and in its upper part the floriferous areola combined, is the same in all stages of development; only it is smaller on the lower part of each joint, and bears fewer or often no spines, and rarely if any flowers or new shoots; while the uppermost *pulvilli* have the longest and most numerous spines and bear the flowers as well as the young branches. The *pulvilli* of *Opuntiæ* continue to grow year after year, and the bristles become longer and more numerous, and in many species the spines themselves grow stouter; sometimes new spines are developed between the bristles, indicating a low degree of continued vegetative activity on the rudimentary axis represented by the floriferous areola.

Subgen. 2. PLATOPUNTIA.

Articuli complanati, lanceolati, elliptici, obovati seu suborbiculati. Aculei nunquam vaginati.

Flores majores seu magni. Petala latiora, obovata seu orbiculata, flava seu rarius miniata, rarissime purpurascentia.

Stigmata plura (5–10) obtusa.

Bacca floris rudimentis dejectis late umbilicata, pulposa seu succosa, et inermis, rarius sicca et aculeata.

Semina margine latiore seu angustiore cincta.

Embryo plus quam circularis circa albumen parcum spiraliter convolutus. Cotyledones semper contrariæ, incumbentes.

This is the well-known form of *Opuntiæ*, with compressed and more or less elliptic joints, decumbent or erect, with fibrous or sometimes tuberous roots, mostly with spines only on the upper, or in one section (*Xerocarpeæ*) on all the pulvilli, rarely (principally the *Pubescentes*) spineless. Flowers commonly 2–3 inches and sometimes even 4 or 5 inches, in diameter; stigmata, as far as my observation goes, always from 5 to 8, or at most 10, in number, whitish, yellowish, or green, patulous or mostly erect. Fruits often edible, so that some species are cultivated for their fruits, and have been introduced into the warmer parts of the other continents; in the section *Xerocarpeæ* the fruits are spiny and dry. Seeds among the largest in the whole genus, or even in the whole family, in some species over 3 lines in diameter.

2. O. STRIGIL (sp. nov.): suberecta; articulis ovatis obovatis seu orbiculatis obtusis seu subinde subacutis tenuibus; pulvillis confertis, junioribus albido-villosis mox setis difformibus stramineis stipatis, omnibus aculeiferis; aculeis rufis fuscisque versus apicem flavidis, 5–8 radiantibus deflexis, versus margines articuli cum 1–2 robustioribus longioribus erectis patulis seu deflexis; bacca parva subglobosa late umbilicata areolis 25–30 minutis stipata rubra; seminibus parvis crassis obtuse marginatis. (Tab. LXVII.)

Western Texas, west of the Pecos, in crevices of flat limestone rocks, *Wright*, *Bigelow*.—About 2 feet high, pale green; joints covered with numerous pulvilli, each with a bunch of bright red-brown spines, paler at the tip, which give this plant a very showy appearance. Joints 4–5 inches long, 3½–4 inches wide; pulvilli 4–6 lines apart, prominent; their whitish wool soon disappears, leaving them covered with fine pale-yellow bristles, a dozen of which are longer than the rest, radiating upwards and laterally, and by joining the lower radiating spines forming with them a complete circle. Spines on most areolæ 5–8, on the lower ones (as usual) fewer, shorter and paler, on the upper and marginal ones more perfect; exterior radiating spines 3–4 lines, lower ones 5–8 lines long; the 1 or 2 stouter somewhat compressed spines on the upper areolæ are nearly an inch long, deep-brown below, light red-brown in the middle, gradually fading into yellow at the point. Flower unknown. Fruit 6–7 lines long, about 6 lines thick, with a broad and flat umbilicus; areolæ small, with grey wool and a few bristles. Seed 1½ line in diameter, rather irregular, very thick in proportion.—It would be desirable to obtain living specimens of this showy species, which could be easily done by travellers on the now well-frequented road between San Antonio and El Paso.

3. O. ENGELMANNI, Salm: erecta, grandis; caule demum lignoso tereti cortice cinereo rimoso obducto; articulis orbiculato-obovatis seu obovatis magnis pallide viridibus; pulvillis

remotis griseo-tomentosis; setis flavis rigidis valde inæqualibus sparsis; aculeis paucis (in areolis superioribus plerumque 2–3) validis compressis seu angulatis rectis seu subinde curvatis deflexis seu varie divergentibus stramineis corneisve basi rufis, cum adventitiis inferioribus 1–2 gracilioribus pallidioribus sæpe deficientibus; floribus flavis intus rubellis; ovario obvato-subgloboso seu rarius elongato subclavato sepalis e basi lata subulatis et pulvillis 20–25 griseosue fulvo-tomentosis parce setosis instructo; sepalis tubi sub-13, exterioribus ovato-lanceolatis acuminatis, interioribus orbiculato-obovatis cuspidatis; petalis 8–10 obovatis subspathulatis obtusis mucronatis; stylo crasso parum tumido; stigmatibus 8–10 erectis; bacca globoso-obovata seu rarius pyriformi late umbilicata; seminibus minoribus sub-irregularibus plerumque anguste marginatis. (Tab. LXXV, fig. 1–4.)

From the Canadian river, *Bigelow*, to New Braunfels, in Texas, *Lindheimer*, and to the mouth of the Rio Grande; westward to the Pecos and Presido, *Bigelow*, El Paso, *Wright*, and perhaps to the Pacific, *Parry*, south to Chihuahua, *Wislizenus:* fl. May and June.—A stout, coarse-looking plant, 4–6 feet high; lower part of old stems woody with loosely reticulated ligneous fibres, and with grey bark often covered with lichens, about 6 inches in diameter. Joints, in the larger specimens, one foot long, 9 inches in diameter; leaves subulate, 3–4 lines long, patulous; pulvilli 1¼–1½ inch apart, 3–4 lines in diameter; bristles coarse, sparse and very unequal; longer ones on the upper edge of the pulvillus sometimes 4–6 lines long; spines 1–1½ inch long, lower smaller ones 6–9 lines long. Flower 2½–3 inches in diameter, characterized by the usually quite short ovary, and the comparatively narrow and not emarginate petals; ovary commonly 1–1¼ inch long, almost globose; in some instances, however, I have seen it clavate and nearly 2 inches long, (perhaps then sterile and inclined to become proliferous.) Fruit subglobose, somewhat contracted at base, nearly 2 inches long; umbilicus about an inch in diameter, flat or a little depressed; fruit dirty purplish, usually with a bright purplish pulp, of an insipid or even nauseous taste. Seeds usually less than 2 lines, in most specimens only 1.5–1.7 line in diameter, of a regular (from Matamoras) or commonly more irregular twisted shape, with an obtuse or acutish, rather narrow margin. Young plants, raised from seed, are characterized by the fascicles of very long (¾–1 inch) fine woolly hairs on the pulvilli, which appear in the second season, and remain for several years. Among the numerous varieties of this species, the var. *cyclodes*, from the Upper Pecos, has been described in Capt. Whipple's Pacific Railroad Report; another one was collected, by Mr. Wright, on the Limpia, with 1–6 stout, curved spines on the upper pulvilli, and none at all on the lower ones.

Dr. Bigelow distinguishes from this species another plant, which he has frequently observed near Presidio del Norte and Eagle Pass. From his notes, and from the meagre material on hand, I venture to describe it, without asserting its specific difference from the last species.

O. DULCIS (sp. nov.): adscendens, patula; articulis obovatis; pulvillis remotis; setis fulvis difformibus, exterioribus confertis tenuioribus brevioribus subæqualibus, interioribus uniseriatis robustioribus multo longioribus; aculeis 2–3 angulatis sæpius tortis pallidis deflexis, sæpe cum 1–3 gracilioribus; bacca ovata late umbilicata pallida; seminibus minoribus regularibus anguste marginatis. (Tab. LXXV, fig. 5–7.)

A sub-erect, spreading bush, lower and with smaller joints than the last species, and always with a very sweet and pleasant-tasted fruit. Plant about 2 feet high; joints ½ foot long; spines 1–1¾ inch in length, almost white; a semicircle of short spines or long bristles distinctly separates the spiniferous from the bristly part of the pulvillus; the bristles themselves are much more numerous, finer, and more crowded than in *O. Engelmanni;* this arrangement of the bristles I find again only in *O. chlorotica*, Eng. & Big., from the Western Colorado The spines resemble *O. tortispina*, Eng. & Big., the flower and fruit *O. Engelmanni*, and the seed seems different from all these. Fruit 1½–1¾ inch long, one inch in diameter; umbilicus ¾ inch wide, shallow. Seeds 1.5–2.0 lines in diameter.

O. OCCIDENTALIS, E. & B. in P. R. R., found by *Dr. Bigelow*, "in immense patches, 40 miles east of Los Angeles," California, was also observed by *Mr. Schott* in the high valleys of San Pascual and Santa Isabel, northeast of San Diego, "covering extensive tracts of land." It is probably a good species, and quite distinct from *O. Engelmanni;* young plants, raised from Dr. Bigelow's seeds, do not show the peculiar capillary spines of that species mentioned above.

Another *Opuntia* grows on the hillsides and plains near San Diego, *Parry*, and on the sea beach there, *Schott;* an erect plant, 4–6 feet high; spines 2–4, stout, compressed yellowish or brownish, also forming large thickets; joints 6–8 inches long and 4–6 inches wide; ovary subglobose, with 16–20 bristly pulvilli; 15–18 broadly obovate cuspidate sepals; about 8 (?) orbiculate petals; 8–10 stigmata; a large yellowish or purple fruit, of pleasant taste, much relished by the inhabitants. Whether this is a form of *O. Engelmanni* or *O. Tuna*, which, from having for a long while been cultivated about the settlements, may have become naturalized, I cannot at present determine.

4. O. MACROCENTRA (sp. nov.): adscendens; articulis magnis suborbiculatis tenuibus sæpe purpurascentibus; foliis gracilibus lineari-subulatis; pulvillis subremotis orbiculato-ovatis setas graciles breves fulvas tomentum griseum vix superantes gerentibus plerisque inermibus, summis et marginalibus solum armatis; aculeis 1–2 rarius pluribus prælongis rectis seu varie flexuosis fusco-atris sursum pallidoribus sæpe annulato-notatis, superiore terete inferiore subbreviore compresso seu canaliculato; flore flaro; ovario ovato; pulvillis 20–25 villosis et fulvo-setosis versus superiorem ovarii partem congestis; sepalis tubi 13 lanceolatis seu interioribus obovatis acuminatis cuspidatisve; petalis sub-8 obovatis obtusis mucronatis; stigmatibus 8; seminibus majusculis late obtuseque undulato-marginatis. (Tab. LXXV, fig. 8.)

Sandy ridges in the bottom of the Rio Grande near El Paso, also on the Limpia, *Wright:* fl. in May.—A remarkably striking plant 2–3 feet high—with large, almost rounded, thinly compressed, often purplish joints, and very long nearly black spines—of which it would be very desirable to obtain living plants, as none of those sent home by Mr. Wright have survived. Joints 5–8 inches long, 4–7 inches wide; leaves 2½–3 lines long, remarkably slender; pulvilli ¾–1 inch apart; lower ones smaller and closer together, unarmed; spines on the upper ones 2–3 inches long, lower half almost black; ovary 1¼ inch long, 8 lines in diameter; flower 3 inches in diameter when fully open. The seeds sent by Mr. Wright as belonging to this species are 2.0–2.2 lines in diameter, much twisted, their border undulating, very similar to seeds of some form of *O. phæacantha*. From this species our plant seems to be distinguished by its larger, thinner, more orbicular joints, the closer and more woolly pulvilli, the slenderer leaves, and the small number of very long spines; the ovary also is more elongated, the sepals narrower, the flower larger.

5. O. PHÆACANTHA, E. in Pl. Fendl.: diffusa, adscendens; articulis obovatis seu suborbiculatis crassis glaucescentibus; foliis e basi crassa subulatis; pulvillis subremotis orbiculato-ovatis setas graciles stramineas seu fuscatas tomento griseo plerumque longiores gerentibus

plerisque armatis; aculeis 2–5 rectis superiore teretiusculo porrecto, cæteris brevioribus inæqualibus plus minus angulatis seu compressis deflexis fuscis seu fusco-atris sursum pallidioribus; flore flavo; ovario brevi pulvillis sub-20 tomentosis et fulvo-setosis versus superiorem ovarii partem congestis; sepalis tubi sub-13 exterioribus late oblanceolatis cæteris late obovatis cuspidatis; petalis 8–10 late obovatis obtusis submucronatis; stigmatibus 8 erectis; bacca cuneato-pyriformi late umbilicata vix pulposa; seminibus plerumque majusculis sub-regularibus crasse marginatis. (Tab. LXXV, fig. 9–13.)

Var. *α*. NIGRICANS: obovata, viridior; pulvillis magis approximatis; aculeis brevioribus acute angulatis nigricantibus.

Var. *β*. BRUNNEA: obovata, glaucescens; pulvillis remotis; aculeis longioribus obtuse angulatis infra brunneis.

Along the Rio Grande near Santa Fé, var. *α*. *Fendler;* var. *β*. common about El Paso, on the sandy ridges in the immediate valley of the river, *Wright*.—The northern plant has been correctly described in *Plantæ Fendlerianæ*, with the exception of the flower, which probably refers to *O. Missouriensis*, or some allied species. The variety from El Paso has remarkably thick and glaucous joints, which in fall and winter often assume a purplish hue; they are commonly 4 or 5 inches long, and 2½–3 inches wide; the largest ones were 7 inches long, and 4½ inches broad; sometimes they are more orbicular and shorter; leaves 2½–3 lines long, thick in proportion; pulvilli 1–1½ inch apart, with dirty yellowish or brownish bristles; only the lowest ones without spines; spines usually 2–4, sometimes 4 or 5, and even more, in one bunch, 1–2 or sometimes 2½ inches long, terete or more or less flattened, but without sharp angles, often striate, light or dark brown below, whitish above; lower spines often entirely whitish. Flower 2¼–2½ inches in diameter; ovary 10 lines long, 8 lines in diameter; fruit 1¼–1½ inch long, with the lower part contracted, solid and seedless; umbilicus rather shallow; seeds very variable, usually over 2 lines in diameter, but sometimes smaller.

6. O. TENUISPINA, (sp. nov.): diffusa seu adscendens; articulis mediis seu majusculis obovatis basi attenuatis læte viridibus; foliis gracilibus subulatis parvis, pulvillis subapproximatis setas breves graciles fulvas rufasve gerentibus, plerisque armatis seu inferioribus inermibus; aculeis singulis binisve teretiusculis rectis gracilibus flexilibus albidis non raro basi apiceque fuscatis annulatisque, adjectis sæpe inferioribus tenuioribus albis, superiore in areolis superioribus porrecto, cæteris deflexis; ovario clavato gracili pulvillis 25 versus apicem aggregatis griseo-villosis et fulvo-setosis stipato; sepalis tubi sub-13 obovato-orbiculatis abbreviatis cuspidatis; petalis 13 obovatis sub-emarginatis mucronulatis flavis basi aurantiacis; stigmatibus 7–8 erectis virescentibus; bacca minore oblonga profunde umbilicata, seminibus minoribus irregulariter angulatis anguste marginatis. (Tab. LXXV, fig. 14.)

Sand-hills on the Rio Grande, near El Paso, from Doña Ana to San Elizario, *Wright;* fl. May.—About a foot high, spreading; joints 3–6 inches long, 2–4 inches wide; leaves 2 lines long, or less, ½ line in diameter; pulvilli ½ inch, or, in the largest specimens, almost an inch apart, with short grey wool, and bright, reddish-brown, slender bristles, 1–1½ line long; spines stiff and very straight, but flexible; lowest ones ½–1¼ inch long; upper ones 1½–2½, or rarely even 3 inches long, whitish, or, in some species, brown towards the base, or on the lower half, always darkish at tip; flower 2½–3 inches in diameter; ovary 1–1¼ inch long, slender; sepals remarkably short; petals rounded or somewhat emarginate, 1–1¼ inch long, 6–9 lines broad, yellow, with orange-red at base, turning all red on the second day of flowering. Fruit 1–1¼ inch long, with a very deep umbilicus, and without any contraction at base; seeds 1.5–2.0 lines in diameter, deeply notched at the hilum, very irregular. Distinguished from the nearly allied *O. phæacantha* by its thinner joints, slenderer and longer spines, larger flowers, different fruit, &c.

7. O. FILIPENDULA, (sp. nov.): adscendens, glauca; radicibus nodoso-incrassatis tuberiferis; articulis minoribus diversissimis orbiculatis seu obovatis seu oblanceolatis tenuibus; foliis minutis subulatis; pulvillis approximatis in tomento albo setas numerosas tenuissimas penicillatas demum elongatas virescenti-stramineas gerentibus, plurimis armatis seu omnibus plus minus inermibus; aculeis 1–2 albidis elongatis setaceis non raro subangulatis tortisque, 1–2 minoribus sæpe adjectis; ovarii subcylindrici gracilis pulvillis 16–20 villo albo et setis parcis stramineis munitis; sepalis tubi sub-8 lanceolatis, interioribus obovato-cuspidatis; petalis 8 late obovatis retusis purpurascentibus margine pallidioribus; stylo purpurascente; stigmatibus 5 erectis flavidis; seminibus minoribus tumidis anguste crasseque marginatis. (Tab. LXVIII.)

Alluvial bottoms of the Rio Grande, in rather fertile soil, near Doña Ana, above El Paso, and at San Elizario, below it; also on alluvial prairies between El Paso and the Limpia, *Wright:* fl. May and June.—The tubers of the root, ½–1 inch thick, are long and cylindric, or oval, or globular swellings of the roots, strung upon thick fibres; these tubers will sprout when planted. The stems are 6–12 inches high and spreading; joints of a bluish glaucous hue, more so than any other of our species, very variable in shape, orbicular, or even transverse to obovate and lanceolate, often on the same plant, 1½–3 inches long, 1–2 inches wide, very much compressed; leaves 1¼–1¾ line long; pulvilli 4–6 lines apart, with a perfectly white tomentum, becoming grey when old, and numerous slender, greenish-yellow bristles, which finally become 2–3 lines long and very conspicuous. Sometimes the joints are entirely spineless, but usually they are armed with long, deflexed, very slender, white spines; the longer ones 1–2 inches, the lower and shorter ones less than 1 inch in length; ovary slenderer than in any other species known to me, an inch long, at top hardly more than 3 lines wide; flowers about 2½ inches in diameter, purplish, without any mixture of brick-red or yellow, as in the allied species. The only other purple one of our *Platopuntiæ* is *O. basilaris*, which is of a yet purer and deeper purple color. Fruit unknown; seeds have been sent which have germinated and produced plants which already after the first year showed the characteristic glaucous hue and the tuberous roots. These seeds also differ from all our other *Opuntia* seeds by their great thickness, and their remarkably narrow but thick and obtuse margin; they are only very slightly notched at the hilum, and have a diameter of 1.7–2.0 lines, with a thickness of 1.2 lines.

8. O. MACRORHIZA, E. in Pl. Lindh., from between San Antonio and Austin, *Lindheimer*, is apparently well distinguished by its large tuberous roots, which even the young seedlings very soon begin to show; but without these it is hardly distinguishable from *O. Rafinesquii*, E. of the Mississippi valley. I find the flower bud long-acuminate, and the stigmata always 5. (Tab. LXIX.)

9. O. RUFIDA (sp. nov.): erecto-patula; articulis late obovatis seu suborbiculatis pubescentibus; foliis e basi lata subulatis longe acuminatis; pulvillis confertis griseo-villosis setas rufidas graciles numerosissimas penicillatas gerentibus inermibus; floris flavi ovario obovato pulvillis 40–50 instructo; sepalis tubi 20–30 exterioribus lineari-lanceolatis acuminatis, interioribus obovatis cuspidatis; petalis (8?) orbiculato-obovatis obtusis erosis sæpe mucronulatis; stigmatibus sub-7 abbreviatis in capitulum globosum congestis.

Common about Presidio del Norte, on the Rio Grande, on rocks and mountains, *Bigelow*; in the lower valley of the Nazas, southeastern Chihuahua, *Gregg*: fl. May.—Stems 2–4 feet high; joints 2–6 inches long, pale green, without any red or colored spots surrounding the pulvillus, as is said to be constantly the case in the allied *O. puberula* and *O. decumbens*; leaves very slenderly acuminate, 2½ lines long, about twice the length of the axillary wool; pulvilli thickly tomentose, and with an abundance of very delicate brown-red bristles, almost entirely covering the surface of young or not fully-grown joints; in adult ones about 4 lines apart. The flower described above was obtained south of the Rio Grande, in the Bolson de Mapimi; ovary 10 lines long, flower 2½ inches in diameter, stigmata (green?) about one line in length. This species is nearly allied to *O. microdasys*, which is common in cultivation, and specimens of which from Saltillo I have been able to compare. Our plant has more rounded and larger joints, more distant pulvilli, which bear reddish-brown (not yellow) bristles, and longer leaves; from *O. puberula*, which seems to be yet nearer allied to it, it differs by the absence of spines, larger leaves, etc. Mr. Schott has noticed a pubescent *Opuntia* on the dividing ridge of the California Cordilleras, near the boundary line, and a suberect species in the Santa Cruz valley, in Sonora, about 3 feet high, both without spines. It is impossible to form any opinion where they belong, as no specimens have been saved.

10. O. BASILARIS, E. & B. in Pacif. R. R.: found by *Mr. Schott*, in the Gila valley, and up the eastern slope of the Californian Mountains; fl. in May.

11. O. ARENARIA (sp. nov.): diffusa, adscendens; radicibus crassis elongatis sæpe stoloniferis; articulis minoribus obovatis crassis tumidis seu subcompressis tuberculatis nitide virentibus; foliis minutis pulvillo vix longioribus; pulvillis subconfertis parce albo-tomentosis setas plurimas gracillimas pallidas demum in articulis vetustis numerosissimas pulvinatas fulvas gerentibus, omnibus fere armatis; aculeis superioribus 1–4 sæpe subangulatis, summo validiore porrecto albido seu fusco-variegato, cæteris brevioribus divergentibus seu deflexis albidis; aculeis inferioribus 2–6 brevibus setaceis albis radiantibus; floribus sulphureis; ovario obovato pulvillis 20–30 setosis aculeolatisque instructo; sepalis tubi 12–14, inferioribus late obovatis cuspidatis, superioribus obtusis; petalis sub-8 obcordatis seu emarginatis sæpe mucronatis; stigmatibus 5 mucronatis viridibus in capitulum collectis; bacca oblonga ovata; umbilico infundibuliformi aculeolis 3–6 inæqualibus deflexis armata; seminibus magnis irregularibus late crasseque marginatis. (Tab. LXXV, fig. 15.)

Sandy bottoms of the Rio Grande near El Paso, *Wright*: fl. May.—Roots 3–5 lines thick, at last ligneous, far spreading in the loose sand, and sometimes stoloniferous, which I have also noticed in some forms of *O. Missouriensis*; stems spreading 2 or 3 feet, ½–1 foot high; joints 1½–3 inches long, 1–2 inches wide, often terete or rather oval, or clavate, (a specimen before me is 2½ inches long and ¾ inch thick,) and always strongly tuberculate. Leaves about a line long; pulvilli smaller than in *O. fragilis*, very sparingly tomentose, very bristly; the tawny bristles of the old joints covering almost the whole surface. Upper and longer spines 9–15, or even 18 lines long, white, with a yellow tip, or brown, yellow, or reddish at base and tip; other spines 2–6 lines long, white. Flower 2–2½ inches in diameter; ovary 9–12 lines long; filaments greenish-yellow; stigmata nearly 2 lines in length. Fruit dry, 10–14 lines long, contracted at top, with a deeply immersed umbilicus, and with spines of 1–5 lines in length; seeds 2½–3 lines in diameter. This species is nearly allied to the northern *O. fragilis*, but is distinguished by the larger and more strongly tuberculated joints, smaller pulvilli set with numerous bristles, the longer and slenderer spines, and the spinose fruit.

Subgen. 3. CYLINDROPUNTIA.

Articuli teretes, clavati seu cylindrici. Aculei plerumque vaginati.

Flores parvi seu majores. Petala obovata seu orbiculata, rubra seu purpurea, rarius flava.

Stigmata 5–8, obtusa.

Bacca umbilicata, sicca seu subsicca, rarissime pulposa; inermis, seu setosa, seu aculeata; floris rudimentis dejectis seu persistentibus.

Semina sutura commissurali cincta, plerumque immarginata.

Embryo circa albumen copiosius subcircularis. Cotyledones contrariæ, incumbentes, haud raro obliquæ, interdum parallelæ, accumbentes.

The species forming this subgenus have an appearance so striking, and at the same time so distinct from the common type of *Opuntiæ*, that a generic separation has been attempted; but the flowers are so entirely identical, and in the fruit so little difference is observed, that it had to be abandoned; the only real distinction, and a permanent one, as far as my observation goes, I find in the embryo; in *Cylindropuntia* it is less curved, not completing an entire circle, and surrounds a more copious albumen; in *Platopuntia*, on the contrary, it is somewhat spirally coiled, and the space for the albumen is thereby much smaller. It is worthy of remark, that in *Cylindropuntia* the direction of the cotyledons is by far less constant than in other *Cactaceæ*; though usually incumbent, as in all other *Opuntiæ*, they are very often oblique, and not rarely accumbent, like to those of *Echinocactus;* in *O. echinocarpa* I have found them invariably so.

§. 1. *Clavatæ.*

Stems prostrate; joints short and clavate, tuberculate, proliferous near the base; the ligneous tissue loosely reticulated much like that of *Platopuntia;* spines more or less compressed and striate, the epidermis not or but slightly separating from them; flowers yellow and rather large; fruit always dry, crowned by the persistent remains of the flower, beset on the pulvilli with numberless spiny bristles.

12. O. PARRYI, E. in Sill. Journ. *Dr. Parry* observed this species on the eastern slope of the Californian Mountains near San Felipe, and sent notes about it, an extract of which I published in Silliman's Journal. Since then *Dr. Bigelow* has collected it 80 or 100 miles northeast of that place, near the Mojave river, and in his report a full account of the plant is given. Dr. Parry describes the joints as 4–8 inches long, ascending, with white spines only 6 lines long; flowers greenish yellow, 1½ inch in diameter; stigmata green.

13. O. EMORYI, (sp. nov.): prostrata; articulis cylindricis basi clavatis glaucis adscendentibus; tuberculis elongatis; pulvillis magnis setas paucas rigidas gerentibus; aculeis plurimis rufis seu fuscis demum cinerascentibus; interioribus 5–9 validioribus triangulatis subcompressis porrectis seu deflexis, superioribus solum suberectis; aculeis exterioribus 10–20 sæpe pluriserialibus undique radiantibus, superioribus gracilioribus teretiusculis, inferioribus rigidioribus compressis; floribus flavis extus rubellis; bacca ovata basi clavata flava pulvillis 35–50 stipata setosissimis, omnibus seu solum inferioribus aculeatis; seminibus numerosissimis valde inæqualibus plerumque transversis indistincte commissuratis. (Tab. LXX—LXXI.)

Arid soil south and west of El Paso, especially between the Sand hills and Lake Santa Maria, *Wright*, *Bigelow*, in Sonora, *Wright*, and on the lower Gila and in the Colorado desert, *Schott:* fl. August and September.—This is the largest and stoutest of our clavate *Opuntiæ*, with very numerous and long spines, spreading largely and growing 6–12 inches high; forming a welcome retreat for the smaller Rodentia, snakes, &c., which, under the protection of its powerful spines, are secure against the attacks of their enemies. Joints curved, 4–6 inches long, 1–1½ inch in diameter; the tubercles are 1–1½ inch long, very prominent, and might be termed cylindric if they were not longitudinally attached to the stems. The upper tubercles of each joint and their spines are more fully developed than the others in this, as in all *Opuntiœ*. In those we distinguish four larger central spines; the upper one more erect, the lower one stouter, longer, broader, and deflexed. We often find a second upper one above, and a second lower one below the other, or the four central spines are surrounded by a circle of 6 or 8 somewhat smaller spines, which may be considered as an interior series of radiating ones. The exterior series consists of 10–20 shorter and more slender spines; but the arrangement of spines in this genus is never so regular as it is in other genera, especially in *Echinocactus*. Stoutest spines 1½–2½ inches in length, ¾–1 line wide, striated, flat on the upper, strongly carinate on the lower surface, so as to appear triangular; other interior spines 1–2 inches, exterior ones ¾–1½ inch long. Fruit 2–2½ inches long, an inch in diameter; larger pulvillis 2–2½ lines in diameter; bristles whitish or reddish 3–4 lines long; 10 or 12 spines, 4–8 lines in length, are mixed with the bristles on all or only on the lower pulvilli. Seeds in the same fruit 2½–3 lines in diameter, or more; often transverse, or angular, blunt or beaked; cotyledons generally oblique, sometimes accumbent, contrary to the usual arrangement in this genus. The specimens from the lower Gila and the Colorado must, I have little doubt, also be referred here. Plant 12–18 inches high, far-spreading, of a dull greyish-green color; joints similar to those described above; spines only 1–1½ inch long; flowers sulphur-yellow, externally tinged with purple, 2 or 2½ inches in diameter; pulvilli of the ovary over a line in diameter, white-tomentose, supported by subulate leaves (2 lines long), bearing short white bristles and reddish spines; exterior sepals oblanceolate, cuspidate, red-brown; interior ones with yellow and red petaloid margins; petals yellow, with red tips; fruit not as large, but even more spiny than in the specimens from El Paso. This species, also, has been named in honor of *Col. Wm. H. Emory*, who, in his different expeditions to the extreme southwestern parts of our territory, always exerted himself for the advancement of our knowledge of the natural history of these regions.

14. O. Schottii (sp. nov.): articulis breviter clavatis adscendentibus; tuberculis elongatis; pulvillis paucisetosis; aculeis scaberrimis rubellis, interioribus 4 cruciatis, superiore triangulato erecto, cæteris ancipitibus supra planis subtus convexis, inferiore latiore; aculeis exterioribus 8–10 radiantibus valde inæqualibus; bacca ovata clavata pulvillis 35–40 setas suberectas aculeosque paucos gerentibus; seminibus angulatis rostratis transversis, commissura lineari indistincta. (Tab. LXXIII, fig. 1–3.)

Abundant on the arid hills near the Rio Grande, between the San Pedro and Pecos rivers, *Wright, Schott.*—The specimens gathered in July and September were all in fruit. Joints 2 inches, tubercles 8–9 lines long; pulvilli even in the oldest joints with few bristles; spines rougher than in any other allied species, red; the broader ones with a white margin, 1½–2 inches long; smaller radiating spines 4–9 lines long, almost surrounding the inner one. Ovary with white-tomentose pulvilli and short bristles; those in the fruit become a little longer, but are confined to the upper half of the pulvillus and are erect, while in all the allied species they are much more numerous and stellately spread in all directions. Seed a little over 2 lines in the transverse diameter; cotyledons in all the seeds examined oblique. Dedicated to one of its discoverers, whose name I have often had occasion to mention.

Dr. Gregg has sent a similar plant from San Luis Potosi, Mexico, which, though growing 7 or 8 degrees farther south, I must consider the same as *O. Schottii*. Its joints 2 inches long; tubercles 10–12 lines long; 4 central spines ancipital or triangular, 12–20 lines long, much less rough, 8–12 exterior spines of very different sizes. (Tab. LXXIII, fig. 4.)

15. O. GRAHAMI (sp. nov.): radicibus crassis fusiformibus; articulis breviter clavatis adscendentibus læte viridibus; tuberculis oblongis; folii e basi ovata abrupte acuminatis; pulvillis albo-tomentosis setas demum numerosas elongatas rigidas gerentibus; aculeis gracilibus scabris rubellis demum cinereo-fuscis, interioribus 4–7 robustioribus scabris teretiusculis seu 4-angulatis seu rarius compressis, exterioribus 4–6 multo minoribus; flore flavo; ovarii pulvillis sub 30 albo-tomentosis setosis; bacca ovata setosissima; seminibus regularibus vix rostratis, commissura lineari indistincta. (Tab. LXXII.)

Sandy soil in the bottom of the Rio Grande, near El Paso, and for a distance of about 100 miles along the river, *Wright*, *Bigelow*; fl. June.—Roots often 6 inches long and an inch thick, tapering, single or divided; joints 1½–2 inches long, ¾ or at most 1 inch in diameter; tubercles 6–7 lines long; leaves similar to those of *O. vulgaris*, short and thick; nearly a line in diameter at base and about twice as long. Larger spines 1½–2 inches long and spreading, scabrous, slenderer than in any allied species. Flowers apparently 2 inches in diameter, and, like the fruit, very similar to those of *O. clavata*; seeds 2.5–2.8 lines long, with a linear and often very indistinct commissure; cotyledons in the seeds examined regularly incumbent. This species, peculiar to an interesting part of our boundary, has been named in honor of the gentleman who was for a time chief of the scientific corps of the Commission, and by whose orders this, with many other species of *Cacti*, has been sent to me.

16. O. BULBISPINA (sp. nov.): radicibus fusiformibus; articulis parvis ovatis vix clavatis sæpius ex apice proliferis fragilibus; pulvillis parce setosis, junioribus laxe villosis; aculeis teretiusculis scabrellis basi bulbosis, interioribus 4 cruciatis, inferiore longiore, exterioribus 8–12 radiantibus. (Tab. LXXIII, fig. 5–6.)

Near Perros Bravos, north of Saltillo, *Gregg*.—Spreading masses 2–4 feet in diameter; joints 9–12 lines long, 6 lines in diameter, often proliferous at the upper end; tubercles 3–4 lines long; interior spines 4–6 lines, exterior ones 1½–3 lines in length. This species has the subcylindric joints, the reticulated ligneous texture, and the scabrous spines of the clavate *Opuntiæ*, but its mode of ramification is rather different, and the form of the joints is more ovate than clavate. Perhaps it belongs rather to Prince Salm's section *Glomeratæ*, and near *O. pusilla* from South America.

### § 2. *Cylindricæ*.

Stems ascending or usually erect, much branched; joints cylindric or tumid, tuberculate or sometimes almost smooth; the ligneous tissue is compact, and either (in spec. 17–24) forms a reticulated hollow tube, in which the meshes correspond with the tubercles, and which by age becomes more and more solid and massive, or it is (in spec. 25–28) reticulated only when quite young, and soon becomes quite dense. The spines are almost always terete, and are always covered with a loose glistening sheath. Flowers purple or rarely yellow, large, or usually middle sized or (in the two last species) quite small. The fruit is unarmed, somewhat fleshy or leathery, rarely pulpy, throwing off the dead flower, or very rarely retaining it. In a few species it is dry and spiny.

17 O. ECHINOCARPA, E. & B. in Pacif. R. R. Var. β. MAJOR: elatior; articulis elongatis basi attenuatis; tuberculis oblongo-linearibus; setis tenuibus penicillatis; aculeis longioribus laxius vaginatis paucioribus; bacca globosa seu basi clavata pulvillos pauciores gerente.

In the deserts on both sides of the Colorado, and in Sonora, *Schott.*—This form looks very different from the plant collected by Dr. Bigelow, and described in the report of Captain Whipple; but the very peculiar seeds which fortunately have been obtained by both collectors prove them to be identical. Dr. Bigelow's plant is a low straggling shrub; but Mr. Schott's is 4 or 5 feet high, with divaricate branches, joints 8–10 inches long, with elongated tubercles, (6–9 lines in length,) fine long bristles, and longer spines with looser sheaths. The 4 central larger spines are 1–1¾ inch long; the 4–8 radiating spines on the contrary shorter; the first is longer and bears only about 25 pulvilli, as spiny as in the original form.

18. O. SERPENTINA, E. in Sill. Journ., 1852: diffusa; ramis elongatis subverticillatis divaricatis adscendentibus; tuberculis prominentibus ovatis; pulvillis albido-setosis; aculeis 7–9 vaginatis albidis seu rufescentibus porrectis, infimis deflexis; floribus minoribus flavis extus rubellis; ovario depresso pulvillis sub-20 stipato; sepalis 10 late obovatis breviter cuspidatis; petalis sub-5 obovatis integriusculis mucronatis; stigmatibus 8 erectis; bacca sicca subhemisphærica villosa aculeatissima late et profunde umbilicata flore emarcido sæpe coronata.

Dry hills near San Diego, California, *Parry*, generally nearer the seacoast than *O. prolifera*, and not gregarious, nor so common as that species, *Schott.*—Stems 1–1½ inch in diameter, suberect, 4–5 feet high, or almost prostrate; joints 6–12 inches long, ¾–1¼ inch thick, somewhat verticillate, divaricate; spines 3–9 inches long, sheathed, light yellowish, or rusty, upper ones stellate-divaricate, lower one closely deflexed. A single flower was collected by Mr. Schott in October; it is not quite 1½ inch wide, the ovary depressed, about 8 lines high with 20 areolæ bearing dirty yellowish wool, yellow bristles, and 5–7 reddish brown sheathed spines, 2–4 lines in length; sepals externally yellowish-green, tinged with purple; even the lower ones unusually obtuse or short cuspidate; petals rounded scarcely 9 lines long, yellow above, red at tip, ascending and forming a cup-shaped corolla; stigmata (green ?) 2 lines long. Fruit saucer-shaped, deeply and broadly umbilicate, yellowish-brown, very spiny, and "long woolly."

19. O. PROLIFERA, E. l. c.: caule arborescente; ramis numerosis horizontalibus divaricatissimis; articulis ovatis seu ovato-cylindricis tumidis fragilibus versus ramorum apicem congestis perviridibus, inferioribus demum refractis brunneis; tuberculis obovato-oblongis prominulis; pulvillis ovatis tomentosis, vetustioribus stramineo-setosis; aculeis 8–10 obscuris stramineo-seu rufo-vaginatis, singulo subcentrali, cæteris patulis stellatis, inferioribus brevioribus; flore rubro; sepalis late ovatis; petalis oblongo-obovatis; stigmatibus erectis; bacca ovata umbilicata aculeolata sæpissime sterili proliferaque.

On arid hills about San Diego, California, near dry beds of streams, forming impassable and extensive thickets, *Parry, Schott.*—These thickets are likened by Mr. Schott to unapproachable coral reefs. Stem 2–4 and sometimes even 6–7 inches thick, and 3–10 feet high; the wood forms a reticulated hollow tube with short meshes, which in old plants finally become obliterated. The tumid joints are 3–6 inches long, 1½–2 inches in diameter, clustered at the end of the branches; the younger ones easily break off and stick to the skin of men or animals. The tubercles are obovate, narrowed below, and about 6 lines in length, arranged in 5 or 8 spirals; areolæ oval, somewhat immersed, with bunches of fine straw-colored bristles at the upper edge. Spines very variable, always with large loose sheaths; in a specimen before me I find 7–8 radiating spines; the upper ones and the central one equal, about 12–14 lines long; the lower ones 6–8 lines long, with a few still smaller ones below; in other specimens the upper spines are reduced in size or are wanting; flowers dark-red, salverform, about 1½ inch in diameter; fruit said to be spinulose, but always abortive, as Dr. Parry has often satisfied himself, and usually proliferous. This species somewhat resembles *O. arborescens*, but is easily distinguished by the short and tumid joints, short tubercles, spiny fruit, etc. The alliance with the next species and with *O. Bigelovii* is much closer. They represent the same type east of the California mountains that this does on the Pacific coast; just as *O. echinocarpa* in the Colorado valley represents another type which has on the coast its representative in *O. serpentina.*

20. O. FULGIDA (sp. nov.): caule erecto arborescente flexuoso; ramis numerosis divaricatis; articulis ovatis seu ovato-cylindricis tumidis glaucescentibus ad ramorum apicem congestis; tuberculis ovato-oblongis sub-prominulis; foliis ovatis cuspidatis; pulvillis pulvinatis ovatis tomentosis setas pallide stramineas et aculeos 7–9 subæquales laxe vaginatos undique porrectos stellatos gerentibus; floris parvi purpurei ovario ovato pulvillis 25–30 albo-tomentosis prædito setis aculeisque destituto; sepalis tubi 8–10 orbiculatis obtusis crenulatis; petalis 8, exterioribus cuneatis retusis crenulatis, intimis lanceolatis acutis cætera superantibus; stigmatibus 5 erectis; bacca ovata pulposa vix tuberculata plane umbilicata sæpissime sterili et fasciculatim prolifera; seminibus parvis irregulariter angulatis rostratis anguste commissuratis; cotyledonibus regulariter incumbentibus. (Tab. LXXV, fig. 18.)

Throughout all the Sierras in western Sonora, named by the inhabitants "Vela de Cojote," whence the specific name, which however would be just as appropriate for most other cylindric *Opuntiæ*, which are often visible for several miles when the sun strikes the glistening sheaths of their spines: fl. in July and August.—Stems 5–12 feet high, flexuous with few divaricate branches; joints clustered at their ends, 3–8 inches long and often 2 inches in diameter; "dull grayish, inclined to olive"; tubercles ovate-elongate, 6–7 lines long; leaves thick and only about 1 line long; spines almost equal in length, (1–1¼ inch,) stellate and not much deflexed; completely hiding the surface of the young joints; ovary about 10 lines long; flower cup-shaped, mostly less than an inch in diameter; fruit a plump fleshy berry, oval, rounded, not or only slightly tuberculated, 1–1¼ inch long, a little less in diameter, and entirely spineless; characterized by the large white tomentose pulvilli. Seeds 1–1½ line in diameter, or with the beak often 2 lines long, much compressed, and thin and very angular, often oddly shaped. The fruit is not rarely sterile and proliferous, and becomes pendulous from the weight of the young sprouts attached to it.

21. O. WHIPPLEI, E. & B. in Pacif. R. Rep., var. β SPINOSIOR: elatior, erecta; articulis cylindricis; tuberculis ovatis confertis; pulvillis parce tomentosis, vix setosis; aculeis 12–14 stramineo-vaginatis stellato-porrectis; flore rubro; ovarii ovati tuberculati pulvillis 20–30 albo-tomentosis setas stramineas et aculeolos paucos mox deciduos gerentibus; sepalis 8 orbiculatis cuspidatis; petalis 8–10 spathulatis cuspidatis; bacca subglobosa leviter tuberculata inermi; seminum commissura lineari.

From the Gila south to the Santa Cruz river and Tucson, and further east, *Schott:* fl. in June.

—Stems 6–10 feet high; joints 4–12 inches long, ½–¾ inch thick, covered with ovate or rather rhombic tubercles. Spines much more numerous in this variety than in the original form, found by Dr. Bigelow farther north, 6–9 lines long. Flowers 1¼–1½ inch wide, cup-shaped; seeds nearly 2 lines in diameter, larger than in the northern form, with a very sharply marked linear commissure.

22. O. ARBORESCENS, E. in Wisl. Rep.: caule arborescente erecto reticulato-lignoso; ramis verticillatis horizontaliter divergentibus seu pendulis; articulis verticillatis plerumque ternis quaternisve cylindricis perviridibus; tuberculis elongatis cristatis; foliis teretibus elongatis patulis; pulvillis ovatis pulvinatis breviter tomentosis vix setosis; aculeis 8–30 corneis seu fuscis stramineo-vaginatis undique stellato-porrectis, 1–8 interioribus longioribus laxius vaginatis, centrali sub-deflexo, exterioribus debilioribus arcte vaginatis; flore purpureo magno; ovarii subglobosi tuberculati pulvillis 20–25 breviter tomentosis setas minutas et aculeolos paucos erectos deciduos gerentibus; sepalis tubi 8–13 obovatis obtusis medio virescentibus margine purpureis; petalis 1012 obovatis obtusis retusisve; filamentis purpureis; stigmatibus 8; bacca globosa seu hemisphærica tuberculis prominentibus cristata late umbilicata inermi subsicca flava; seminibus regularibus anguste commissuratis; cotyledonibus incumbentibus seu rare obliquis. (Tab. LXXV, fig. 16–17.)

This species extends from the upper waters of the Arkansas and the Platte rivers deep into Mexico, and from the plains east of the Llano Estacado (200 miles east of the Pecos) to Zuñi, 150 miles west of the Rio Grande, about 15 degrees of latitude and 8 of longitude: fl. May and June.—North and east this species is only about 5 feet high, but further south it is said to become 20 or 30 feet high. Even the old trunks continue greenish and spiny; the massive ligneous skeleton is always characterized by the elongated-rhombic meshes and the verticillate insertions of the branches; in very old specimens the cavity of the tube and the meshes become almost obliterated by the filling in of ligneous layers. The roots are often somewhat tuberous by a swelling of the fibres. Joints 2–6 inches long, less than an inch in diameter; tubercles compressed-cristate, elevated, 7–9 lines long; leaves 6–10 lines long, hardly a line in diameter; spines very variable in number and size; sometimes we find only 8–12 spines, not half an inch long, so that the plant from a distance appears spineless; but more frequently 20–25, or even more spines occur, the longest middle ones deflexed, and 8–10, or rarely 12–14 lines in length, other spines spreading all around, 4–8 lines long. The beautiful purple flowers are 2½–3 inches in diameter, and often profusely cover the tree; the stigmata have a length of 3 or 3½ lines. The fruit is about an inch long in all dimensions; umbilicus wider or narrower, shallower or deeper, according to the greater or smaller prominence of the upper tubercles of the fruit. Seeds 1½–2 lines in diameter, usually of a regular shape, with little or no beak; the commissure distinct, and between 0.1 and 0.2 line broad; cotyledons almost always regularly incumbent, rarely somewhat oblique. Sometimes 3 cotyledons are observed in the seeds of this species, as is also the case in many others.

23. O. MAMILLATA, A. Schott in litt.: caule arborescente reticulato-lignoso divaricato-ramosissimo; articulis ovato-cylindricis crassis abbreviatis retusis perviridibus; tuberculis ovatis tumidis prominentibus; foliis ovatis abbreviatis cuspidatis; pulvillis ovatis albo-tomentosis setas brevissimas seu nullas gerentibus; aculeis 4–6 gracilibus brevibus arcte vaginatis stramineis, plerisque deflexis; flore parvo purpureo; ovarii ovati pulvillis 18–24 pulvinatis albo-tomentosis; sepalis tubi sub-8 orbiculatis; petalis 8 late obovatis abbreviatis; filamentis exterioribus

dilatatis (sterilibus?); stigmatibus 7–8 erectis; bacca ovata plane umbilicata pulvillis magnis albo-tomentosis inermibus notata; seminibus parvis angulatis vix rostratis anguste commissuratis valde compressis. (Tab. LXXV, fig. 19.)

South range of the Sierra Bubuquibari, in Sonora, and southeastward, in fertile valleys, *Schott:* fl. July and August.—This peculiar species is more tree-like than any other Sonorian *Opuntia.* It has a distinct trunk and a dense top, much like any other ordinary tree, though only 5 or 6 feet high; the joints are 3 or 4 inches long, and 1½ inch in diameter; the swelling tubercles much resemble those of a *Mamillaria,* whence the name; the thick leaves are scarcely a line long; spines few, 3–9 lines long, sometimes almost wanting. The flowers are hardly an inch in diameter, and of a bright pink or purple color; the ovary is 8 or 9 lines long, and the fruit of the same length, slightly tuberculate, in all the specimens before me unarmed, (according to Mr. Schott's notes, "spiny.") Seeds 1–1½ line in each dimension, often higher than broad, very irregular, remarkably similar to those of *O. fulgida,* but scarcely beaked, and still more compressed; cotyledons incumbent, or often somewhat oblique.

24. O. Thurberi (sp. nov.): frutescens, erecta; articulis cylindricis gracilioribus tuberculatis; tuberculis oblongo-linearibus minus prominulis; pulvillis sub-orbiculatis breviter fulvo-tomentosis vix setosis; aculeis 3–5 brevibus obscuris stramineo-seu fulvo-vaginatis lateraliter divergentibus, infimo robustiore deflexo; flore miniato; ovarii clavati tuberculati pulvillis 18–20 tomentosis brevissime setosis et parce aculeolatis; sepalis tubi obovatis cuspidatis; petalis erectiusculis obovato-spathulatis obtusis retusisve; stigmatibus 7 brevibus crassis erectis.

Near Bacuachi, Sonora, *G. Thurber:* fl. in June.—Similar in some respects to *O. arborescens;* but the slender joints only about 6 lines in diameter; tubercles 9 lines long, spines 3–8 lines long, the lowest one the stoutest! and deflexed. The ovary is about 10 lines long and bears on some of the pulvilli 1 or 2 spines, which are evidently deciduous, as we see them in *O. arborescens* and *O. Whipplei;* the flower is 1½ inch in diameter, dull brick red, salver form, and opens much less than that of *O. arborescens,* which is pure purple; stigmata 1–1½ line long. This species I have named for its discoverer, Mr. George Thurber, who, in Mr. Commissioner Bartlett's party, traversed Sonora, and gathered many interesting plants in that then almost unknown country.

25. O. Wrightii (sp. nov.): caule frutescente erecto, juniore reticulate, seniore compacto-lignoso; ramis adscendentibus; articulis cylindricis gracilibus sub-tuberculatis; tuberculis elongatis depressis; foliis elongatis subulatis patulis; pulvillis orbiculatis albo-tomentosis setas gracillimas penicillatas gerentibus; aculeis singulis (seu rarius 1–2 superioribus minoribus adjectis) porrectis seu paullo deflexis e cinereo rubellis vagina straminea decidua indusiatis; flore miniato; ovarii obovati pulvillis 15–18 albo-tomentosis setosisque; sepalis tubi 9–12 orbiculatis, exterioribus cuspidatis, interioribus obtusis; petalis sub-8 late obovatis emarginatis; styli crassi stigmatibus 6–7 brevibus adpressis.

Common on steep rocky mountain sides on the Limpia, *Wright,* and along the Rio Grande from Presidio del Norte to the Pecos, *Parry, Bigelow;* also southward, in Mexico, *Gregg:* fl. June and July.—A shrub, 2–4 feet high, about 1 or 1½ inch thick below, intermediate between *O. arborescens* and *O. frutescens* in size, structure of stem, and arrangement of spines; branches few; joints 4 lines in diameter; tubercles flat, 7–9 lines long; leaves about 5 lines long; spines 8–10 lines in length, generally single or with 1 or 2 small and divergent ones above; in one specimen before me those upper spines are almost as stout and long as the lower one; flowers about 1 or 1¼ inch in diameter; ovary 7–8 lines long; fruit unknown.—This pretty species of *Opuntia* bears a name which has been often mentioned in these pages, and which is forever inseparably connected with the botany of our Southern boundary.

26. O. ARBUSCULA, (sp. nov.): caule erecto arborescente dense lignoso apice ramosissimo capitato; ramis divaricatis elongatis teretibus etuberculatis; articulis junioribus læte viridibus leviter tuberculatis; tuberculis oblongo-linearibus depressis; pulvillis magnis orbiculatis albo-tomentosis; setis parcis gracillimis penicillatis; aculeis singulis (seu subinde binis lateralibus) porrectis demum deflexis stramineo- seu fulvo-vaginatis, rarius une alterove breviore inferiore deflexo adjecto; flore flavo-virescente; ovarii clavati pulvillis 16–18 albo-tomentosis vix setosis; sepalis tubi sub-8 orbiculatis cuspidatis seu mucronatis; petalis sub-5 spathulatis, staminibus extus in staminodia latiora subulata transeuntibus; stigmatibus 5 brevibus erectis.

On the desert heights, near Maricopa village, on the Gila, *Schott*: fl. in June.—A truly arborescent species, 7–8 feet high, with a solid, ligneous trunk, 4–5 inches thick, smooth green bark, and a top formed by the numerous slender and divaricate branches; ultimate joints 2–3 inches long, about 4 lines in diameter; tubercles flat and indistinct, about 6 lines long; spine 9–12 lines long. Ovary, in my specimen, 10 lines long and only 4 lines in diameter, without any spines; but the fruit is described by Mr. Schott as "bristly, crowned by the persistent flower." Flower apparently nearly 1½ inch in diameter; petals few, 9 lines long and 4 lines broad, greenish-yellow, tinged with red. Stamina and staminodia (perhaps what I consider so are but the broader filaments of the exterior fertile stamens) finally breaking off near their base, leaving a rough surface. The name of this species indicates a small tree.

27. O. FRUTESCENS, E. in Pl. Lindh. was collected abundantly in all western Texas and southern New Mexico. For a fuller account and a figure, see Engelmann and Bigelow's paper on the *Cactaceæ* of Captain Whipple's Pacific Railroad Exploring Expedition Report.

28. O. TESSELLATA, E. in Pacif. R. R. (O. ramosissima, *E. in Sill. Journ.* 1852).—This curious species was first noticed by *Dr. Parry*, and described, as above cited, in an account of his Californian *Cactaceæ*, under the name of *O. ramosissima*, which being deemed an improper name in a section where all could claim it with equal, and some with greater justice, it was changed in the account of *Dr. Bigelow's* plants, who brought specimens of the wood, the branches, and the fruit. Mr. Schott, the third botanist who collected it, was fortunate enough to find the flowers. Living plants are yet a desideratum in our gardens.

This species grows in arid sandy soil, from the Sierra Madre south of the Gila to the lower Colorado, Bill Williams's fork, and the Californian Mountains. Mr. Schott found it in September with flower and ripe fruit. The flower is purple, about 6 lines in diameter; the clavate ovary is of the same length, and bears 40 or 50 very tomentose but scarcely spiny or bristly pulvilli; the 5 petals are almost orbicular; the exterior filaments are broad and persistent (sterile staminodia?); 5 stigmata short and erect. The fruit resembles very much those of the clavate *Opuntiæ;* it is 9 or 10 lines long, dry, ovate, and contracted above; the narrow and deep umbilicus contains the remains of the flower, the above-mentioned broad filaments being most conspicuous; externally it is covered with a profusion of hair-like flexuous bristles of a red brown color, 2–3 lines in length, mixed with dense wool. Seeds thick, with a broad spongy commissure, 1.8–2.0 lines in diameter. Mr. Schott collected in May other greenish-yellow flowers, from similar bushes, which he considers as of a distinct variety; the ovary in these flowers appears elongated, and is probably sterile, and would have become persistent and proliferous, as we find it in many other *Opuntiæ;* so that this green-flowered form probably is not a variety of our species, but a degeneration.

# ALPHABETICAL INDEX.

# EXPLANATION OF PLATES.

Remarks.—All the figures are in natural size unless otherwise stated. The seeds of Mamillariæ, Echinocacti, and Cerei are represented in the natural size, and eight times magnified: *a* is a lateral view, natural size; *b*, same, eight times magnified; *c*, part of the surface of the seed still more magnified; *d*, seed after the removal of the outer coat, with endopleura and albumen; *e*, embryo; *f*, another form of same seed; *g*, seedling plant; *h*, back view; *i*, front view; *k*, basal view; *l*, top view of embryo—all eight times magnified.

The seeds of Opuntiæ, being larger, are represented: *a*, side view, natural size; *b*, same, four times magnified, as are all the following ones; *c*, posterior view; *d*, anterior view; *e*, vertical section; *f*, seed after the removal of the testa; *g*, embryo.

The landscape opposite the title-page represents a region near the Colorado river, with several *Cacti*, especially *Cereus giganteus;* one of them decayed, showing the form of the ligneous skeleton. The different plants are accurate copies of nature.

Pl. 1. Mamillaria micromeris: 1, a young plant not yet blooming, without the tuft; 2, a plant in bloom, with the tuft; 3 and 4, different views of a plant of the largest size; several fruits are seen in the tuft; 5, a tubercle with a bunch of spines, eight times magnified; 6, a bunch of spines in natural size, and 7 the same, eight times enlarged.

Pl. 2. *The same:* 1, lateral view of a bunch of spines, and its wool on the flower-bearing part of the plant, eight times magnified, exhibiting the upper elongated clavate spines; 2, flower, four times enlarged; 3, fruit; 4, seed.

Fig. 5–8. Mamillaria micromeris var. Greggii: 5, bunch of spines; 6, same, eight times magnified, showing the ragged ends of the long spines where they are broken off; 7, a bunch of spines, with its wool from the flowering part of the plant, with the long clavate spines, eight times magnified; 8, seed.

Pl. 3. Mamillaria lasiacantha: 1, a plant of the ordinary size in flower; 2, flower, four times magnified; 3, a tubercle with a bunch of spines, showing the pubescence, eight times magnified; 4–5, bunches of spines, natural size, and eight times magnified.

Pl. 4. Mamillaria lasiacantha var. denudata: 1, a fruit-bearing plant; 2, a tubercle, with its bunch of spines, eight times magnified; 3–4, bunches of spines, in natural size, and the same eight times magnified; 5, seed.

Pl. 5. Mamillaria pusilla var. Texana: 1, whole plant in flower; 2, a tubercle, with a bunch of spines and the axillary wool, twice magnified; 3, a bunch of spines, same; 4, flower, same; 5, fruit natural size; 6, seed.

Pl. 6, Fig. 1–8. Mamillaria Grahami: 1, a single plant; 2–4, bunches of spines, with one, two, and three central spines; 5, a tubercle and bunch of spines, magnified twice; 6, a bunch of spines from Dr. Parry's specimen from the Colorado, also magnified twice; 7, a flower from A. Schott's specimen from the Gila; 8 seed.

Fig. 9–12. Mamillaria barbata: 9, a tubercle and bunch of spines, natural size; 10, bunch of spines, magnified twice; 11, fruit; 12, seed.

Pl. 7. Mamillaria phellosperma: 1, a flowerless plant; 2, a bunch of spines; 3, a tubercle with the axillary wool and bristles, and the terminal bunch of spines twice magnified; 4–6, bunches of spines with one or more hooks, twice the natural size; 7–8, fruits of different size; 9, seed.

Pl. 8, Fig. 1–8. Mamillaria Wrightii: 1, a whole plant in fruit, from a sketch of Mr. Moellhausen's; 2, a young, and 3, an old tubercle with spines of the same specimen; 4–6, spines of a specimen from the Copper mines, four from the older part of the plant; 7, flower; 8, seed.

Fig. 9–14. Mamillaria Goodrichii: 9, tubercle with spines; 10, bunch of spines, natural size; 11–12, tubercles with the axillary wool and bristles, and the spines; 13–14, bunches of spines; the last four figures are magnified twice.

Pl. 9, Fig. 1–3. Mamillaria meiacantha: 1, whole plant in flower; 2, fruit; 3, seed.

Fig. 4–14. Mamillaria Heyderi, var. applanta: 4, upper part of plant in flower and fruit; 5–6, different views of flowers; 7, fruit; 8, seed, all from the same specimen from El Paso; 9–14, bunches of spines of different forms, of the same variety, from western Texas.

Fig. 15–17: bunches of spines and seed of the var. hemisphærica, from Matamoras.

Fig. 18–20. Mamillaria gummifera: different views of tubercles and spines.

Pl. 10. Mamillaria Echinus: 1, whole plant in fruit; 2–3, tubercles showing the groove and the wool on the basal areola; 4–7, bunches of spines of younger and older plants; 8–9, same, with the central spine curved; 10, fruit; 11, seed.

Pl. 11. Mamillaria pectinata: 1, whole plant in flower; 2–3, different views of tubercles from the sides of the plant; 4–7, bunches of spines; 8–9, tubercles from the flower-bearing top of larger plants; 10, seed.

Pl. 12, Fig. 1–16. Mamillaria tuberculosa: 1, a large specimen in fruit; 2–11, tubercles and bunches of spines of different specimens; 2–3, from a young plant; 10, a very young tubercle; all the tubercles exhibit the large mass of dense wool at base; 12, flower bud; 13, flower; 14, fruit; 15, seed of the same; 16, seed of another specimen, smaller, and with smaller marks.

Fig. 17–22. Mamillaria dasyacantha: 17–20, tubercles and bunches of spines of different specimens; 21–22, seeds of the same.

Pl. 13. Mamillaria radiosa, var. Neo Mexicana: 1, a plant with several branches in flower; 2 and 3, different tubercles with bunches of spines, the woolly grooves extending more or less down along the upper side of the tubercle; 4, a bunch of spines; 6, a fruit; 7, seed.

Pl. 14. Mamillaria macromeris in flower.

Pl. 15. *The same:* 1, one of the largest bunches of spines; 2, one of the smallest ones; 3, a young tubercle not fully developed; 4, a young, but full-grown tubercle, bearing the flower at the lower end of the woolly groove, far above the axil; a younger tubercle attached to it; 5, a ripe fruit with a few scales; 6 and 7, seeds of the largest and the smallest kind.

Pl. 16. Mamillaria fissurata: 1, a flowering plant; 2, petals; 3, nine tubercles of different size and age, and in different positions; 3, a large tubercle from above; 4, same from below; 5, same from the side; 6, a smaller one, with fewer divisions from above; 7, side view of same;

8, a small tubercle from above ; 9, a young one with the silky wool yet straight and smooth ; 10, a young tubercle bearing a fruit, which becomes visible after separating the wool ; 11, seed.

PL. 17, ECHINOCACTUS SCHEERII: 1, a full-grown plant in flower ; 2, part of a rib, front view, showing the form of the tubercles and their grooves ; 3, part of a rib, side view ; 4–6, bunches of spines ; 7, seed.

PL. 18. ECHINOCACTUS BREVIHAMATUS: a full-grown plant of ordinary size.

PL. 19. *The same:* 1, part of a rib, side view, to exhibit the tubercles and their grooves ; 2, part of a rib almost in front, with a flower ; 3, a tubercle with a flower at the base of the long groove ; 4, a young bunch of spines from a small specimen ; 5–8, bunches of spines from different full-grown specimens.

PL. 20. ECHINOCACTUS SETISPINUS: 1, top of a plant with flower ; 2, another flower ; 3, flower bud ; 4–6, bunches with twelve radial and one central spine of different size and shape ; 7–9, bunches with more radial, and sometimes more central spines ; 10, bunch of spines with two almost straight central spines ; 11, fruit ; 12, several seeds attached to the funiculi, four times magnified ; 13, seed of the usual size and form ; 14, larger seed of a specimen from Eagle Pass, to which spines fig. 8, belong.

PL. 21. ECHINOCACTUS LONGEHAMATUS: part of a rib with a flower.

PL. 22. *The same,* a rib, side view, showing the tubercles, and with their short grooves and their flexuous spines.

PL. 23. *The same:* 1, a bunch of spines of the longest spined variety ; 2, a fruit ; 3, seed ; 4 and 5, bunches of spines of the smaller variety.

PL. 24. *The same:* 1, a bunch of spines of the thick spined Mexican form ; 2 and 3, lower central spines of the same ; 4, seed of the *"Limas agrias,"* the sour cactus-berries of Saltillo, to exhibit the peculiar form of the seed, and the great favosity of the surface.

PL. 25. ECHINOCACTUS WISLIZENI: 1, upper part of a rib with a flower and a flower bud ; 2, pistil ; 3, fruit ; 4 and 5, seeds of different form and surface, from El Paso ; 6, seed of different shape, from the upper Gila.

PL. 26. *The same:* 1–3, bunches of spines of different shape and proportion.

PL. 27. ECHINOCACTUS LE CONTEI: 1, part of a rib with a fruit ; 2, a bunch of spines ; 3, a flower ; 4, section of same ; 5, seed.

PL. 28. ECHINOCACTUS EMORYI: 1, bunch of spines of a large specimen, from Guaymas ; 2, young bunch of spines with flower, from Sonora ; 3, section of flower.

PL. 29. ECHINOCACTUS VIRIDESCENS: 1 and 2, bunches of spines of a young plant ; 3, flower ; 4, pistil ; 5, fruit, not fully ripe and therefore a little shrivelled ; 6, seed.

PL. 30. ECHINOCACTUS CYLINDRACEUS: 1, a bunch of spines of a young specimen ; 2-5, bunches of spines of older, but not yet fully grown specimens.

PL. 31. ECHINOCACTUS HORIZONTHALONIUS, in flower.

PL. 32, fig. 1–5, *the same;* 1, a young plant ; 2–4, spines of different forms ; 5, seed.

Fig. 6–7. ECHINOCACTUS PARRYI, bunches of spines.

PL. 33. ECHINOCACTUS TEXENSIS: 1, a larger ; 2, a smaller bunch of spines ; 3, flower ; 4, fruit ; 5, seed from Texas ; 6, seed from Matamoras, smaller and more distinctly marked than fig. 5.

Fig. 7. Seed of ECHINOCACTUS SANDILLON, *Gay,* from Chili, which has also a woolly fruit.

PL. 34. ECHINOCACTUS INTERTEXTUS: 1, a plant of rather large size, in flower ; 2–5, young bunches of spines, more or less developed; 6–8, old bunches of spines; 9, fruit, with a few scales, with wool at base and the dry flower on top; 10, seed.

Pl. 35, fig. 1–5. Echinocactus intertextus, var. dasyacanthus: 1, 1–2, young bunches of spines; 3–5, old ones.

Fig. 6–8. Echinocactus unguispinus, bunches of spines.

Pl. 36. Cereus viridiflorus: 1, large plant from the Limpia in flower, one flower fully, another one half open; 2, bunch of spines of this plant without, and 3 with a central spine; 4–7, bunches of spines of a specimen collected by Dr. Bigelow on the upper Pecos, with 1 or more central spines; 4, a very young bunch; 5, a full grown one; 6, a similar larger one like the former, with 2 central spines; 7, another one, with the largest central spine curved upwards; 8–10, bunches of spines with and without a central spine, from plants collected by Dr. Wislizenus in northeastern New Mexico; 11, part of a plant in flower, with very obtuse petals and very small spines, collected by A. Fendler at Santa Fé; 14, fruit from Santa Fé; 15, seed of the same; 16, fruit from the Limpia.

Pl. 37. Cereus chloranthus in full bloom.

Pl. 38. *The same:* 1, top view, exhibiting the rays formed by the central spines; 2–7, different bunches of spines; 8, a small fruit; 9, one of usual size; 10, seed of common size; 11, smaller seed.

Pl. 39. Cereus dasyacanthus, a simple, branchless plant, with one flower.

Pl. 40. *The same:* bunches of spines, different in size, number, and proportion of the spines; all twice magnified.

Pl. 41, fig. 1–2. *The same:* 1, fruit; 2, seed.

Fig. 3–5. Cereus Roetteri: 3–4, bunches of spines, magnified twice; 5, a fruit.

Pl. 42. Cereus ctenoides: 1, a large specimen in flower; 2–3, front view and lateral view of a bundle of spines, twice magnified; 4, top part of another specimen, in which the spines are not so closely pectinate; 5–6, spines of this specimen, twice magnified.

Pl. 43. Cereus cæspitosus: a specimen of one of the largest forms; petals unusually curled.

Pl. 44. *The same:* 1–4, spines of the larger form, in different states of development, magnified twice; 5–7, spines of the smaller form, also magnified twice; some of the bunches show rudiments of central spines; 8, a fruit with the rudiments of the flower shrivelled up; 9, a fruit exhibiting yet the tube of the flower very distinctly; 10–11, seed of the larger, and 12, seed of the smaller form; 11, *g*, young seedling soon after germination.

Pl. 45. Cereus longisetus.

Pl. 46. Cereus stramineus: One head out of a plant with numerous heads.

Pl. 47. *The same:* Another head with smaller spines, seen from above; 2–4 bunches of spines; 5, fruit; 6, seed of the same, usual size; 7, seed of another specimen larger than usual.

Pl. 48. Fig. 1. A flower of the same.

Fig. 2–4. Cereus enneacanthus: 2, part of a stem showing the ribs and spines and a flower from El Paso; 3, flower of a specimen from Eagle Pass; 4, bunch of spines from El Paso; which, however, may belong to a form of C. stramineus; lower central spine triangular and much flattened.

Pl. 49. *The same:* 1, head of a specimen from Eagle Pass; 2, another one with longer and stouter spines; 3–10, bunches of spines of plants collected at Eagle Pass and at El Paso; 10, with a curved central spine; 11, fruit, belonging to flower, fig. 3, of last page; 12, seed of same.

PL. 50. CEREUS DUBIUS: 1, part of a rib with a flower; 2, bunch of spines, and 3, seed of same plant; 4–5, bunches of spines of another specimen; 6, same, with flower just closed; 7, fruit, and 8, seed of same.

PL. 51. CEREUS FENDLERI: A vigorous head of a plant brought from El Paso.

PL. 52. *The same:* 1, top of a plant with flower-bud and flower from El Paso; 2, fruit with few and stouter spines; 3, seed of same; 4, fruit with numerous slender spines; 5, seed of same; 6, another form of seed.

PL. 53. *The same:* 1, flower from Santa Fé; 2, young bunch of spines; 3–12, bunches of spines of different shape and size.

PL. 54. CEREUS POLYACANTHUS in flower; usual form with short spines.

PL. 55. *The same:* 1, part of a rib with a flower and a bud; 2–4, bunches of spines; 5, fruit with a bunch of spines; 6, seed of same; 7, fruit of another long-spined form; 8, seed of same.

PL. 56. CEREUS PAUCISPINUS: 1, an entire plant; 2, 5 bunches of spines; 6, seed.

PL. 57. CEREUS ENGELMANNI: 1, a head brought from Sonora by A. Schott; 2, young, and 3–4, older bunches of spines of the same; 5, fruit; 6, seed of same; 7, seed of Dr. Parry's original specimen.

PL. 58. CEREUS BERLANDIERI: 1, part of a plant with flower and flower-bud; 2–4, bunches of spines; 5, fruit; 6, seed.

PL. 59. Fig. 1–11. CEREUS PROCUMBENS: 1, a plant with flower-bud, flowers, and young fruit; 2–9, different bunches of spines; 10, fruit; 11, seed.

Fig. 12. CEREUS TUBEROSUS: seed.

PL. 60. Fig. 1–4. CEREUS EMORYI: 1, a fruit; 2, a bunch of spines of this fruit; 3, another one twice the natural size; 4, seed.

Fig. 5–6. CEREUS VARIABILIS: 5, fruit; 6, seed.

PL. 61. CEREUS GIGANTEUS: 1, part of the rib of an adult plant with two bunches of spines; 2, a bunch of spines; 3, part of a young rib of an adult plant collected in March; spines very short and slender yet; 4–5, bunches of spines of a young plant about eight inches high.

PL. 62. *The same:* 1, flower; 2, fruit; 3, seed; *m*, side view of embryo, cotyledons a little open; *n*, front view of same.

PL. 63. CEREUS GREGGII *α*. CISMONTANUS: 1, a flower; 2, a young plant raised from seed in the third year, showing the tuberous root.

PL. 64. *The same:* 1, lower part of a stem with the large tuberous root; half the natural size; 2–4, sections of the stem; 5–11, spines of different states of development and of different ages; all four times the natural size; 5, a bunch of very young spines imbedded in the wool of the areola; 6–10, full grown spines; 10, shows the lower spines crossed; 11, represents a very old bunch of spines; 12, a fruit; 13, seed.

PL. 65. CEREUS GREGGII, *β*. TRANSMONTANUS: 1, flower; 2–3, spines; four times magnified.

PL. 66. OPUNTIA STENOPETALA: 1, part of a joint; 2, part of another one with two flowers; 3, section of flower.

PL. 67. OPUNTIA STRIGIL: 1, an elongated joint with two fruits, bearing a young joint; 2, an orbicular joint; 3, several seeds.

PL. 68. OPUNTIA FILIPENDULA: 1, a whole plant in flower, half natural size; 2, a joint with flower and young fruit, natural size; 3, seed of this plant from below El Paso; 4, seed of same from Doña Ana, above El Paso, a little smaller.

PL. 69. OPUNTIA MACRORHIZA: 1, a whole plant with flower and buds, half natural size; 2, fruit natural size; 3–4, seeds of different size.

PL. 70. OPUNTIA EMORYI, from the region southwest of El Paso, in fruit.

PL. 71. *The same:* 1, a whole plant, reduced; 2, lateral view of a tubercle with a bunch of spines; 3, front view of one of the largest bunches of spines; part of the central spine, four times magnified; 4, different seeds.

PL. 72. OPUNTIA GRAHAMI: 1, whole plant, with large tuberous roots, and in fruit; 2, a young joint; 3, a bunch of spines of the usual form; 4, another one with broader central spines; 5, seed. The seed, as well as parts of spines, are four times magnified.

PL. 73, FIG. 1–3. OPUNTIA SCHOTTII: 1–2, bunches of spines, with parts four times magnified; 3, seed with an oblique embryo.

FIG. 4. OPUNTIA SCHOTTII, var. GREGGII: a bunch of spines, with part magnified four times.

FIG. 5–6. OPUNTIA BULBISPINA: 5, an entire joint; 6, a bunch of spines, part of central spine four times magnified.

FIG. 7–8. OPUNTIA IMBRICATA: 7, a joint; 8, a bunch of spines, and fragment of central spine, four times the natural size, showing the sheath.

PL. 74. Seeds of—1, *Mamillaria calcarata;* 2, *Mamillaria compacta;* 3, *Mamillaria vivipara;* 4, *Mamillaria radiosa*, var. *borealis;* 5, *Mamillaria radiosa*, var. *Texana;* 6, *Mamillaria nutallis α borealis;* 7, *β cæspitosa;* 8, *Mamillaria robusti spina;* 9, *Echinocactus uncinatus;* 10, *Echinocactus uncinatus*, var. *Wrightii;* 11–14, *Echinocactus sinuatus;* 11, from the San Pedro, Wright; 12, from northern Mexico, Gregg; 13, from the same regions, Poselger; 14, the form sent by Poselger under the name of *Echinocactus robustus;* 15, *Cereus Thurberi;* 16, *Cereus Schottii.*

PL. 75. Seeds of *Opuntia:* 1–4, *Opuntia Engelmanni;* 1, from Chihauhua, Wislizenus; 2, from Matamoras; 3, from Presidio, Bigelow; 4, from Santa Rosa, Bigelow; 5–7, *Opuntia dulcis*, Wright and Bigelow; 8, *Opuntia macrocentra*, Wright; 9–13, *Opuntia phæacantha;* 9, from Santa Fé, Fendler; 10–13, Southern New Mexico, Wright; 14, *Opuntia tenuispina*, El Paso; 15, *Opuntia arenaria*, El Paso; 16–17, *Opuntia arborescens;* 18, *Opuntia fulgida;* 19, *Opuntia mamillata.*

The maps accompanying this memoir represents the geographical distribution of the different species of *cactaceæ* in the United States and adjacent regions, as far as at present known.

DEPARTMENT OF THE INTERIOR,

*Pacific Wagon Road Office, November* 26, 1858.

The foregoing paper on the CACTACEÆ of the Boundary having been printed about two years ago, before the author's visit to Europe, it is deemed advisable, in justice to Dr. Engelmann, to append the following corrections made by him since his return.

ALBERT H. CAMPBELL,

*In charge of Mexican Boundary Report.*

# CACTACEÆ OF THE BOUNDARY.

## CORRECTIONS.

# CACTACEAE OF THE BOUNDARY.

## CORRECTIONS.

A voyage to Europe, since my paper has gone through the press, has afforded me the advantage not only of the personal intercourse with numerous men of science and many cultivators, but also of an actual examination of various large collections of living *cactaceae*. Some of the results of my investigations, as far as they bear upon the *Cactaceae of the Boundary*, have been incorporated with the list of corrections of typographical errors.

Page 2, line 22. *Sepalis petalisque.* It will scarcely be necessary to inform the reader that the numerous foliaceous integuments of the cactus-flower do not very properly range under the divisions of *sepals* and *petals*. For convenience sake, however, the exterior more herbaceous ones are called *sepals*, and the interior ones, with thinner texture and brighter color, are named *petals*. The "*sepals*" usually are more numerous than the "*petals*," and, in most genera, form a complete transition from the organs, which on the stem, represent the leaves, (usually with their spiny appendages) to the petals. On the ovary they usually resemble the former, which, among other reasons, seems to give color to the suggestion of Zuccarini mentioned in the note to page 39, line 29.

Page 2, note, line 10, omit *or*.

Page 2, note, line 15: after *found* omit ,.

Page 4, line 12: I follow De Candolle in giving, as one of the characters of the species, the number of the more distinct spirals of the tubercles in *Mamillariae* and cylindric *Opuntiae*, just as we describe the number of ribs of *Echinocacti* or *Cerei*. It is now well known that no character can be deduced from the direction of the spirals to the right or left. It is also known that the greater or less prominence of one or the other spiral depends on the number and crowded state of the tubercles and the comparative thickness and elongation of the axis. The characters deduced therefrom are not absolute, nor are they quite scientific. It would be more exact to state the phyllotactic law of the arrangement of the tubercles. I would have to say that *M. micromeris* has its tubercles arranged after the $\frac{13}{34}$ or even the $\frac{21}{55}$ system. But I suppose the plan followed by me is more intelligible to most readers, and not much less clear to the scientific phyllotaxist.

Page 5, line 4. *M. microthele* is well distinguished from our species by its much larger tubercles and two unusually stout and short central spines.

Page 5, line 36. The pale yellow spines look like the fibres of raw silk, and form a silk-like tuft, but are not *tipped by a brush*.

Page 6, line 25, for *pluribusve*, read *alterove*.

Page 6, line 29, after *hilum* omit —.

Page 7, line 7, for *umbillicus*, read *umbilicus*.

Page 7, line 15, after *dilatatis* put ;.

Page 7, line 28, for *tuberculata*, read *tuberculosa*. *M. Grahami* is nearly allied to *M. Schelhasii*, Pfr., from Real del Monte, Mexico. The next species, *M. Wrightii*, is closely allied to *M. zephyranthoides*, Scheidw., from Oaxaca, Mexico; without the flower, however, and especially without the fruit and seed, which latter has never been paid attention to. These plants can scarcely be sufficiently well characterized, nor their relationship ascertained.

Page 8, line 19, for GOODRICHII, read GOODRIDGII.

Page 9, line 28, for *interior*, read *exterior*. *M. sphaerica* is almost too closely allied to the Mexican *M. longimamma*, DC.

Page 10, line 41. The plant here described as a variety exactly agrees with some original specimens of *M. Scheerii* preserved in the collection of Prince Salm-Dyck. It will not be useless here to urge the importance of preserving the dead cactus plants, or, as these specimens are fancifully called, the "*skeletons*." I have been materially assisted by being able to examine the skeletons of some authentic original specimens, of which no living ones are now found in the gardens. But generally the dead plants are thrown aside, and a description, often vague or incomplete, or at best an indifferent figure, is all that is left for future identification. Unscrupulous gardeners and traders do their best to increase the confusion.

Page 11, line 7, for *mucranatis*, read *mucronatis*.

Page 12, line 9, for *last*, read *next*. *M. pectinata* is probably not sufficiently distinct from *M. radians*, DC., and with it, and both the following species, *M. Echinus* and *M. scolymoides*, may belong to *M. cornifera*, DC., the two former being the forms without, and the three latter those with, central spines.

Page 14. *M. scolymoides*. A specimen brought by *Dr. Bigelow* has flowered. The flower greatly resembles that of *M. pectinata*, figured on plate 11, but is more of a reddish than yellow tinge. *Dr. Poselger* assures me that they also vary with white or whitish flowers. *M. tuberculosa* is clearly identical with *M. strobiliformis*, Scheer in Salm, Hort. Dyck, (1850,) as I have ascertained by a careful examination of the original specimen (now dead) in the collection of Prince Salm. Mr. Scheer's name, having the priority, must be substituted for mine.

Page 14, line 26, for *X., fig.* 1–6, read *XXII., fig.* 1–16.

Page 15, line 9, for 18, read 22.

Page 15, line 15, for *interior*, read *exterior*.

Page 16, line 5, for *tulis*, read *patulis*.

Page 17, line 9, for *spine*, read *spines*. *M. heteromorpha*, Scheer in Hort. Dyck, 1850, is the same species, to judge from the "skeleton" of the original specimen in Coll. Salm. *Anhalonium*. As the genera of *Cactaceae* are now constituted, *Anhalonium* will probably better be kept distinct from *Mamillaria*. A second section of the genus, with flattened tubercles arranged into ribs, would comprise *Echinocactus Williamsii*, Lem. The tufts of dense wool on this plant do not represent the (absent) spines, but are axillary productions, surrounding and partly including the flower and fruit. The ovary is perfectly naked, as in other *Anhalonia* or *Mamillariae*, which has already been noticed by others. The interesting *Leuchtenbergia Principis*, Fisch., may possibly have to be reduced to a third section of this genus. The flowers being borne just below the tip of the nascent tubercles, (which, when full grown, are three to six or seven inches long, prismatic or awl-shaped, and bear at the tip several flat flexible scales in place of spines,) the plant can have no affinity with *Cereus*. If the ovary should prove to be naked, the large flower and elongated tube would not be sufficient to separate it from *Anhalonium* Mr. Labouret, in his *Monographie des Cactées*, Paris, (without date, probably 1853,) page 162, notices the position of the flower. I have seen the young buds below the apex of the tubercle at Kew, and the scar left by the fallen fruit at Mr. Haage's in Erfurt, but could not meet with either flower or fruit itself. *A. fissuratum* is very nearly allied to the Mexican *A. sulcatum*, Salm, (*A. Kotchubei*, Lem.,) of which it seems no living nor dead specimen is at present extant in Europe. The upper surface of the tubercle of *A. sulcatum* is said to be deeply grooved, the groove being filled with silky tomentum; otherwise the tubercles are said to be smooth.

Page 17, line 36, for *applanta*, read *applanata*.

Page 20, line 24, for *superioribus*, read *mediis*.

Page 20, line 29, before *hilo* put ;.

Page 21, line 21, after *San Pedro*. put (*Tab. XX.*) Fig. 12 exhibits the enlarged *funiculi*, which consist of a loose juicy tissue. It seems that in most *Cactaceae* the *funiculi* towards maturity become large and juicy; usually their cells then burst, and form the so-called pulp, in which the seeds are described as nestling: "*semina nidulantia.*"

Page 21, line 24, for *albo*, read *albo—*.

Page 22, line 12, after *junioribus* insert *plerisque purpureis, adultis.*

Page 22, line 19, for *interioribus* read *superioribus*.

Page 22, line 24, after *crassispinus:* insert *aculeis robustissimis, radialibus* 8–11, *centralibus*, 4 *angulatis, infimo flexuoso plus minus hamato.*

Page 22, line 42, after *spines*, put *in var.* $\gamma$

Page 23, line 1, for *often*, read *when young*.

Page 23, line 14, after *annulated*, put , in place of ;. It ought to have been mentioned that the lower central spine is as long as the others or more commonly greatly exceeds them.

Page 23, line 41, put the ( before *interdum* instead of before *aculeo*.

Page 24, line 22, for *ex* (*Parry*) read *ex Parry*).

Page 24, line 23, for *mimus*, read *minus*.

Page 25, last line, after *addita*, omit ,.

Page 26, line 1, for *angulatis*, read *annulatis*.

Page 26, line 11, after *distinct*, put ;.

Page 26, line 13, after *divergent;* omit ;.

Page 26, line 14, after *stoutest* put ,. *E. horizonthalonius;* numerous original specimens of this plant, living and dead, examined in European collections, leave no doubt of the entire identity of the different forms, which can scarcely be counted as varieties.

Page 28, line 1, after *intertextis* put ,.

Page 30, line 25, for *fig.* 1, read *fig.* 1–2.

Page 31, line 13, after *acutis* put ,.

Page 32, line 4, for *incisota*, read *inciso*.

Page 32, line 9, for ; before 12, put ,.

Page 32, line 42, for *XXXIII–XXXIV*, read *XLIII–XLIV*.

Page 32, last line, after *patulis* put ,.

Page 33, line 14, for *centralibus*, read *setaceis.*

Page 34, line 6, after *curvato.* add (*Tab. LI–LIII.*)

Page 35, line 39, for *those*, read *these.*

Page 37, line 7, for *to tubercles*, read *its tubercles.*

Page 37, line 26, for 6 *lines;* read 6 *lines*,.

Page 38, line 18, after *cultivation*, put *in St. Louis, Cincinnati, etc.*

Page 38, line 31, *C. pentalophus* is *erect* "10–15 inches high" only when so trained. It grows naturally like *C. Berlandieri*, *C. procumbens* and *C. Ehrenbergii*, Pfeif., all of which closely resemble one another in habit. *C. Pentalophus* has a 5-angled stem of bright green color with short spines; *C. Ehrenbergii* is usually 6-angled, pale green, with numerous long and setaceous spines; flower and fruit of either seem to be unknown.

Page 38, line 42, *LXIX*, read *LIX.*

Page 39, line 17, *LXIX*, read *LIX.*

Page 39, line 21. The root of young plants forms a single globose tuber, in older ones it consists of a cluster of several oval or cylindric tubers, sometimes 6 or 8 in number, 1–1½ inch in diameter, and 2–3 inches long.

Page 39, line 29, after *family*, add: or the specimen observed by Dr. Poselger offered one of those rare anomalies (one of which, found by Zuccarini in *Cereus serpentinus*, was figured by him in the Annals of the Munich Academy) where the ovary actually forms the continuation and termination of a branch, by which the sagacious observer just mentioned was induced to consider the so-called ovary of *Cactaceae* itself a branch, with the real ovary immersed in it. But how would he view it in *Mamillaria?*

Page 40, line 18, after *fruit*, omit *flower.*

Page 40, line 31, before *smooth*, insert *nearly.*

Page 40, line 31, before *linear*, put *or.*

Page 41, line 13. This is *C. Pottsii*, Salm, Hort. Dyck, a later name.

Page 42, line 14, after *brevioribus* put ,.

Page 42, line 16, for *albido*, read *albido—.*

Page 46, line 10, for *ovari*, read *ovarii.*

Page 46, line 26. Cultivated specimens of *O. grandis* are erect, because, tied to the stake, they are not permitted to grow otherwise. Their white spines seem to grow dark very soon, and the smaller number and greater distance of the spines may be owing to the influence of cultivation. There is, therefore, scarcely a permanent character left to distinguish the new species from this one.

Page 47, line 6, after *succosa*, omit ,.

Page 47, line 8. This *margin* is the enlarged and indurated *funiculus* itself, which, by a lateral expansion, envelopes the seed proper and forms its exterior bony coating. This dilatation of the *funiculus* takes place long before the flowering period; it covers the *ovulum* so completely that only two small lateral openings remain, which lead to the *orifice.* After Mr. Payen and others had already noticed this expansion of the *funiculus*, Dr. Caspary, of Bonn, lately has more completely investigated its nature. It appears that in many, if not in all other *Cactaceae* the funiculus is bent over the orifice of the *ovulum*, partly covering it; (I have seen it in some *Mamillariae, Echinocacti*, and *Cerei;*) but that only in *Opuntiae* it expands into an exterior seminal coat, which is distinguished from *arillus* proper only by its being already fully formed at the flowering period.

Page 49, line 16, for *Tuna,* read *Ficus Indica.*

Page 49, line 24, for *flaro,* read *flavo.*

Page 51, line 42, after 20–30 put ,.

Page 52, line 29, after *ovata;* omit ; and read: *aculeolis inaequalibus armata; umbilico infundibuliformi; seminibus,* etc.

Page 53, line 37, put *setosissimis* before *stipata.*

Page 54, line 16, for *pulvillis,* read *pulvilli.*

Page 54, line 17, after *Seeds,* insert *very different in size and shape.*

Page 54, line 18, after *fruit* put ,.

Page 54, line 34, for *ovata,* read *obovato—.*

Page 54, line 34, after *clavata* put ,.

Page 55, line 8, for *folii,* read *foliis.*

Page 56, line 13, for *first,* read *fruit.*

Page 57, line 14, omit *numerosis.*

Page 58, line 14, for 1012, read 10–12. *O. arborescens* seems to be very closely allied, if not identical, with *O. rosea,* DC., and *O. imbricata,* DC. The former is described from a figure; the flower and fruit of the latter remain unknown, so that it is difficult, if not impossible at present, to solve these doubts.

Page 59, line 4, for *Bubuquibari,* read *Babuquibari.*

Page 59, line 30. *O. Wrightii* may not be different from *O. Kleiniae,* DC., from Mexico, long cultivated in Europe, the flower of which does not seem to be known.

Page 60, line 21. *O. frutescens* seems identical with *O. gracilis,* Hort. Monac, and *O. virgata,* Hort. Vind., the flower and fruit of which are unknown. It is stated that the spines of *O. gracilis* are not vaginate. This is no doubt a mistake; but the sheath is probably not as loose as in others. It corresponds, therefore, with my var. *brevispina,* Synops. Cact. in Proc. Am. Ac. A. Sc., vol. III. In delicate specimens, and such are usually the cultivated ones, the spines of most of the cylindric *Opuntiae* do not exhibit the sheath very plainly; it usually adheres closely to the body of the spine. This *vagina* consists, like the whole spine, of elongated indurated cells; the barbs of the spine are covered by it and are closely adpressed until the vagina detaches itself which commonly takes place very early.

Page 61, column 2 line 30, for 2, read 64.

Page 61, column 2, line 39, for *Goodrichii,* read *Goodridgii.*

Page 62, column 1, line 25, omit entirely.

Page 62, column 2, line 10, for 6, read 68.

Page 64, line 14, for *Goodrichii,* read *Goodridgii.*

Page 66, line 13, before 14, put 12 *and* 13, *bunches of spines of this variety;.*

Page 68, line 18, for *nutallis* read *Nuttallii.*

Page 68, line 24, for *Chihauhua,* read *Chihuahua.*

Page 68, the *map* (not *maps*) mentioned in the two last lines has been necessarily left out.

Mr. Paulus Roetter, of St. Louis, made the drawings for the plates under the close superintendence of the author. The steel engravings were done partly by Mr. W. H. Dougal, of Georgetown, D. C., a few by Messrs. Maillard & Connor, of St. Louis, and the balance by

European artists, viz: Mr. Weber, of Berlin, Prussia, and Mr. Davesne, Mr. Rebuffet, Mr. Martin Schmelz, and the brothers Picart, all of Paris, France. The high order of excellence of the engravings, especially of those of the Picarts and of Schmelz cannot fail to strike those who examine the plates.

In the figures of the embryos in plate 24, 34, 41 and 47, the line indicating the division of the cotyledons does not show in all the copies. The embryo in plate 24 and 34 resembles that of pl. 74, fig. 9 and 10; and that of plate 41 and 47, is like that on plate 55.

GEORGE ENGELMANN.

St. Louis, *November*, 1858.

Paulus Roetter. James D. Smillie.

VIEW ALONG THE GILA. CEREUS GIGANTEUS.

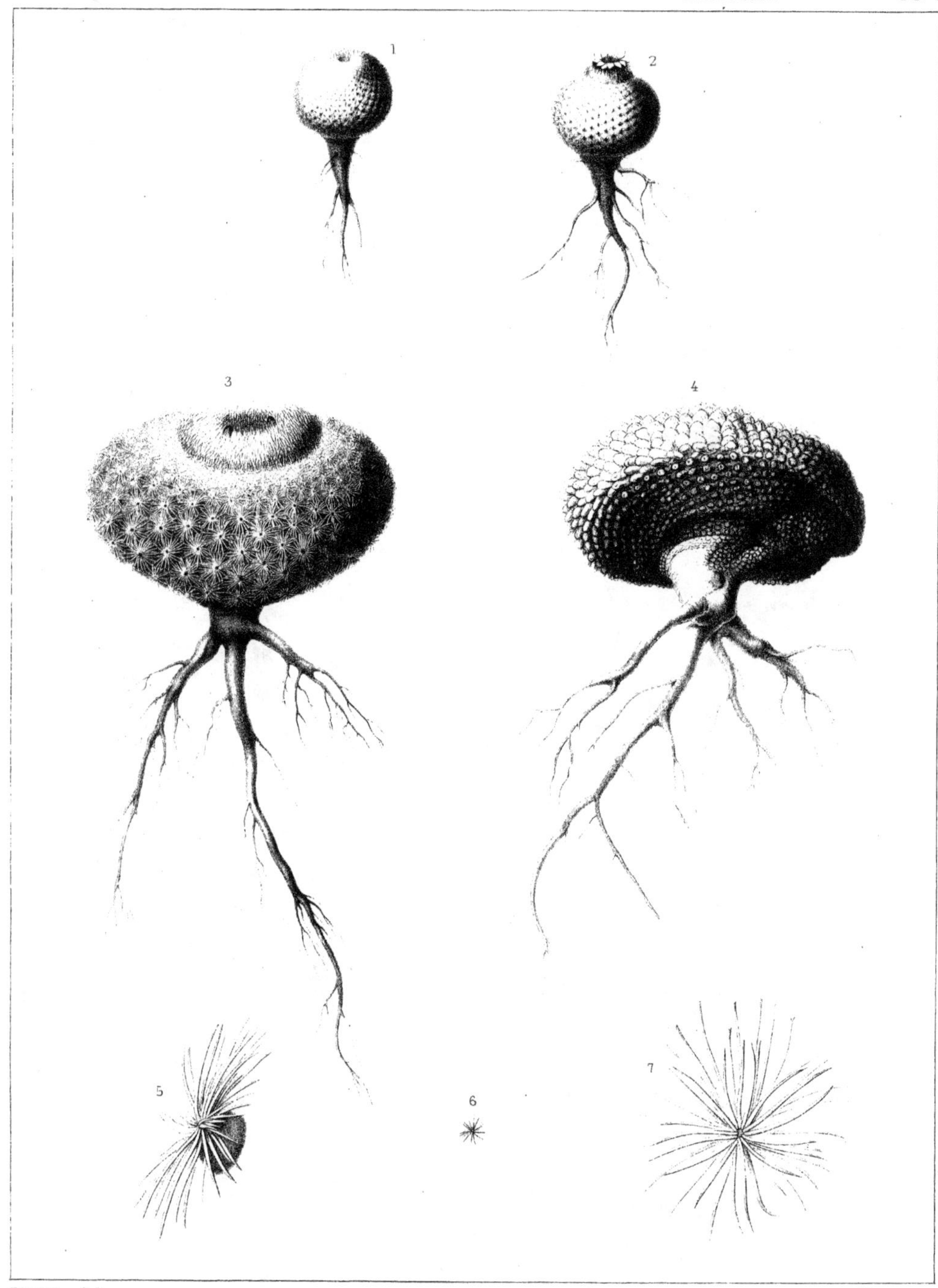


Roetter del. Picart sc.

MAMILLARIA MICROMERIS

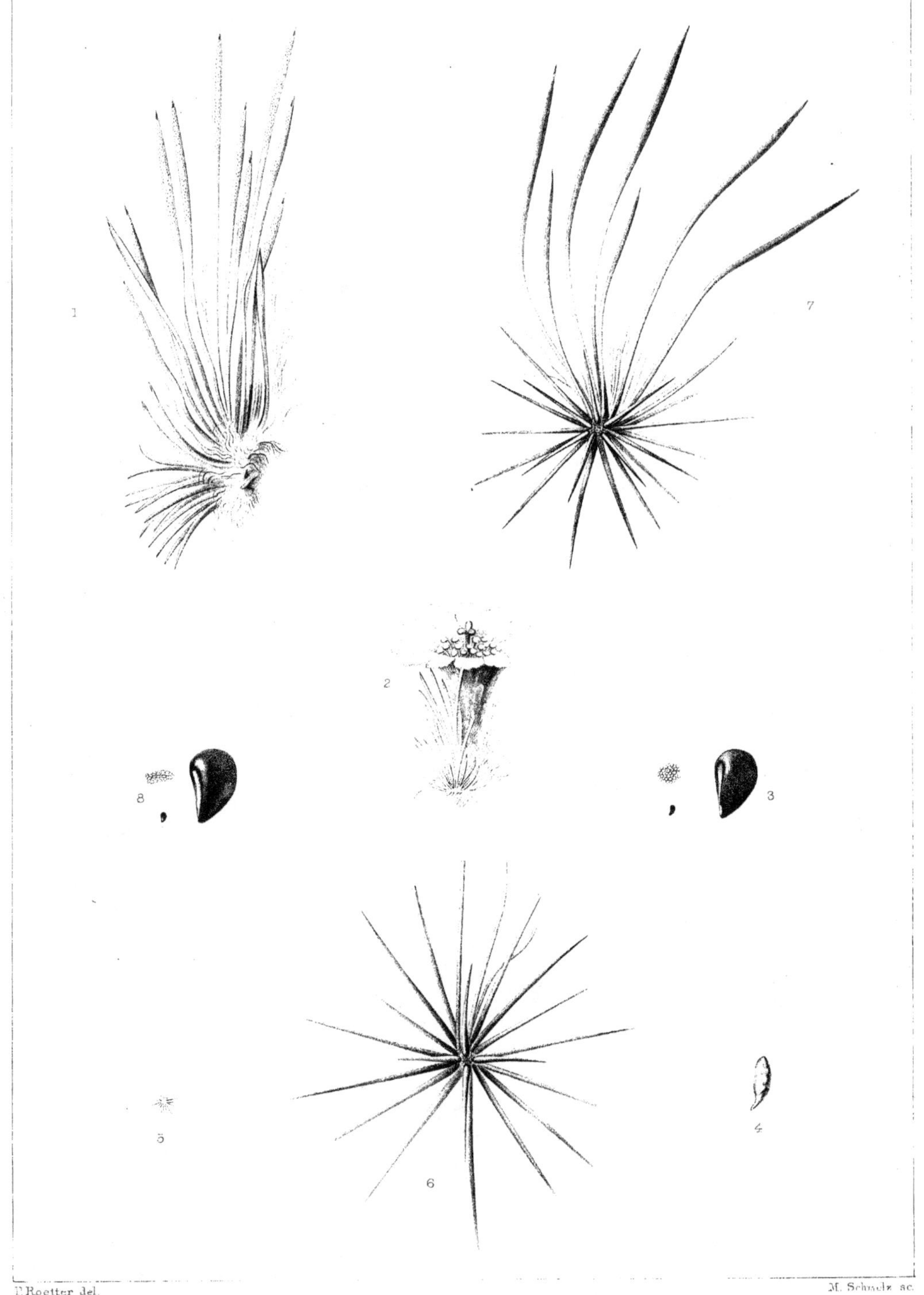


F. Roetter del. M. Schmelz sc.

1-4. MAMILLARIA MICROMERIS

5-8. —"— —"— VAR. GREGGII

Roeuer del. Picart sc.

MAMILLARIA LASIACANTHA

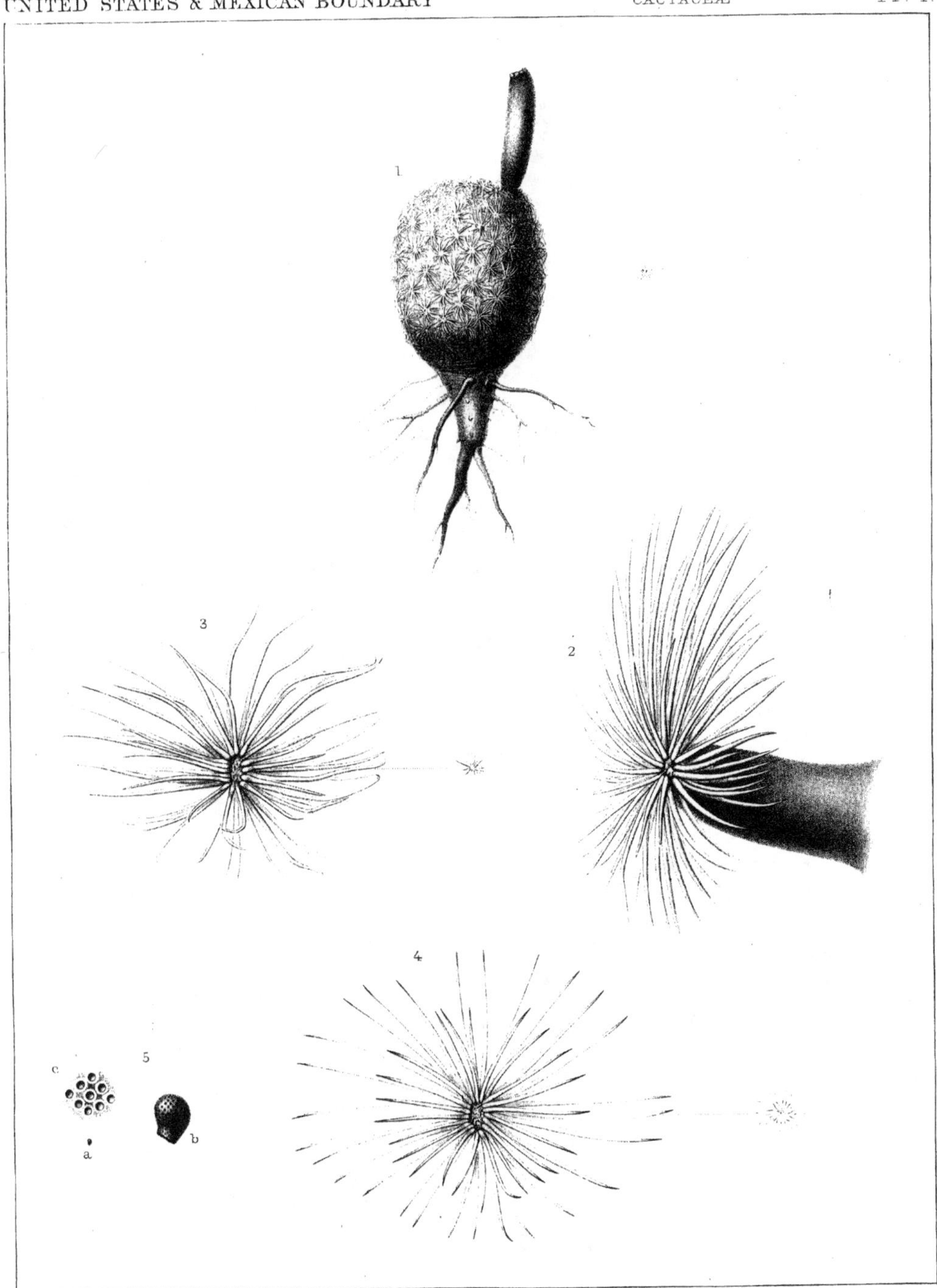


Roetter del. Picart sc.

MAMILLARIA LASIACANTHA, VAR. DENUDATA

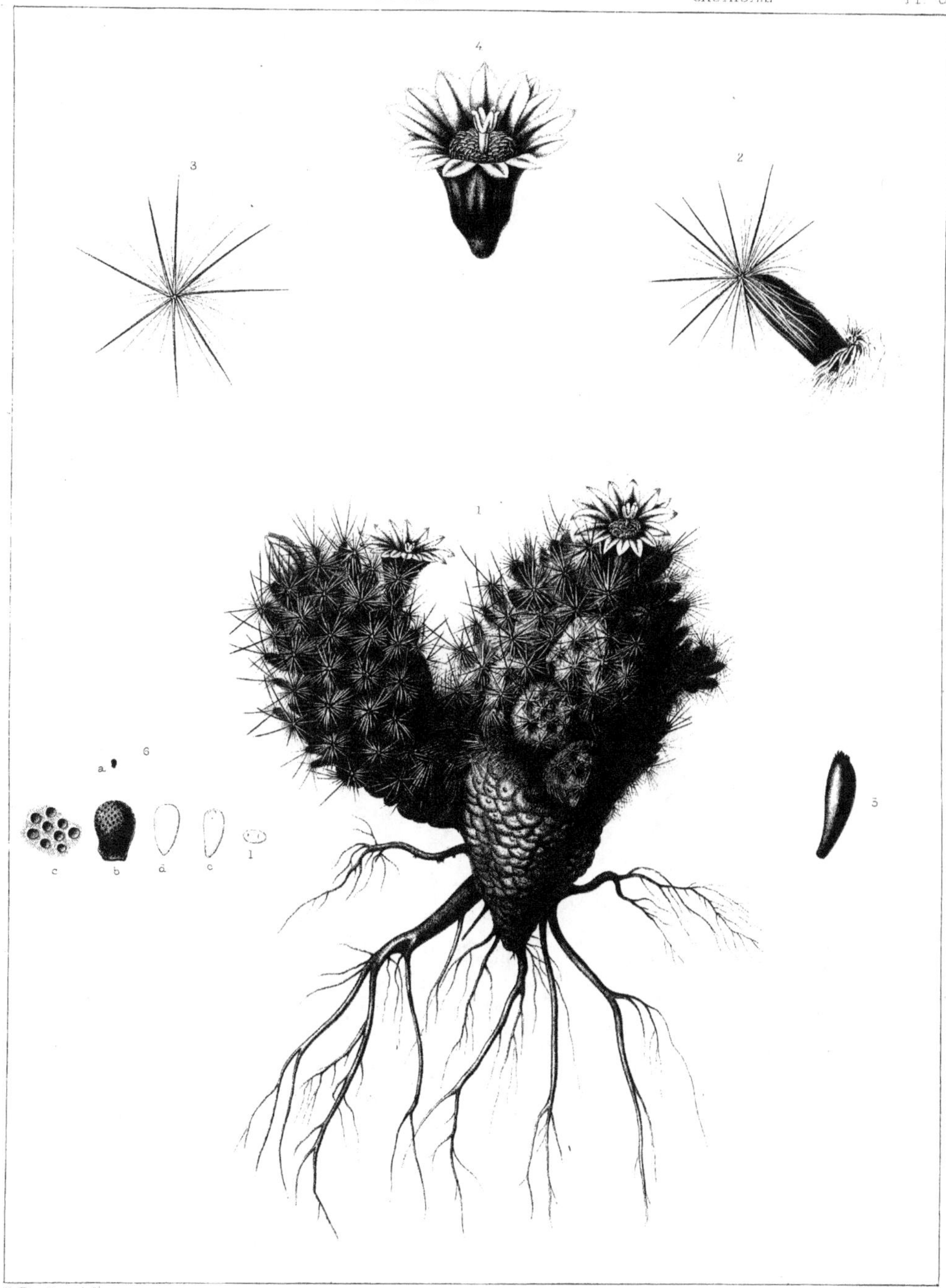


P. Roetter del. Rebuffet sc.

MAMILLARIA PUSILLA VAR. TEXANA

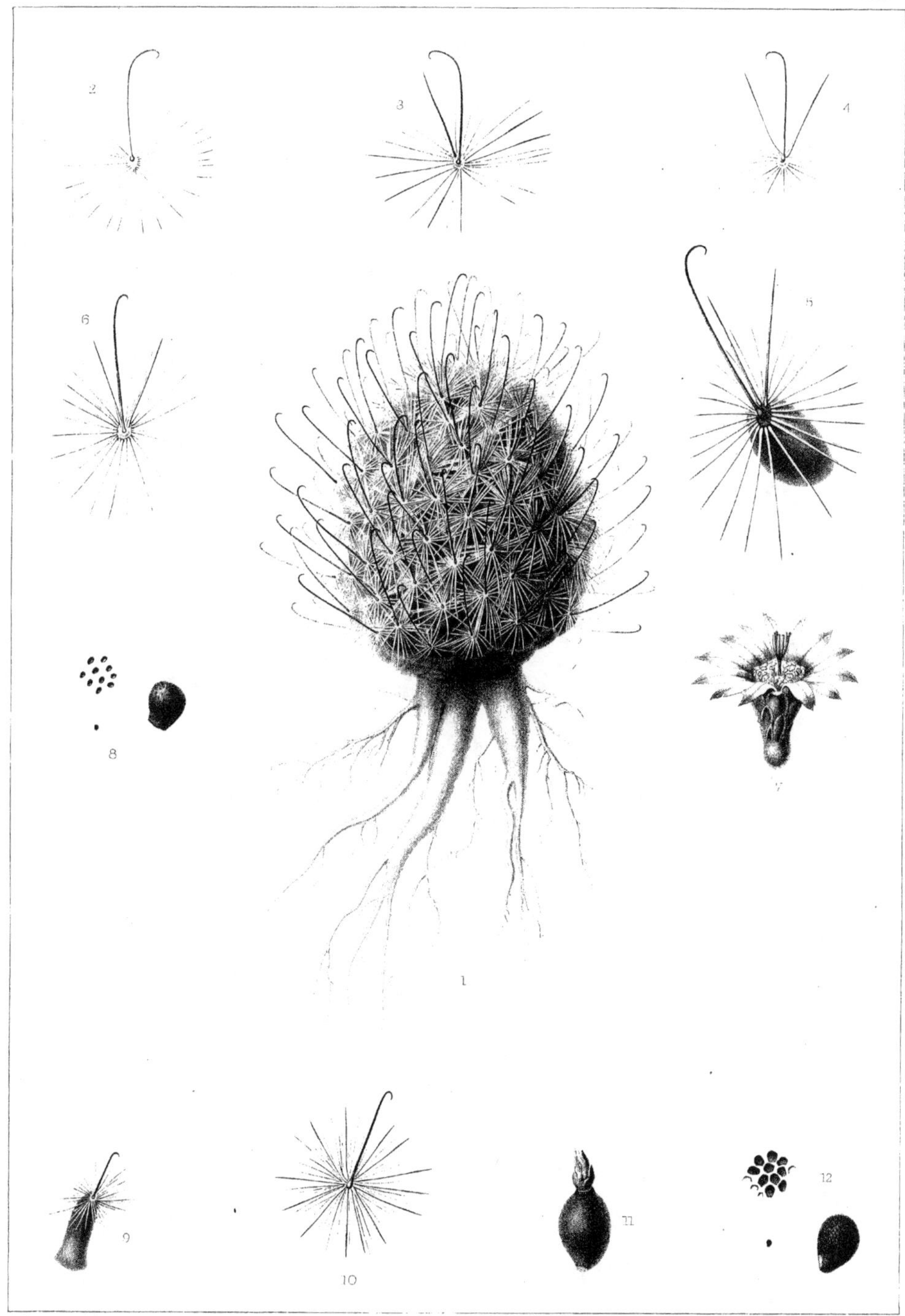


P. Roetter del. Picart sc.

I-8 MAMILLARIA GRAHAMI

9-I2 MAMILLARIA BARBATA

P. Roetter del. Picart sc.

MAMILLARIA PHELLOSPERMA

P. Roetter del. Picart sc.

I-8 MAMILLARIA WRIGHTII

9-14 MAMILLARIA GOODRIDGII

P. Roetter del. Rebuffet sc.

1-3 MAMILLARIA MEIACANTHA 4-14 M. HEYDERI VAR. APPLANATA

15-17 VAR. HEMISPHAERICA 18-20 M. GUMMIFERA

F. Roetter del. W. H. Dougal sc.

MAMILLARIA ECHINUS

P. Roetter del.

R. Connor, A. Maillard scs.

MAMILLARIA PECTINATA E.

Roetter del. Picart sc.

1-16 MAMILLARIA TUBERCULOSA

17-22 " DASYACANTHA

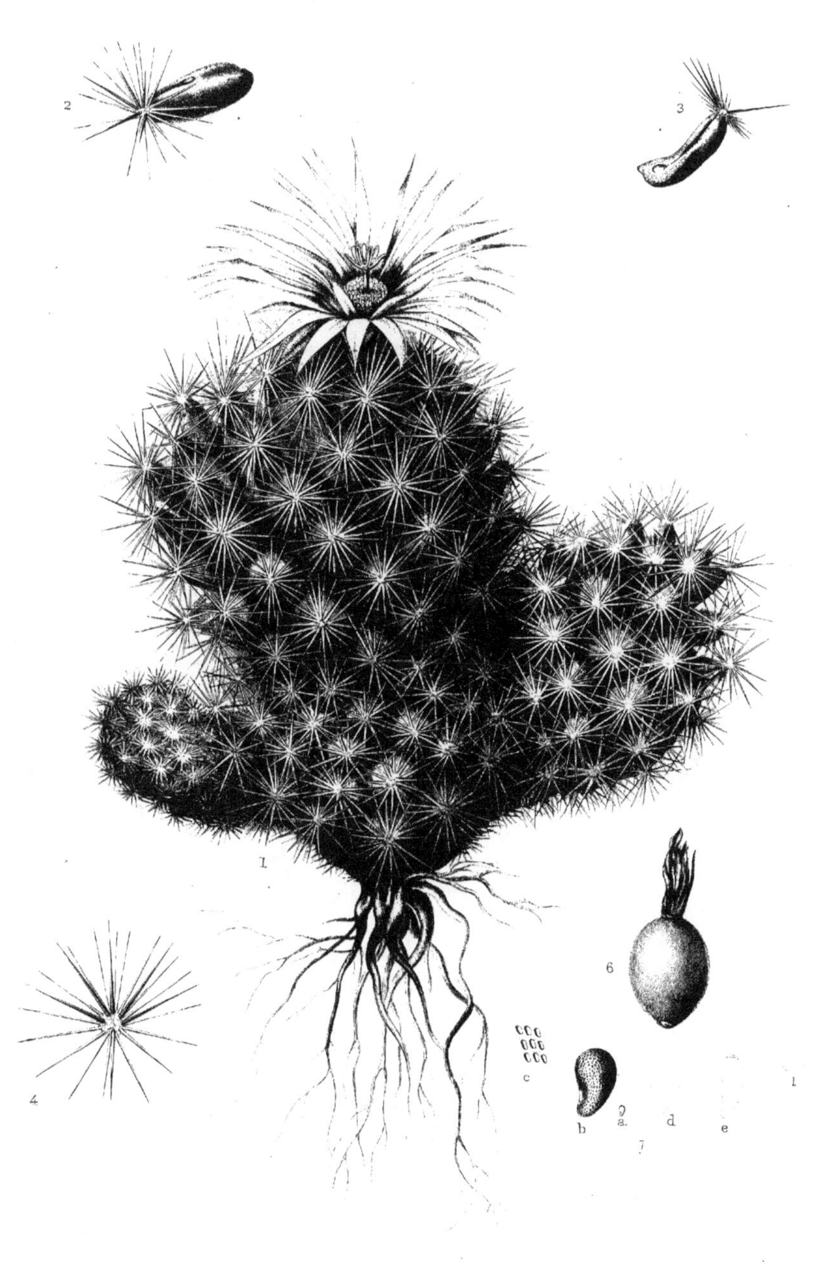


P. Roetter del. W.H. Dougal sc.

MAMILLARIA RADIOSA VAR. NEOMEXICANA

P. Roetter del. Picart sc.

MAMILLARIA MACROMERIS

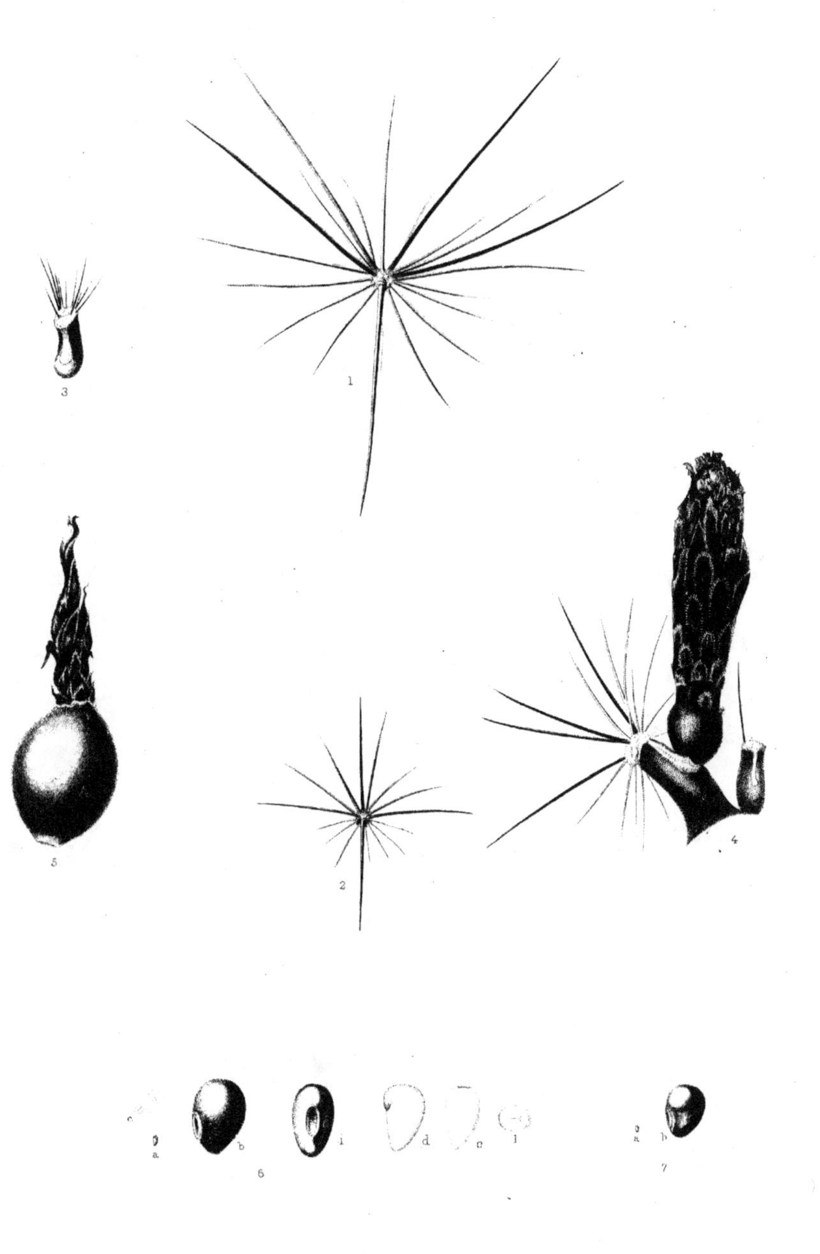


P. Roetter del. Dougal sc.

MAMILLARIA MACROMERIS

P. Roetter del. Picart sc.

MAMILLARIA FISSURATA

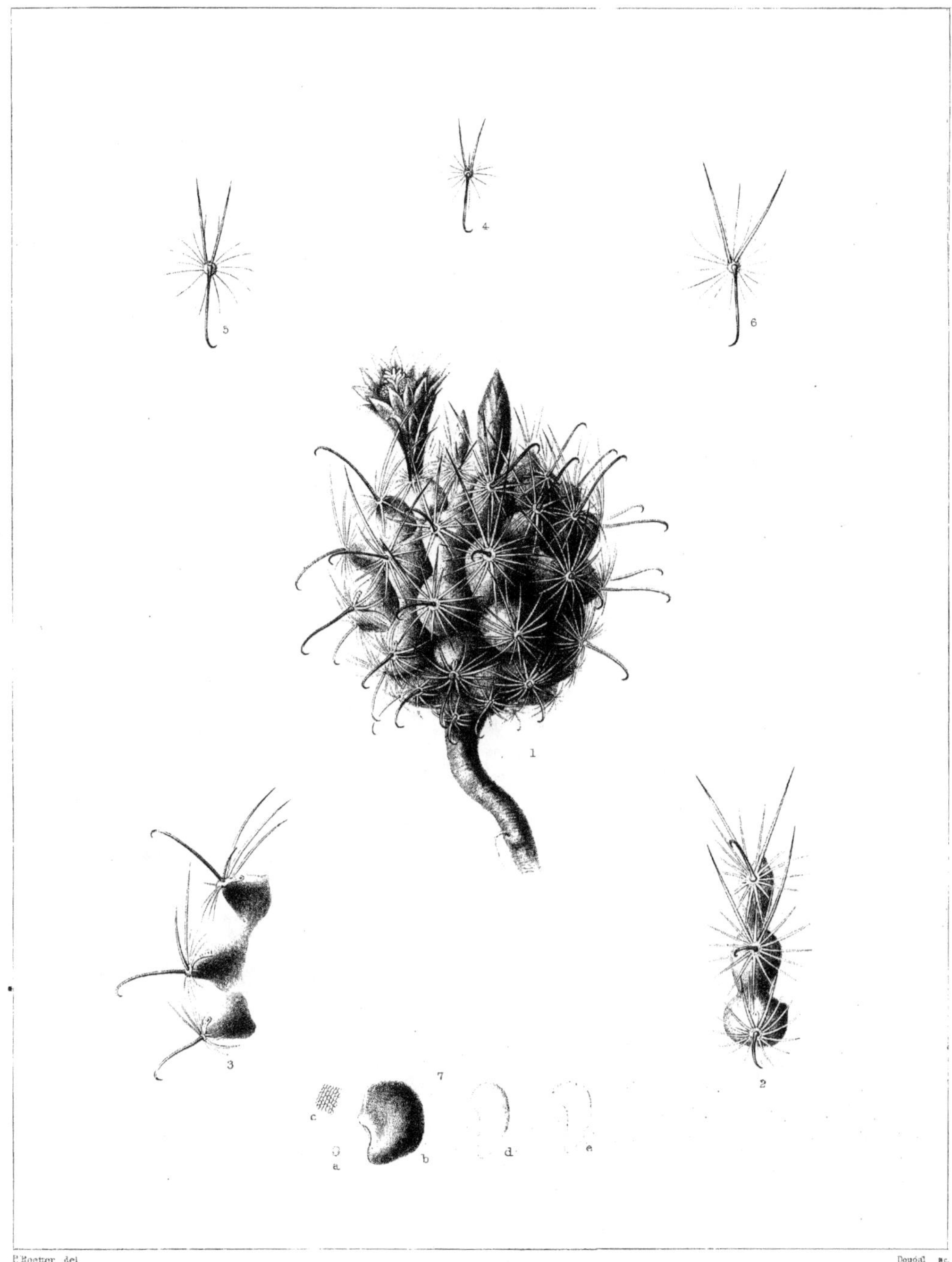


P. Roetter del. Dougal sc.

ECHINOCACTUS SCHEERII

P. Roetter del. W.H. Dougal sc.

ECHINOCACTUS BREVIHAMATUS

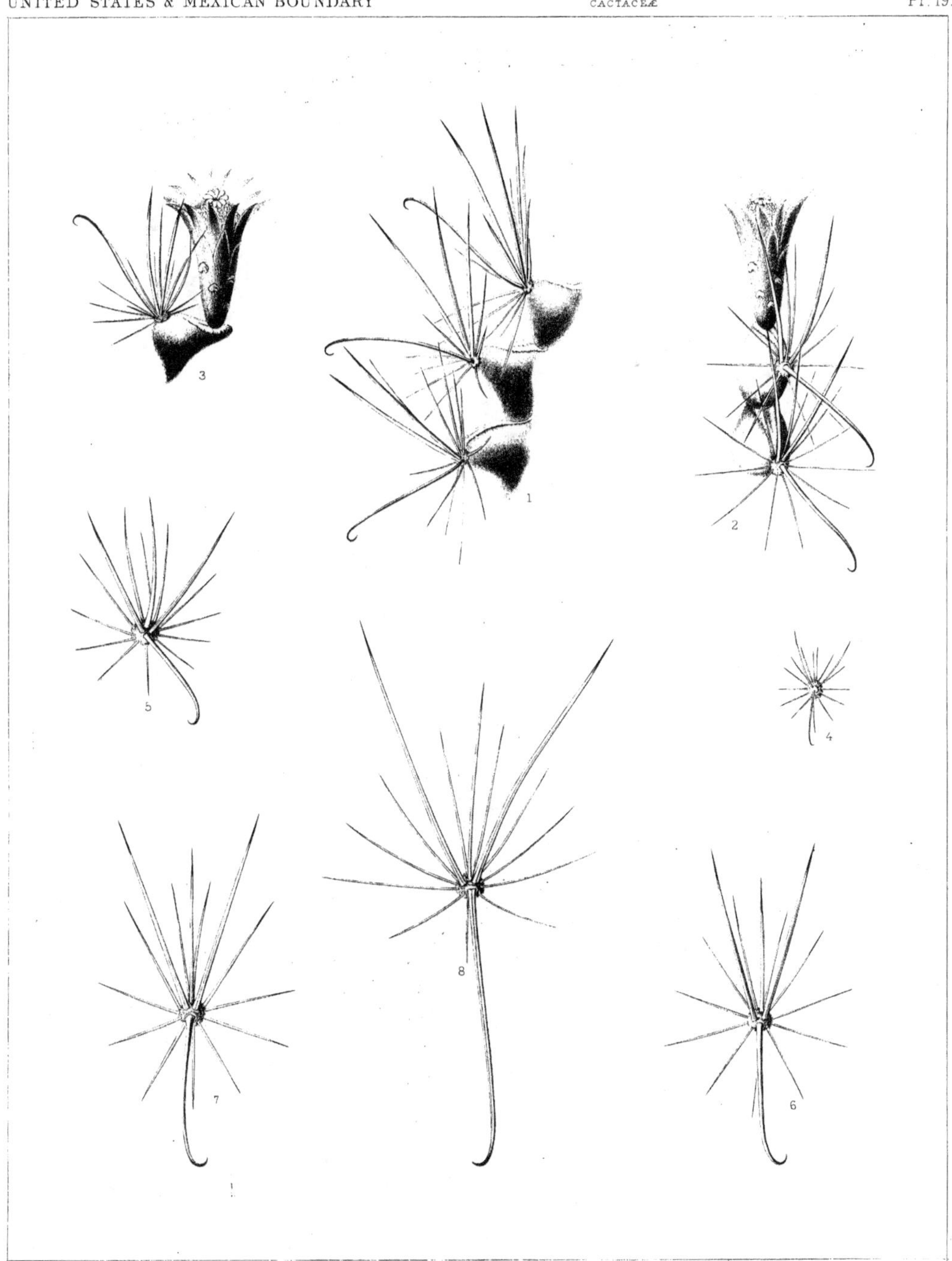


P. Roetter del. W. H. Dougal sc.

ECHINOCACTUS BREVIHAMATUS

P. Roetter del. W.H. Dougal sc.

ECHINOCACTUS SETISPINUS

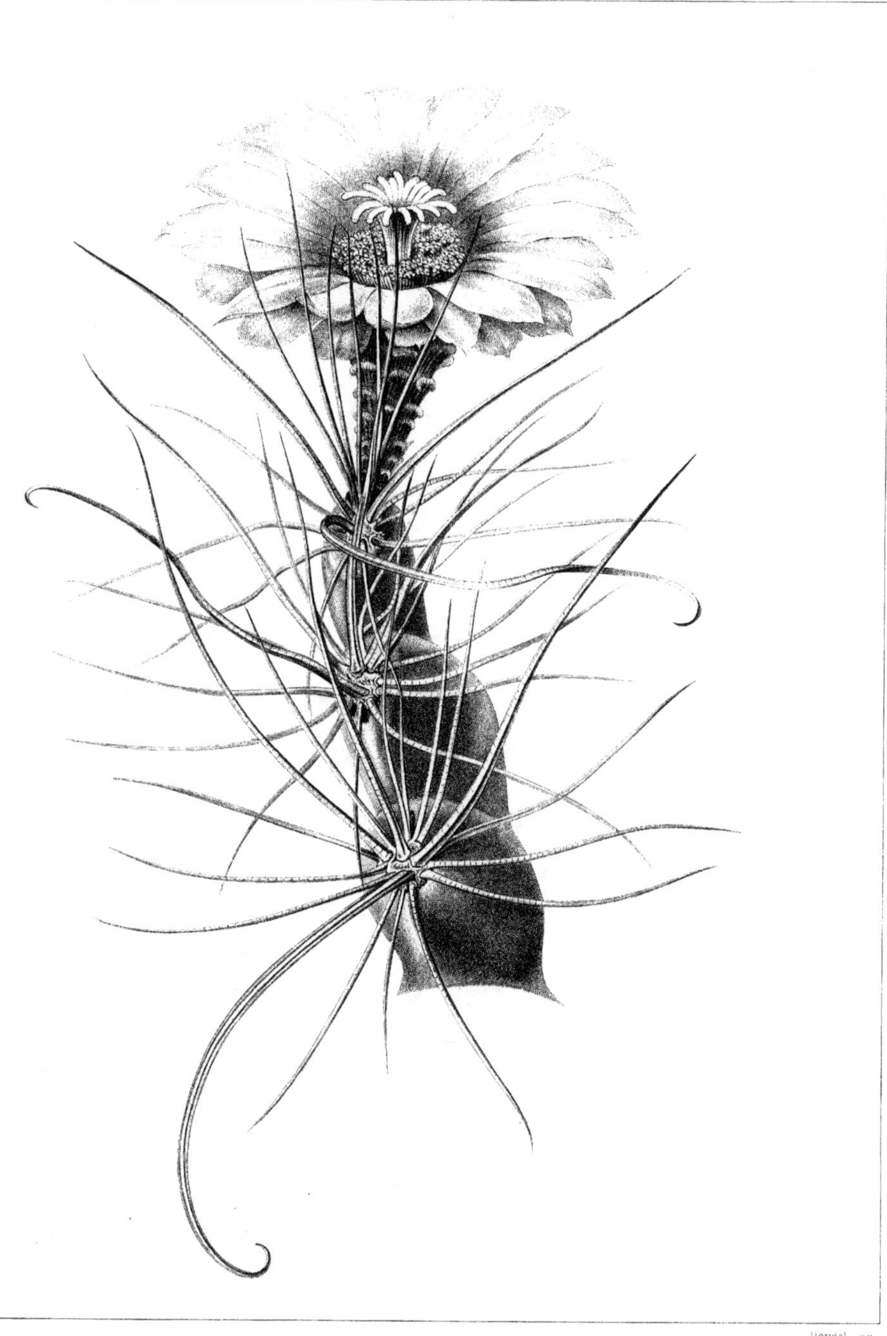

P. Roetter del. Dougal sc.

ECHINOCACTUS LONGEHAMATUS

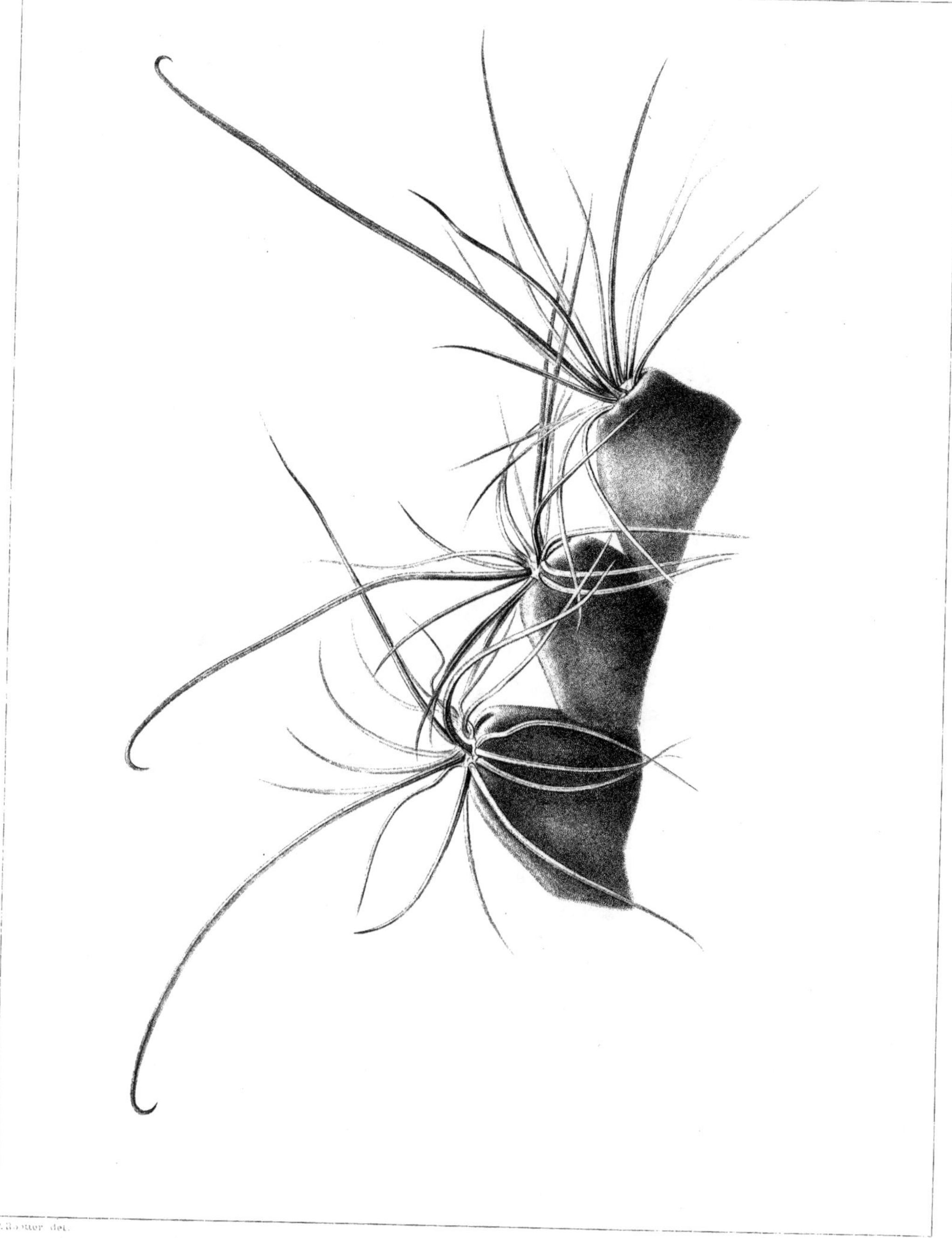

P. Roetter del.

Dougal sc.

ECHINOCACTUS LONGEHAMATUS

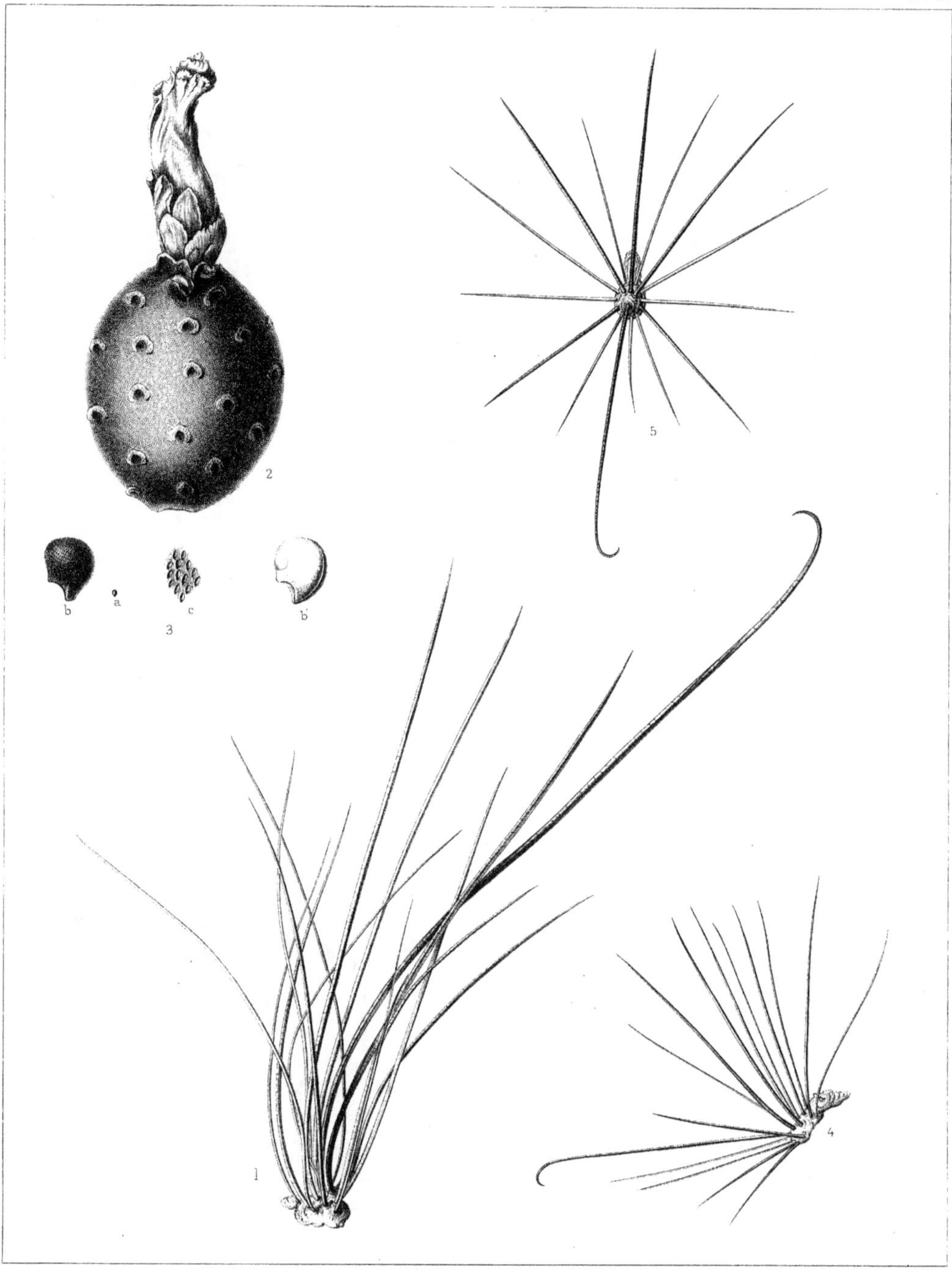


P. Roetter del. Dougal sc.

ECHINOCACTUS LONGEHAMATUS

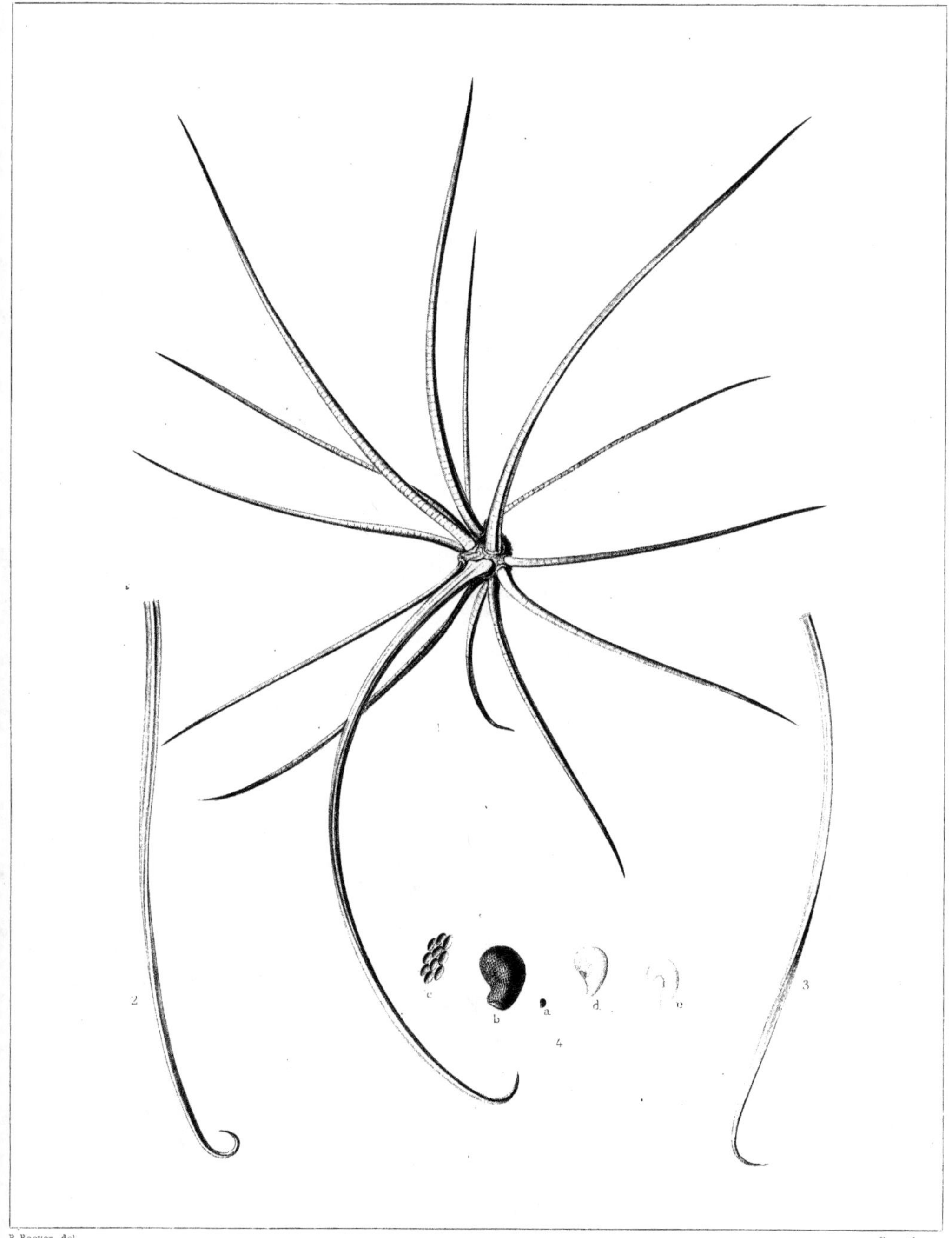


P. Roetter del. Dougal sc.

ECHINOCACTUS LONGEHAMATUS

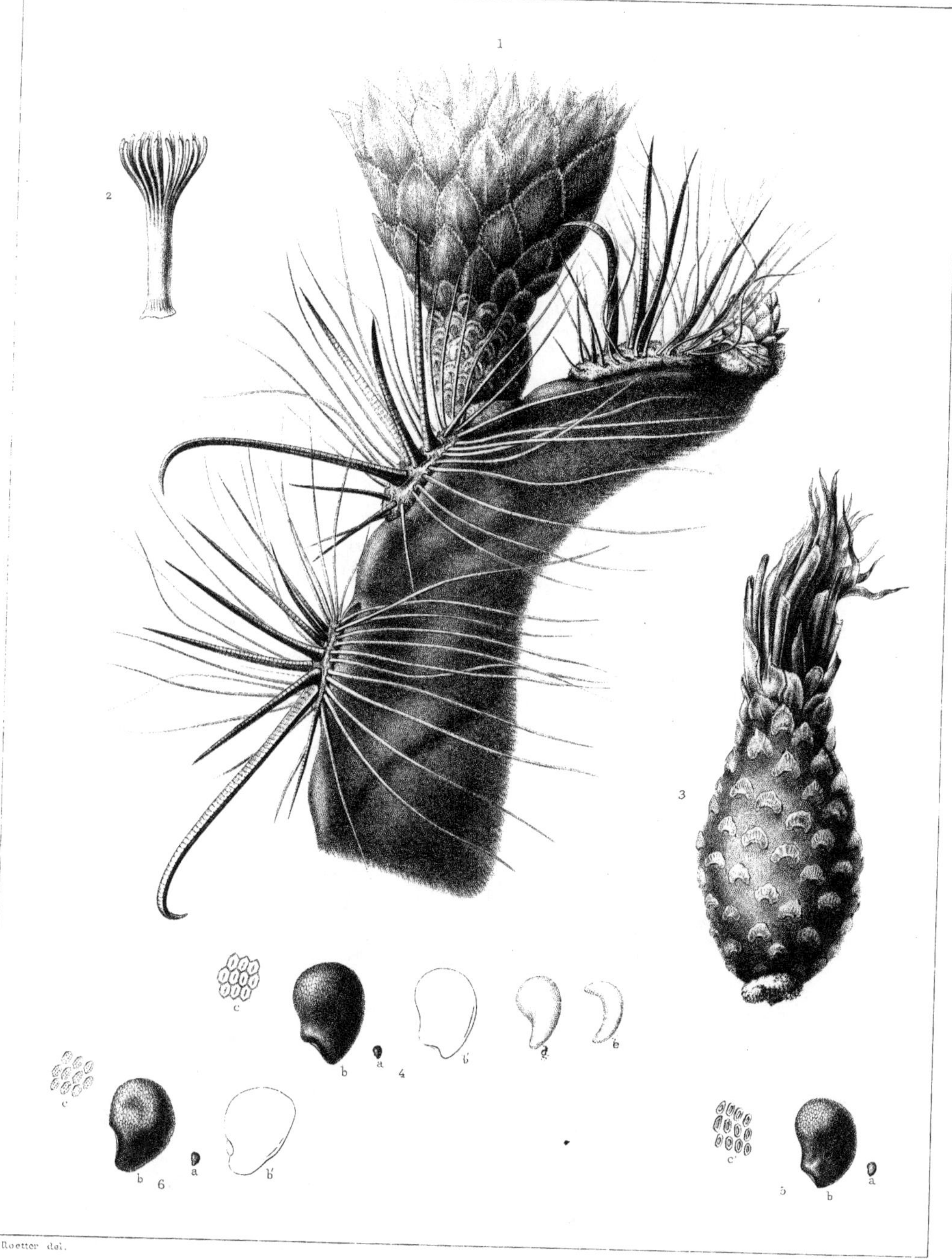


P. Roetter del.

W.H. Dougal sc.

ECHINOCACTUS WISLIZENI

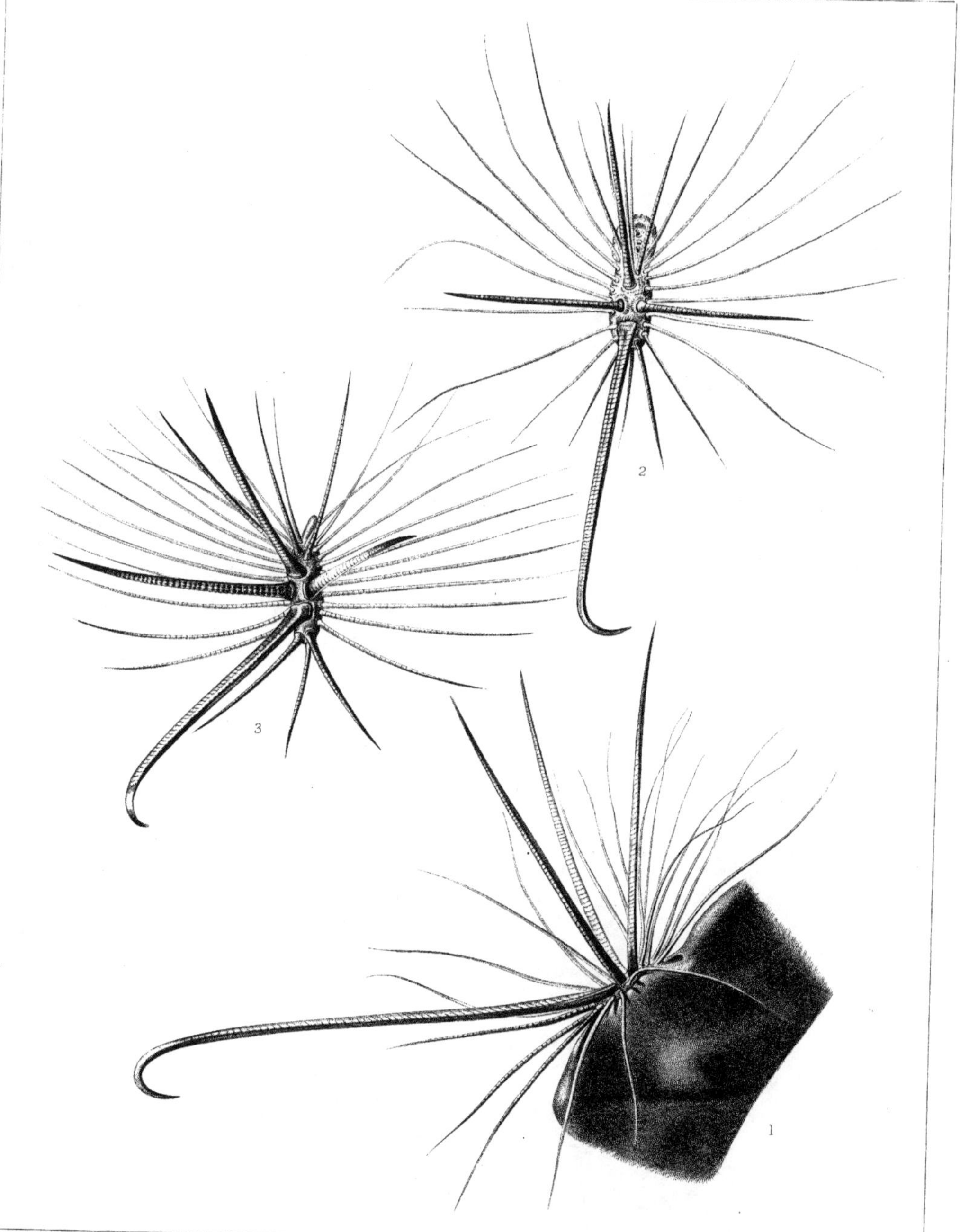

2

3

1

P. Roetter del. W.H. Dougal sc.

ECHINOCACTUS WISLIZENI

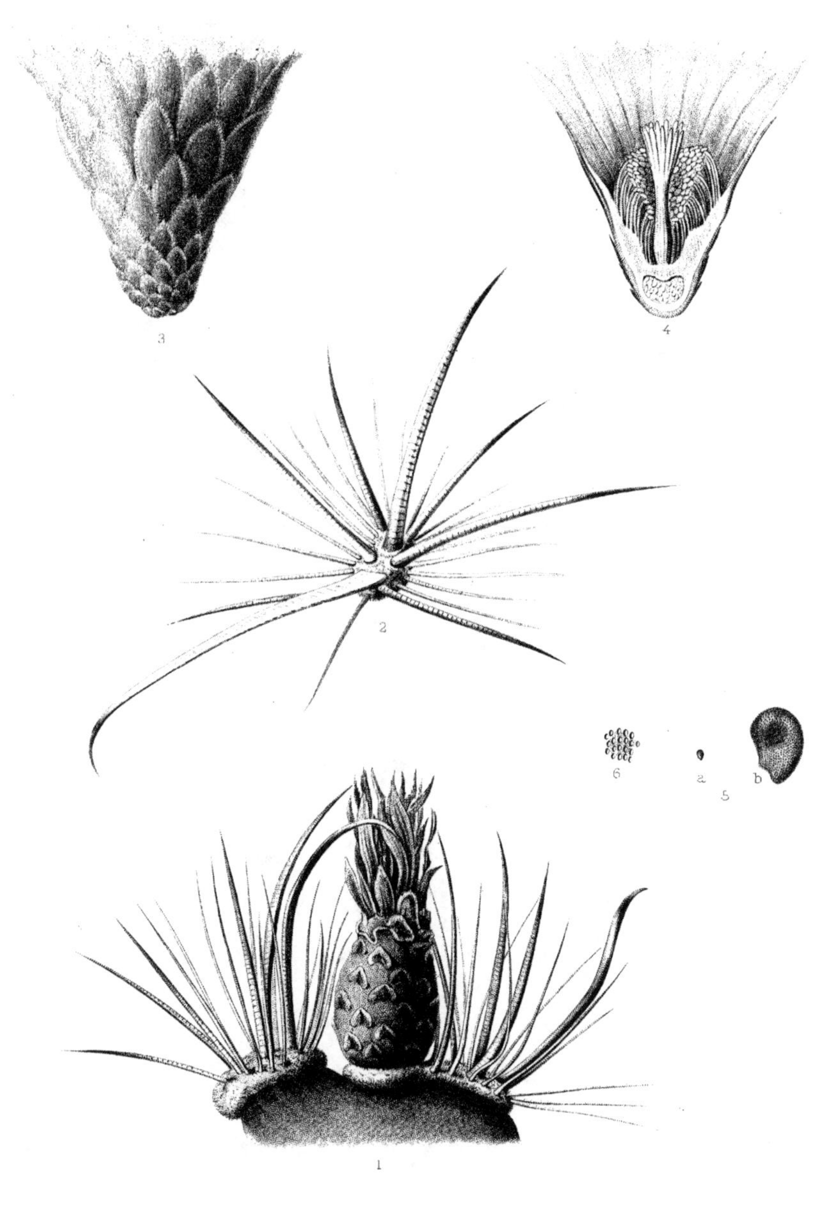


Roetter del. W. H. Dougal sc.

ECHINOCACTUS LE CONTEI

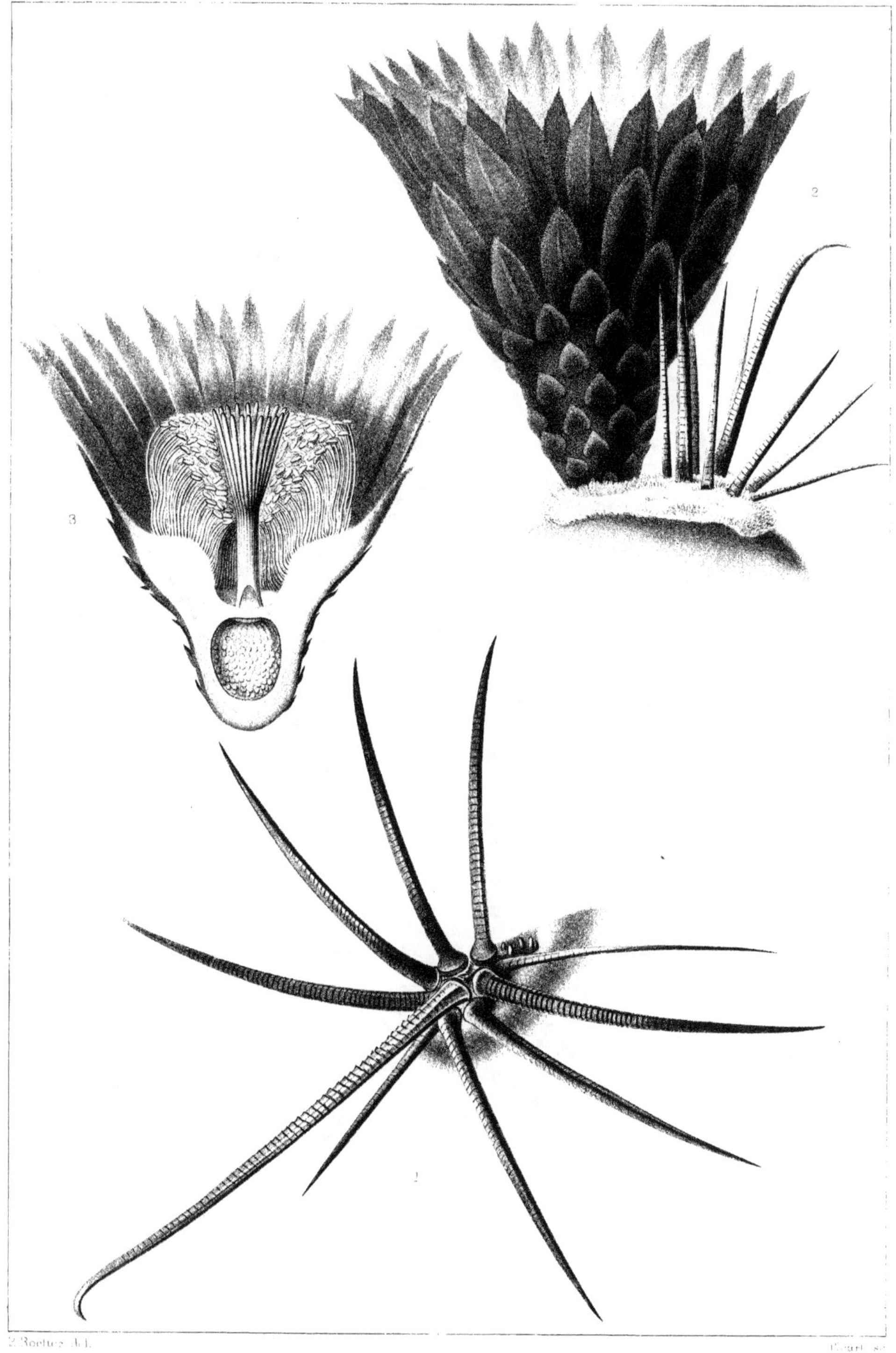


ECHINOCACTUS EMORYI

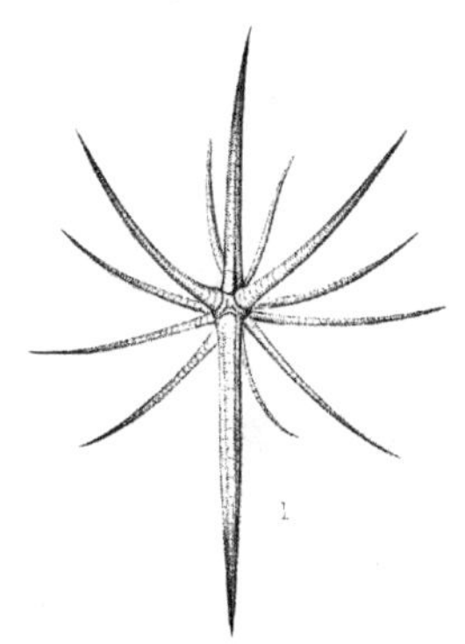


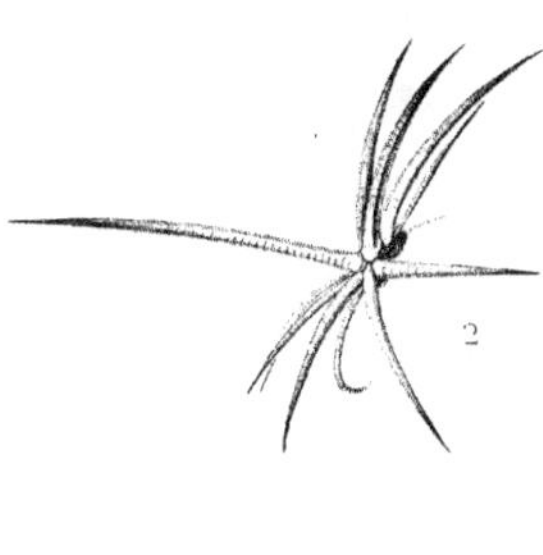


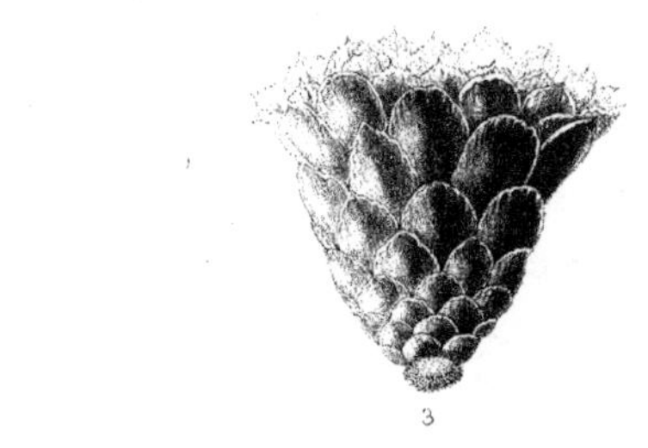

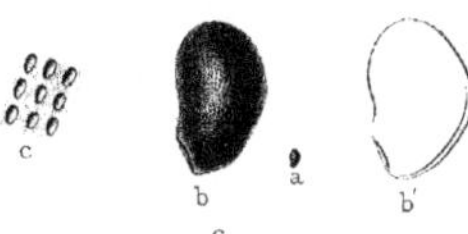


P. Roetter del. Dougal sc.

ECHINOCACTUS VIRIDESCENS

P. Roetter del.

ECHINOCACTUS CYLINDRACEUS

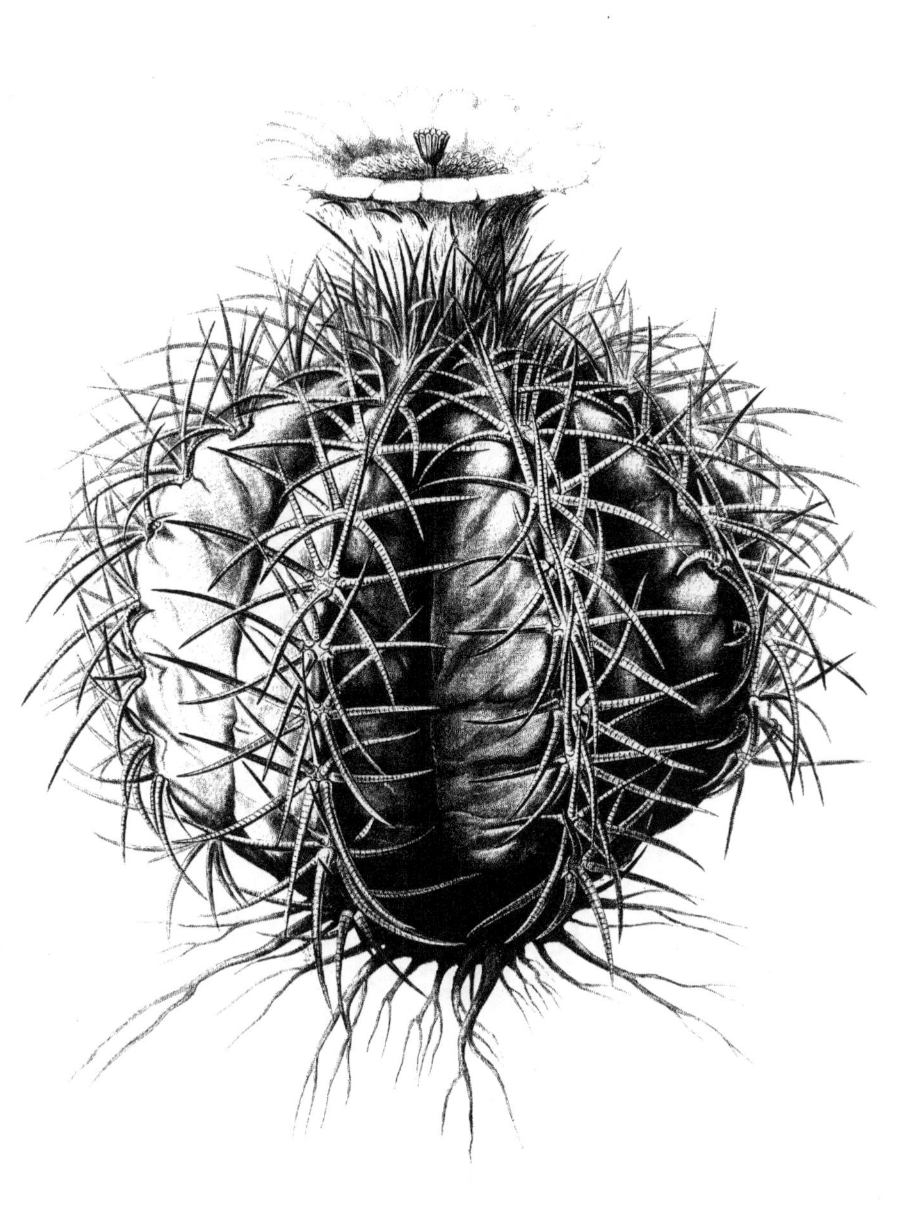

Roetter del. Dougal sc.

ECHINOCACTUS HORIZONTHALONIUS

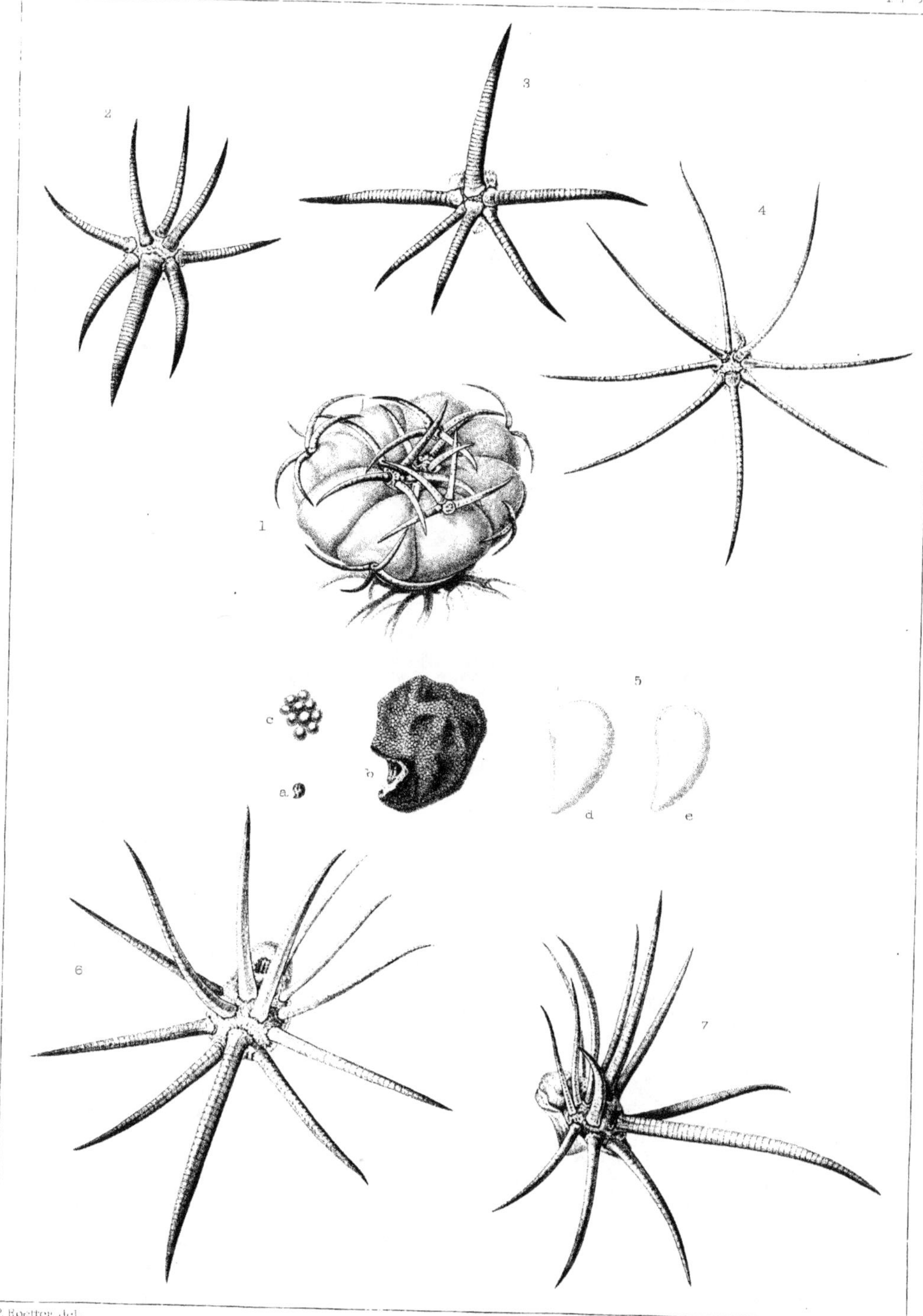


P. Roetter del.

Davesne sc.

1-5 ECHINOCACTUS HORIZONTHALONIUS

6-7 ECHINOCACTUS PARRYI

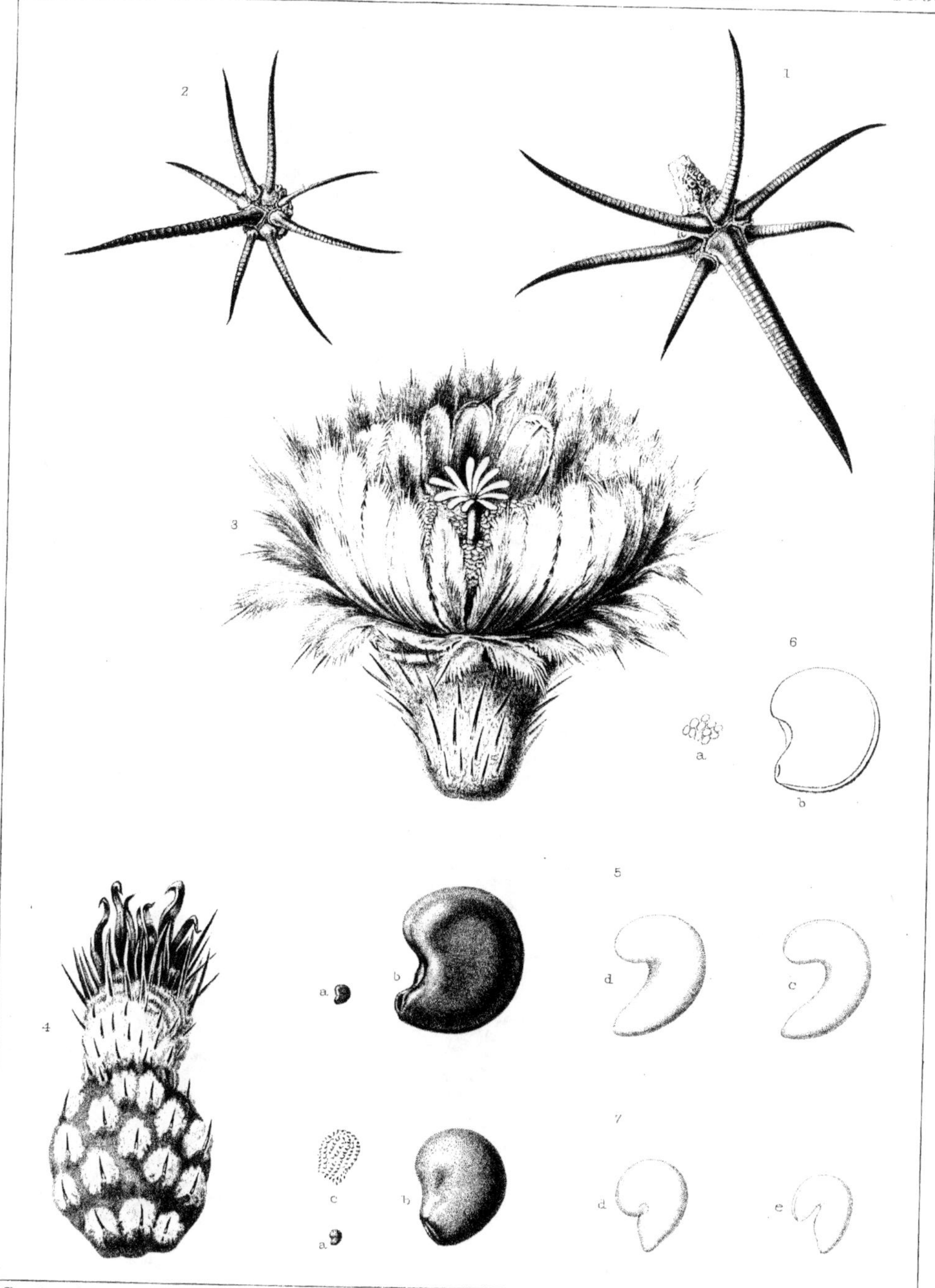


P. Roetter del. Davesne sc.

1-6 ECHINOCACTUS TEXENSIS

7 ECHINOCACTUS SANDILLON

T. Roetter del

W.H. Dougal sc

ECHINOCACTUS INTERTEXTUS

P. Roetter del. W. H. Dougal sc.

1–5 ECHINOCACTUS INTERTEXTUS VAR. DASYACANTHUS 6–8 ECHINOCACTUS UNGUISPINUS

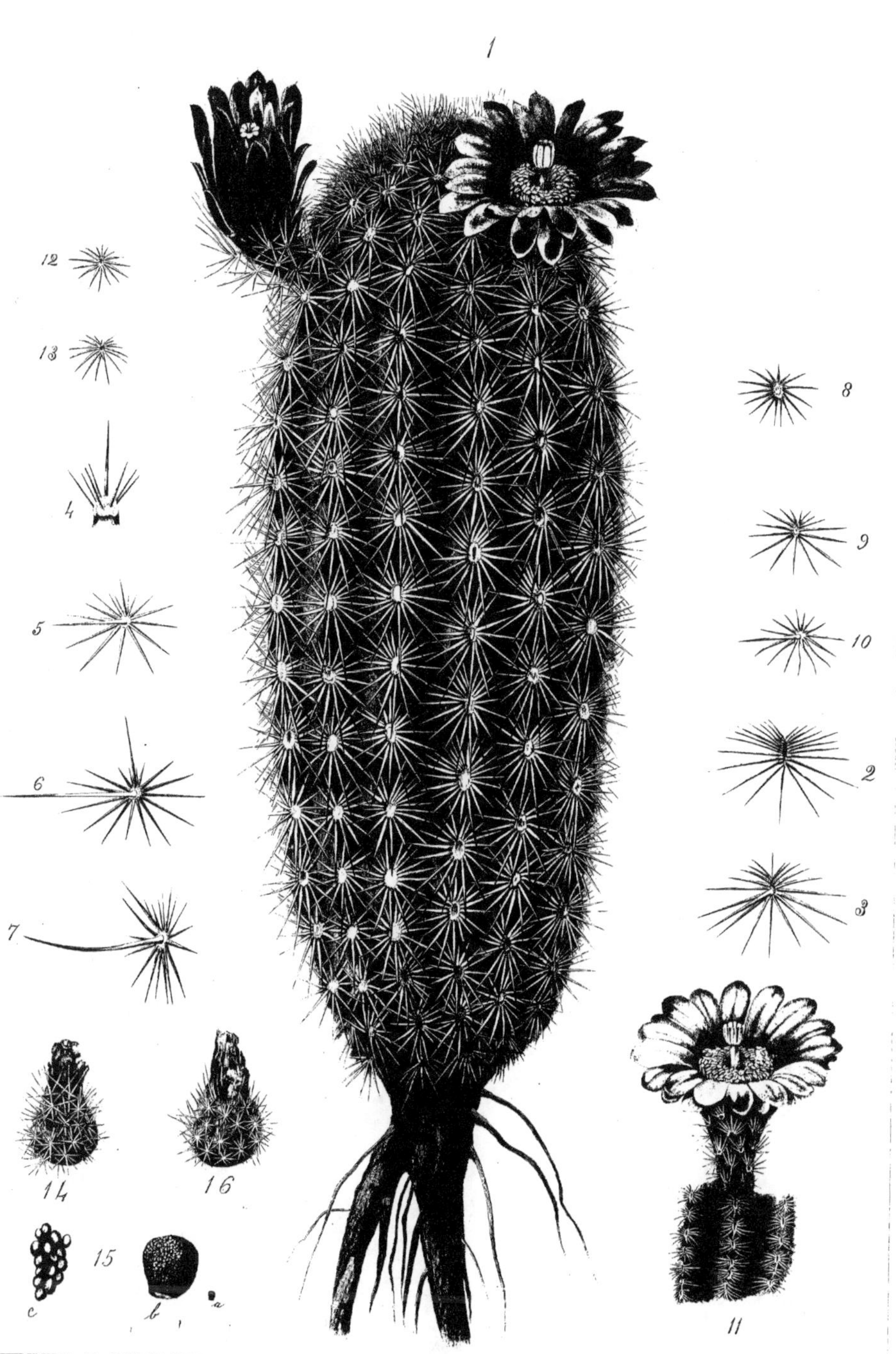


FAULUS ROETTER DEL.

R. CONNOR ENG. ST. LOUIS MO.

CEREUS VIRIDIFLORUS

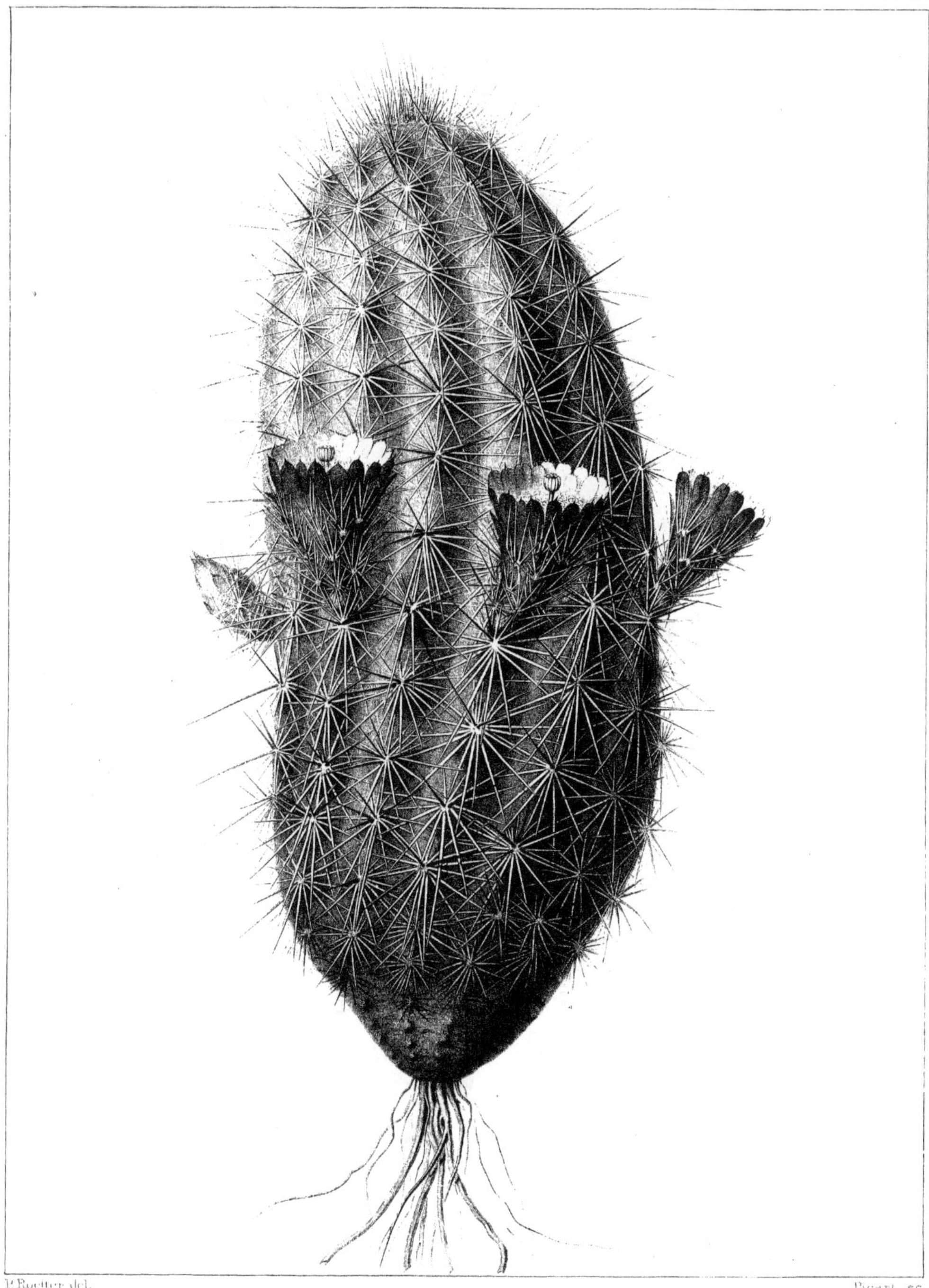

P. Roetter del. Picart sc.

CEREUS CHLORANTHUS

P. Roetter del. Picart sc.

CEREUS CHLORANTHUS

Roetter del. Dougal sc.

CEREUS DASYACANTHUS

P.Roetter del. Dougal sc.

CEREUS DASYACANTHUS

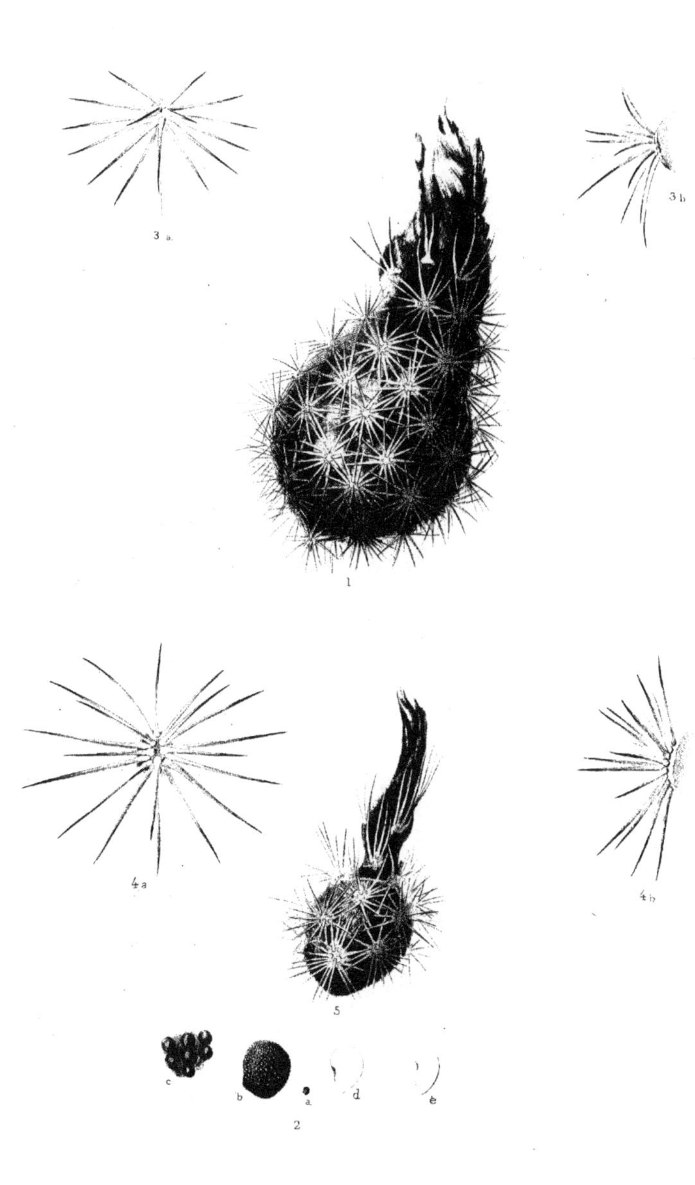


F. Roetter del.
Dougal sc.

1–2 CEREUS DASYACANTHUS
3–5 " ROETTERI

Roetter del. Rebuffet sc.

CEREUS CTENOIDES

P. Roetter del. M. Schmelz sc.

CEREUS CÆSPITOSUS

P. Roetter del.  M. Schmelz sc.

CEREUS CÆSPITOSUS

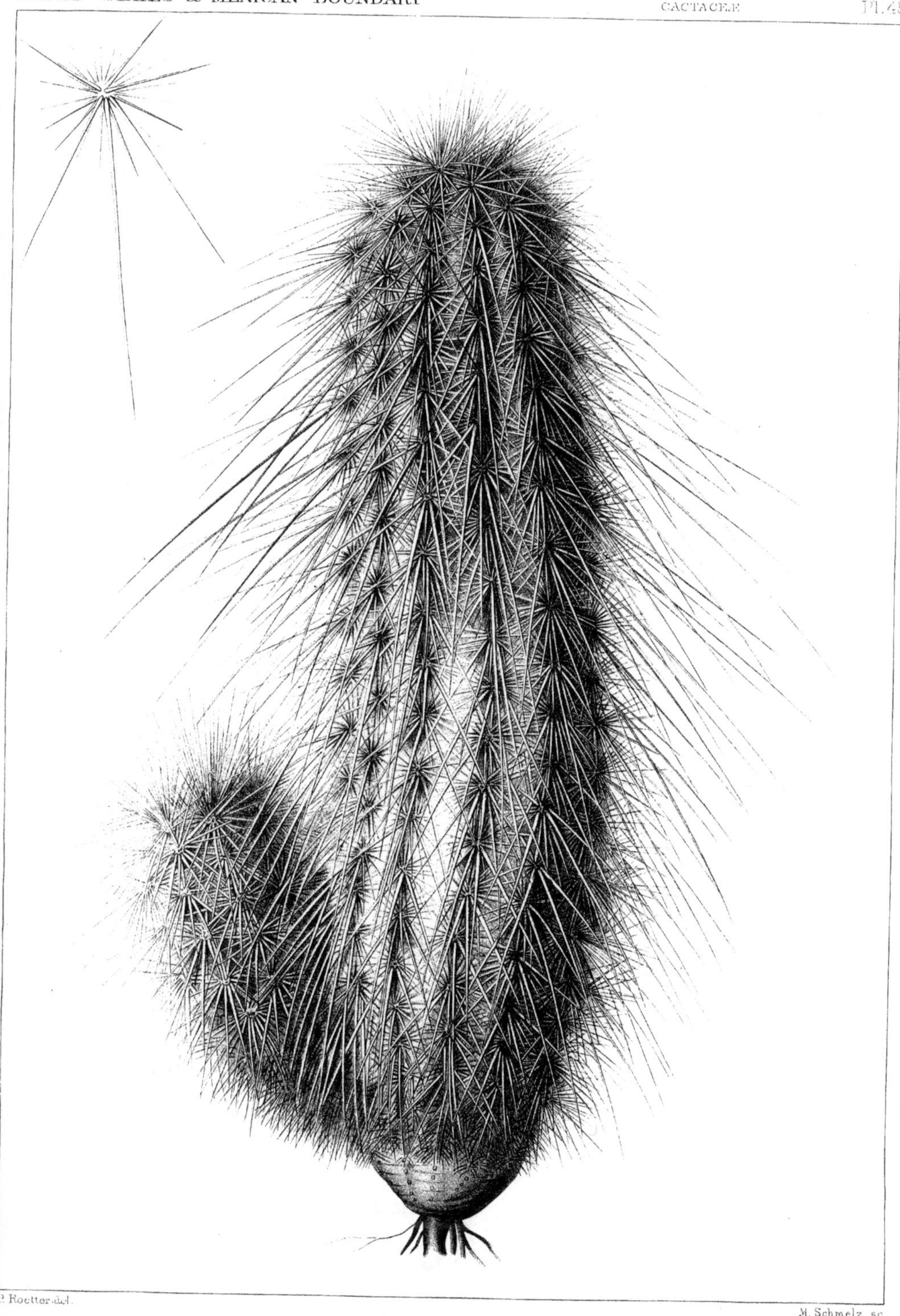

P. Roetter del. M. Schmelz sc.

CEREUS LONGISETUS

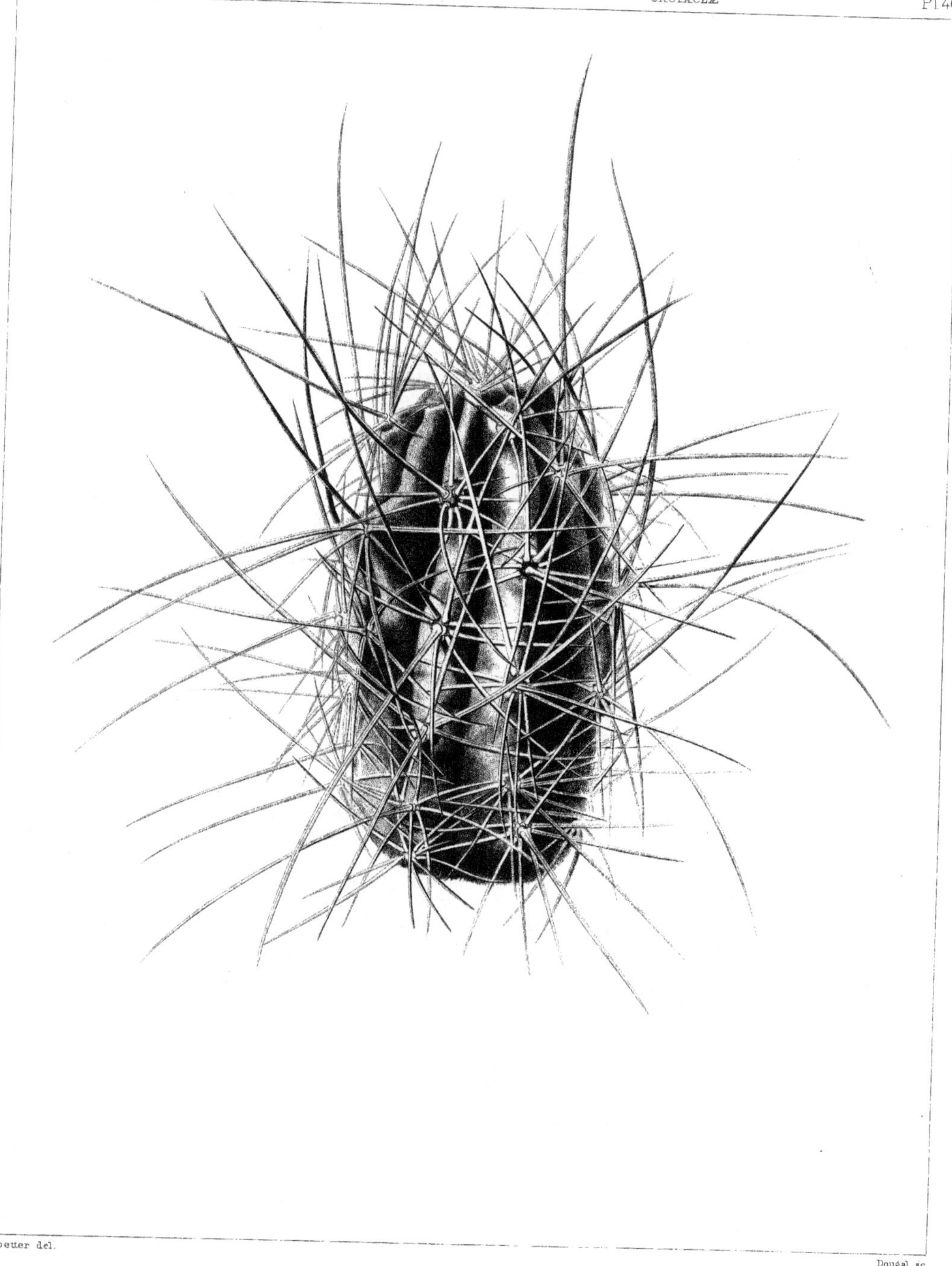

P. Roetter del.

Dougal sc.

CEREUS STRAMINEUS

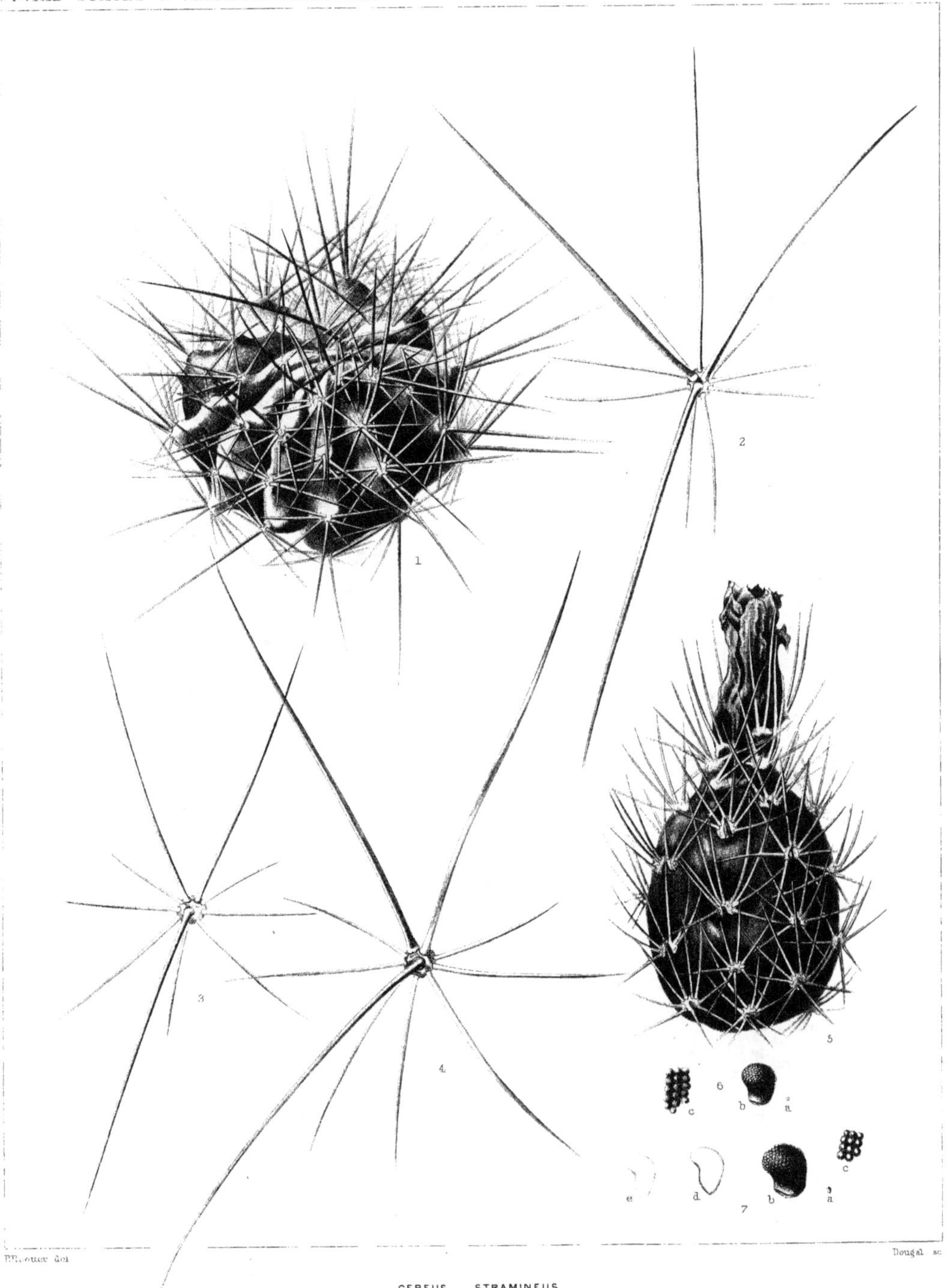


Paulus Roetter del. Dougal sc.

CEREUS STRAMINEUS

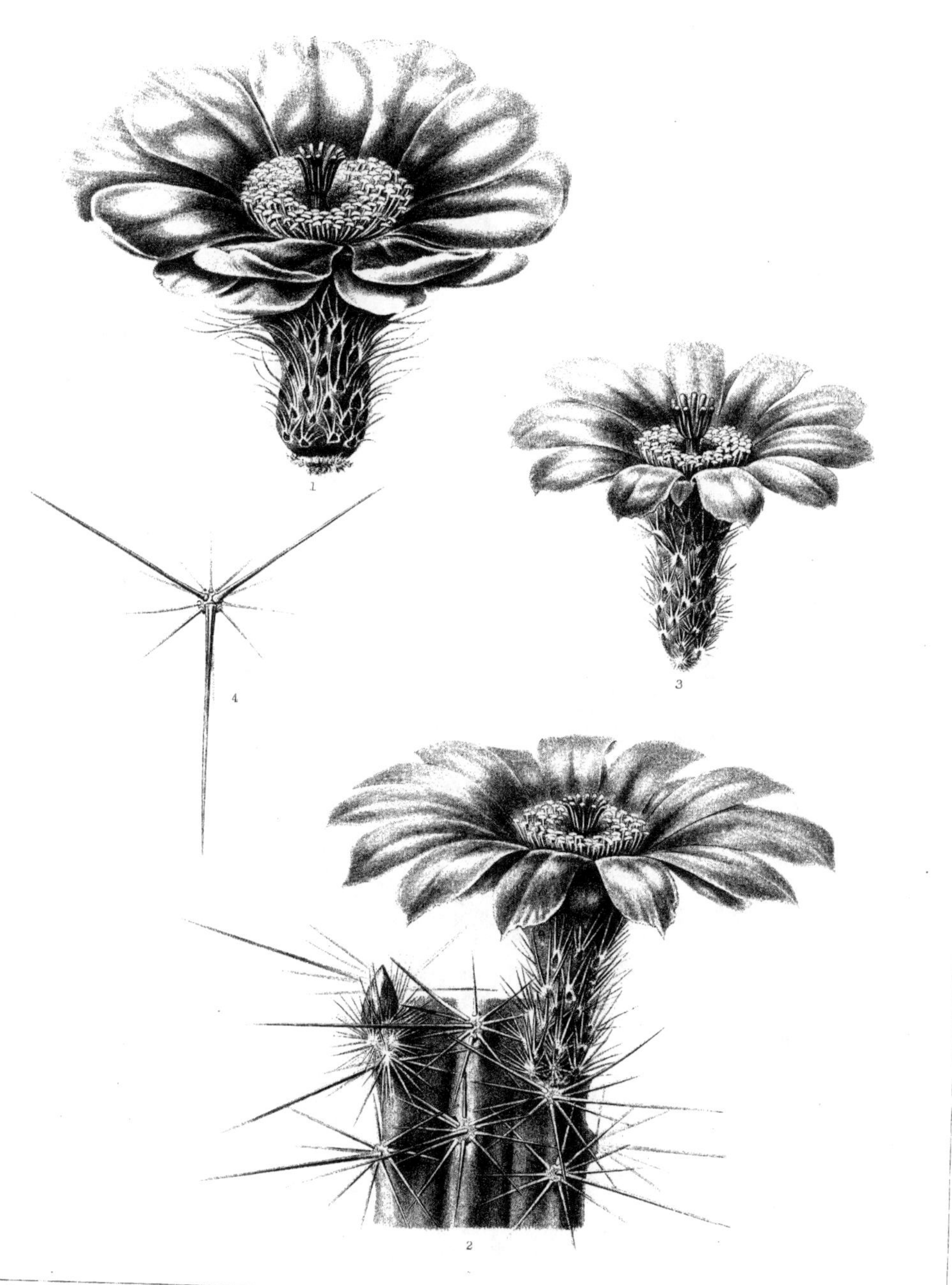


Roeuer del. Dougal sc.

1 CEREUS STRAMINEUS 2 4 CEREUS ENNEACANTHUS

P. Roetter del.
Dougal sc.

CEREUS ENNEACANTHUS

P. Roetter del. Dougal sc.

CEREUS DUBIUS

P. Roetter del.

CEREUS FENDLERI

[illegible] Roetter del.

Weber sc.

CEREUS FENDLERI

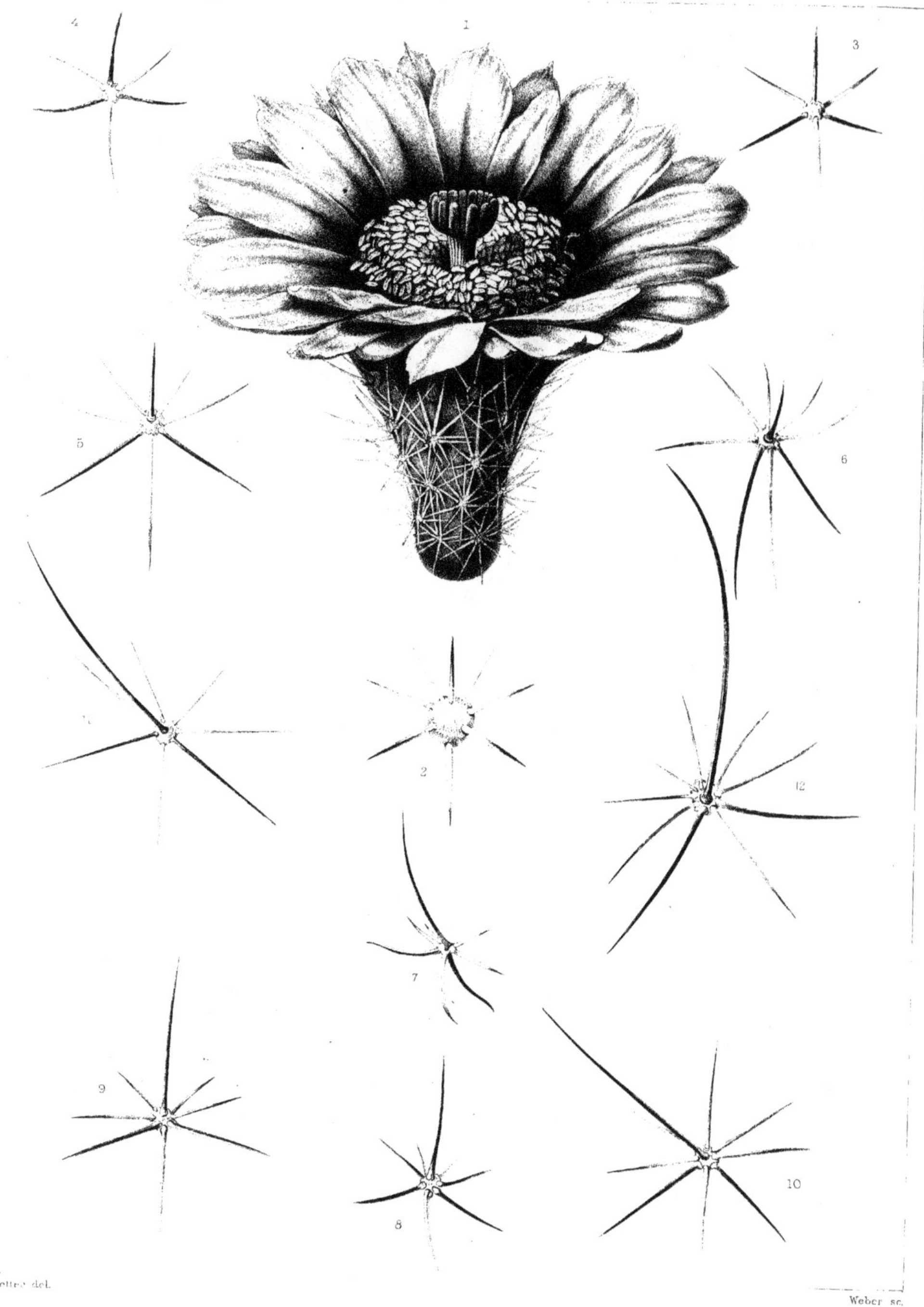


P. Roetter del. Weber sc.

CEREUS FENDLERI

P.Roetter del. Dougal sc.

CEREUS POLYACANTHUS

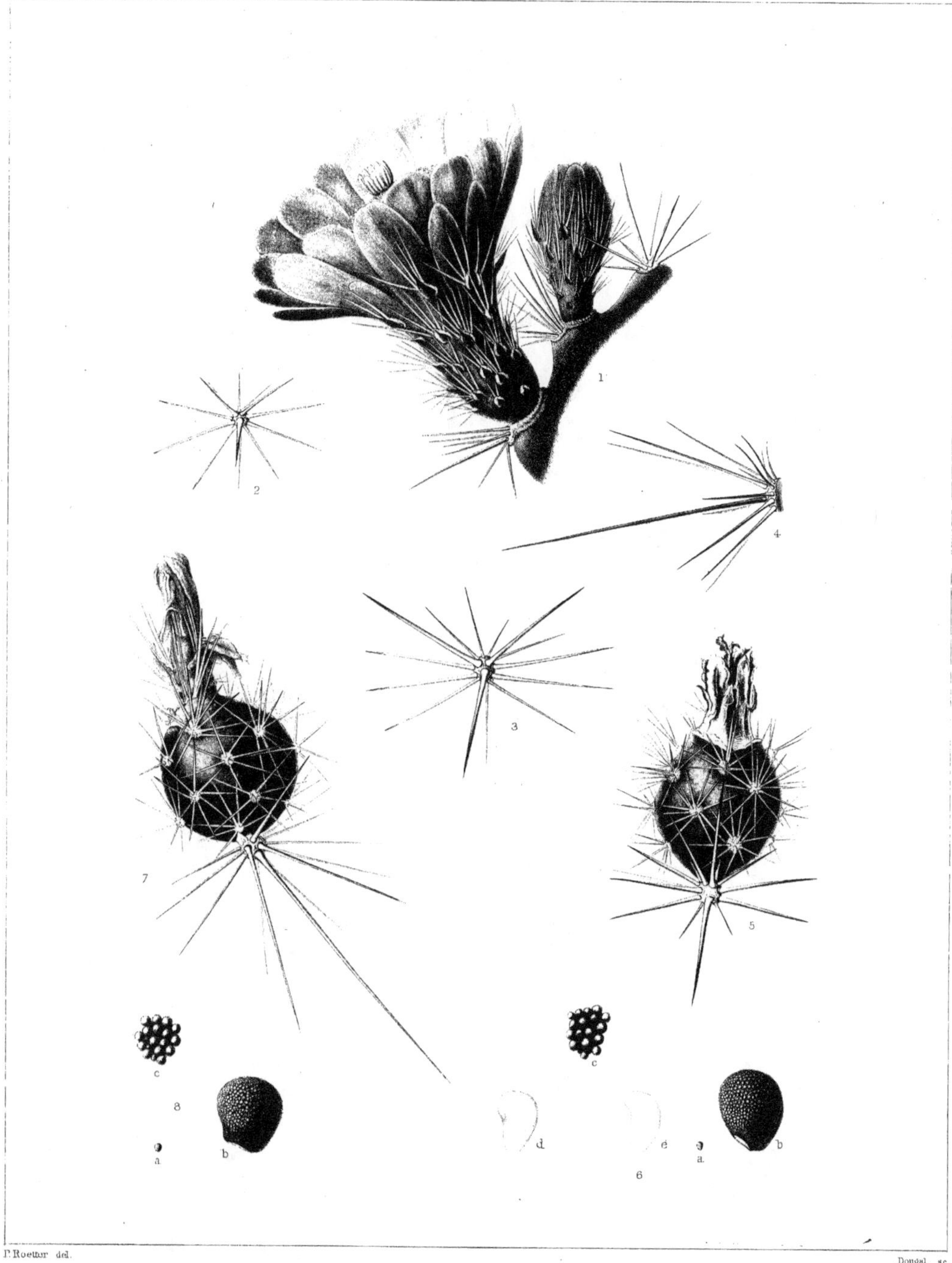


P. Roetter del. Dougal sc.

CEREUS POLYACANTHUS

P. Roetter del. Dougal sc.

CEREUS PAUCISPINUS

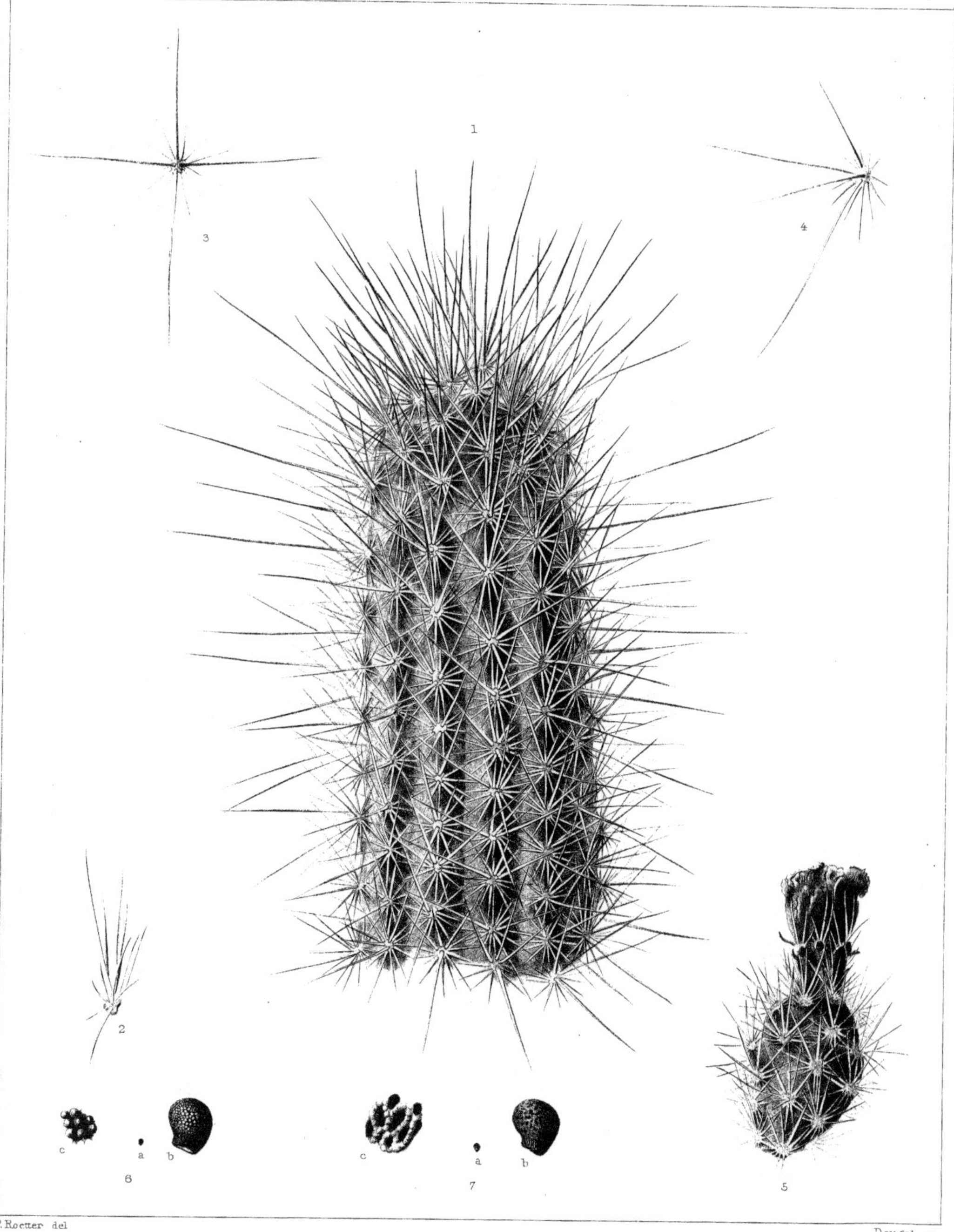


P. Roetter del. Dougal sc.

CEREUS ENGELMANNI

CEREUS BERLANDIERI

P. Roetter del.    Dougal sc.

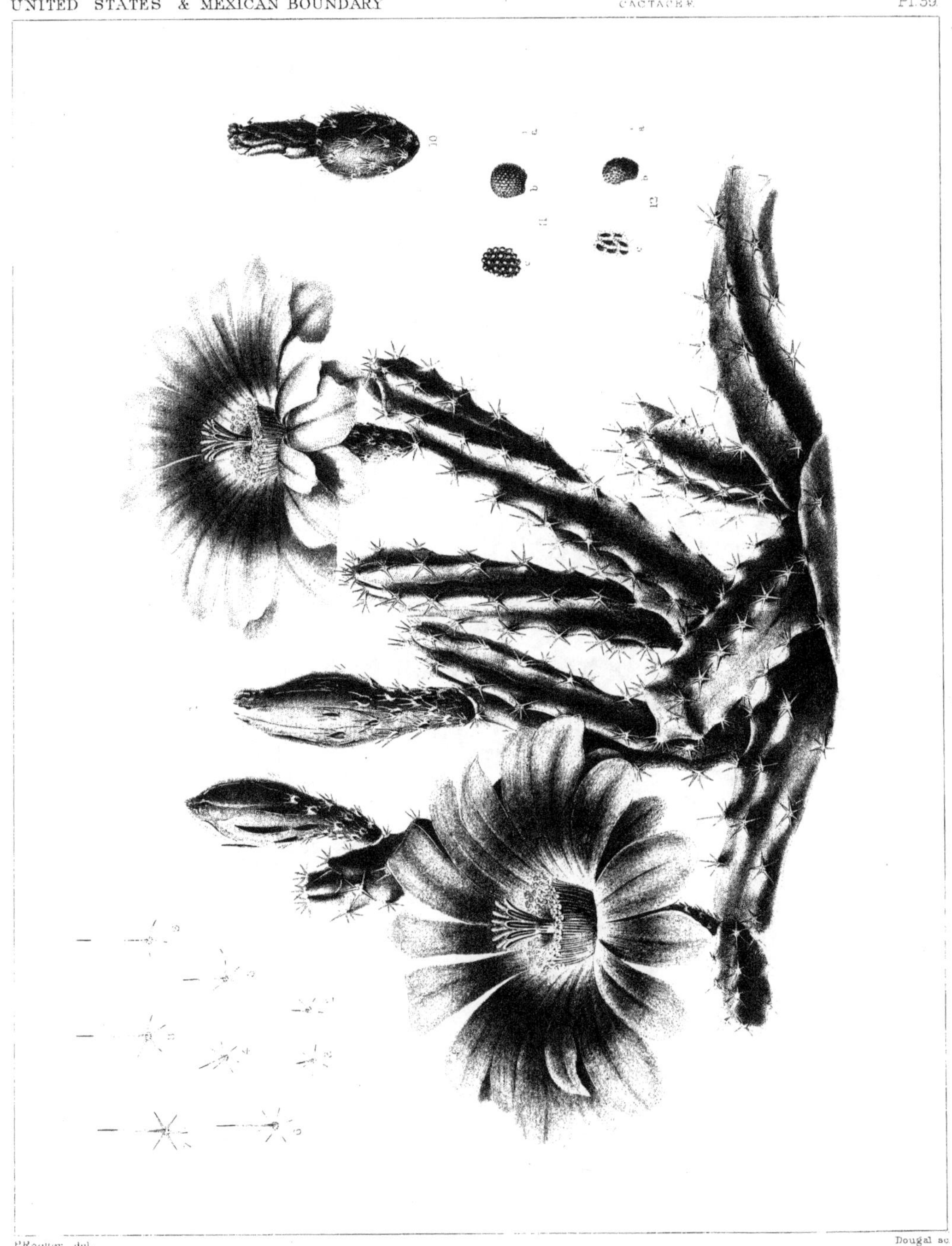


1–11 CEREUS PROCUMBENS

P. Roetter del. Dougal sc

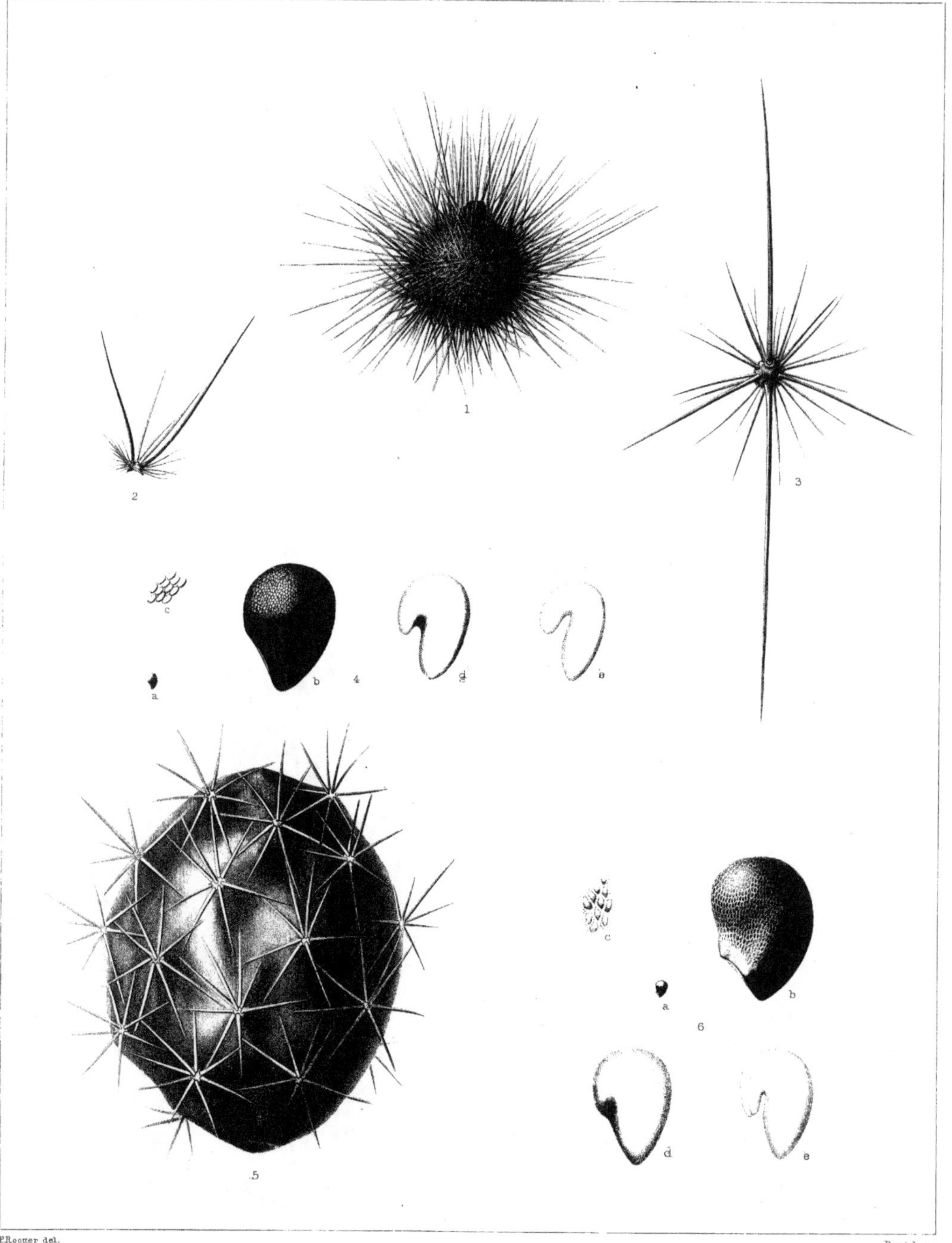


P. Roetter del. Dougal sc.

1 — 4 CEREUS EMORYI 5 — 6 CEREUS VARIABILIS

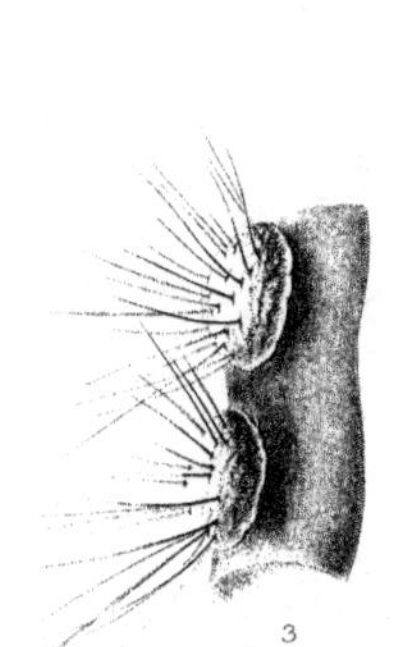

P.Roetter del.

Dougal sc.

CEREUS GIGANTEUS

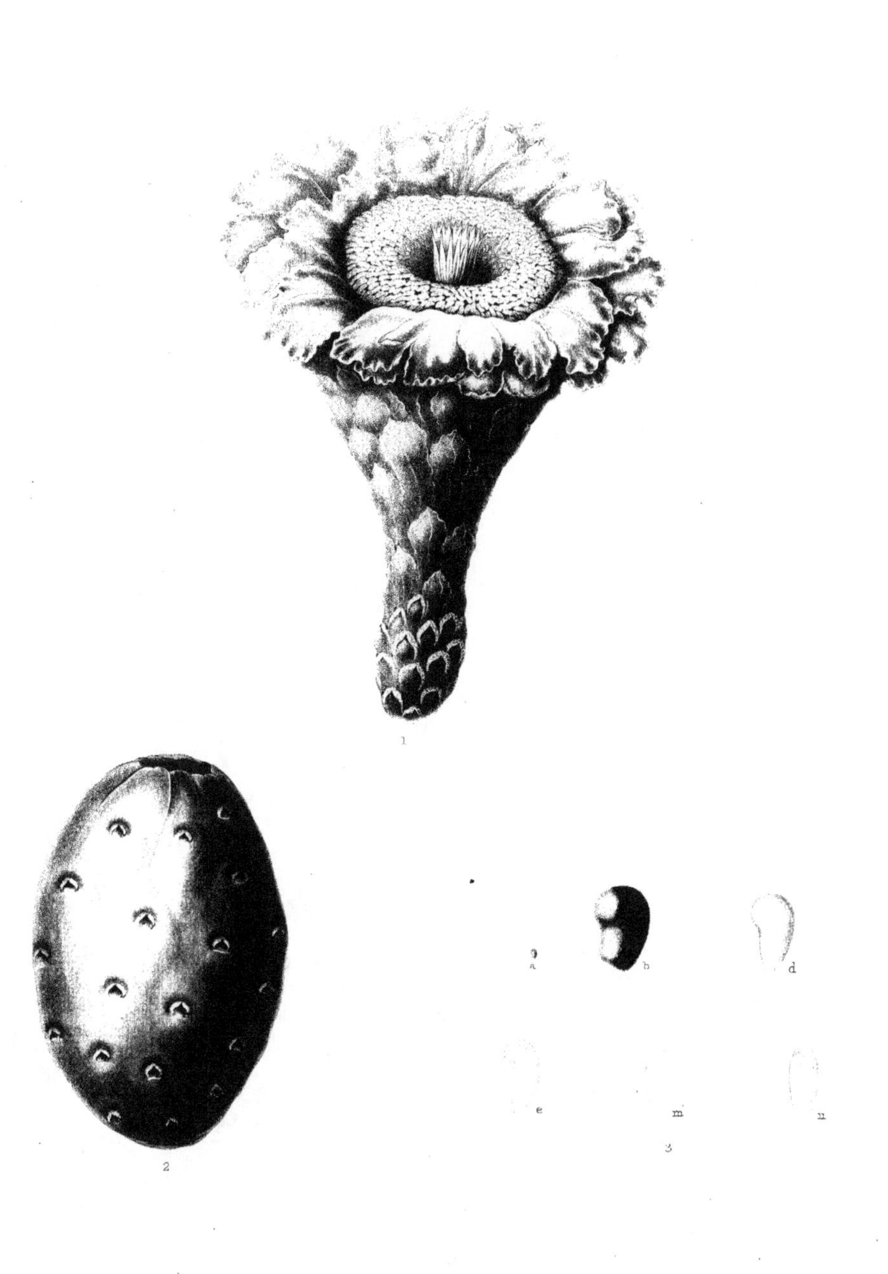


P. Roetter del. Dougal sc.

CEREUS GIGANTEUS

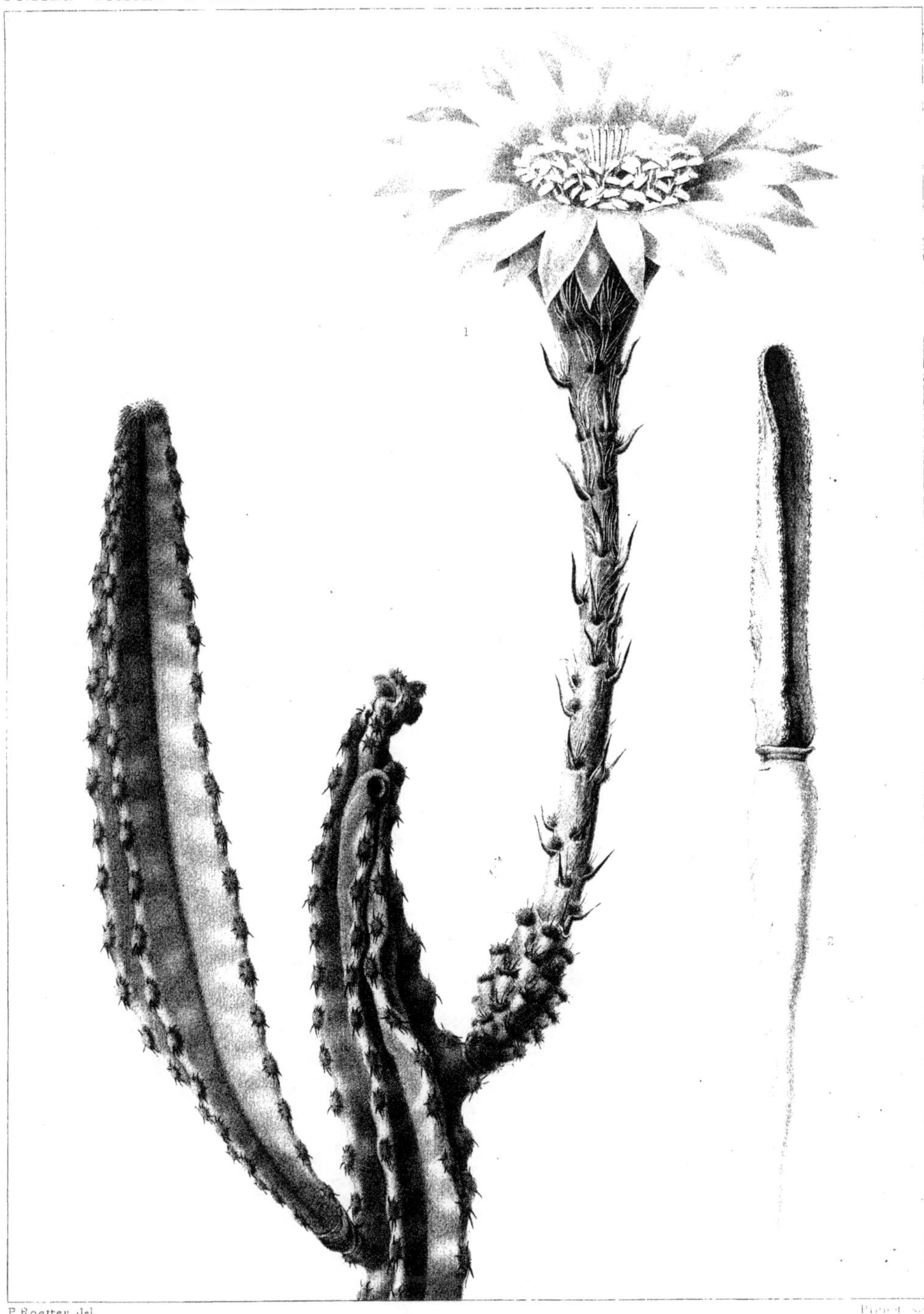


P. Roetter del.

Picart Sc.

CEREUS GREGGII

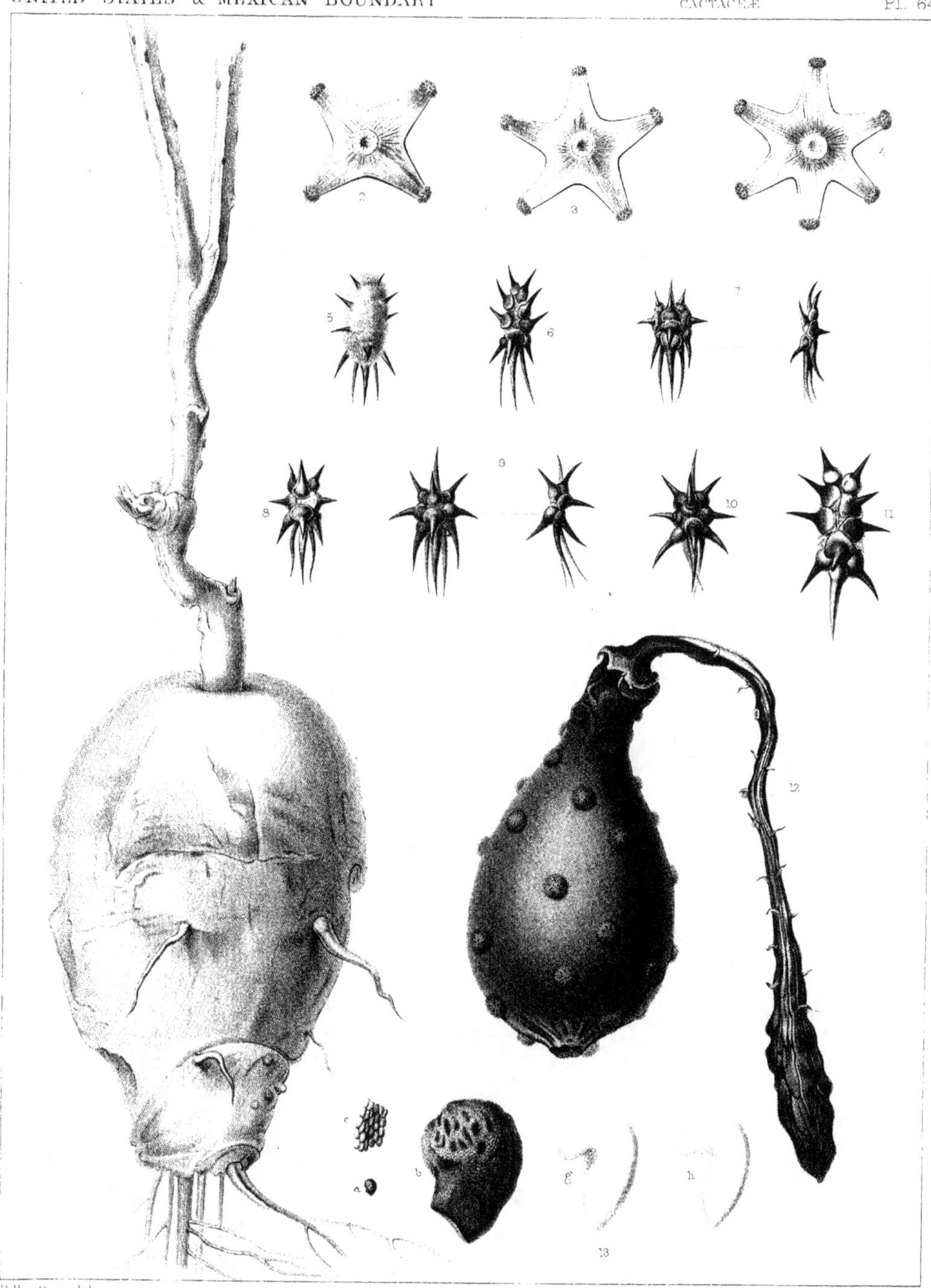


P. Roetter del. Picart sc.

CEREUS GREGGII

P. Roetter del. Picart sc.

CEREUS GREGGII β TRANSMONTANUS

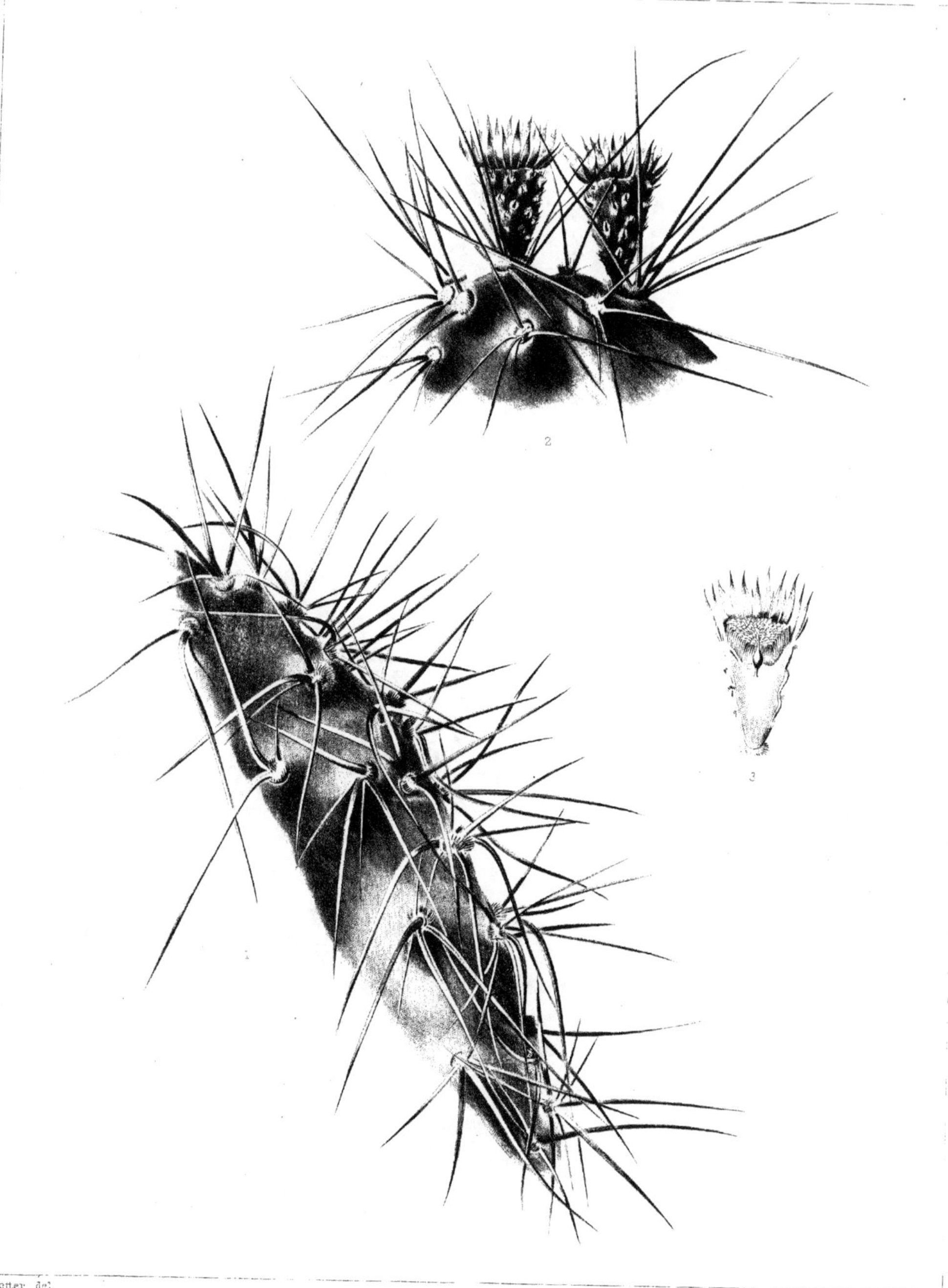


Roetter del.

OPUNTIA STENOPETALA

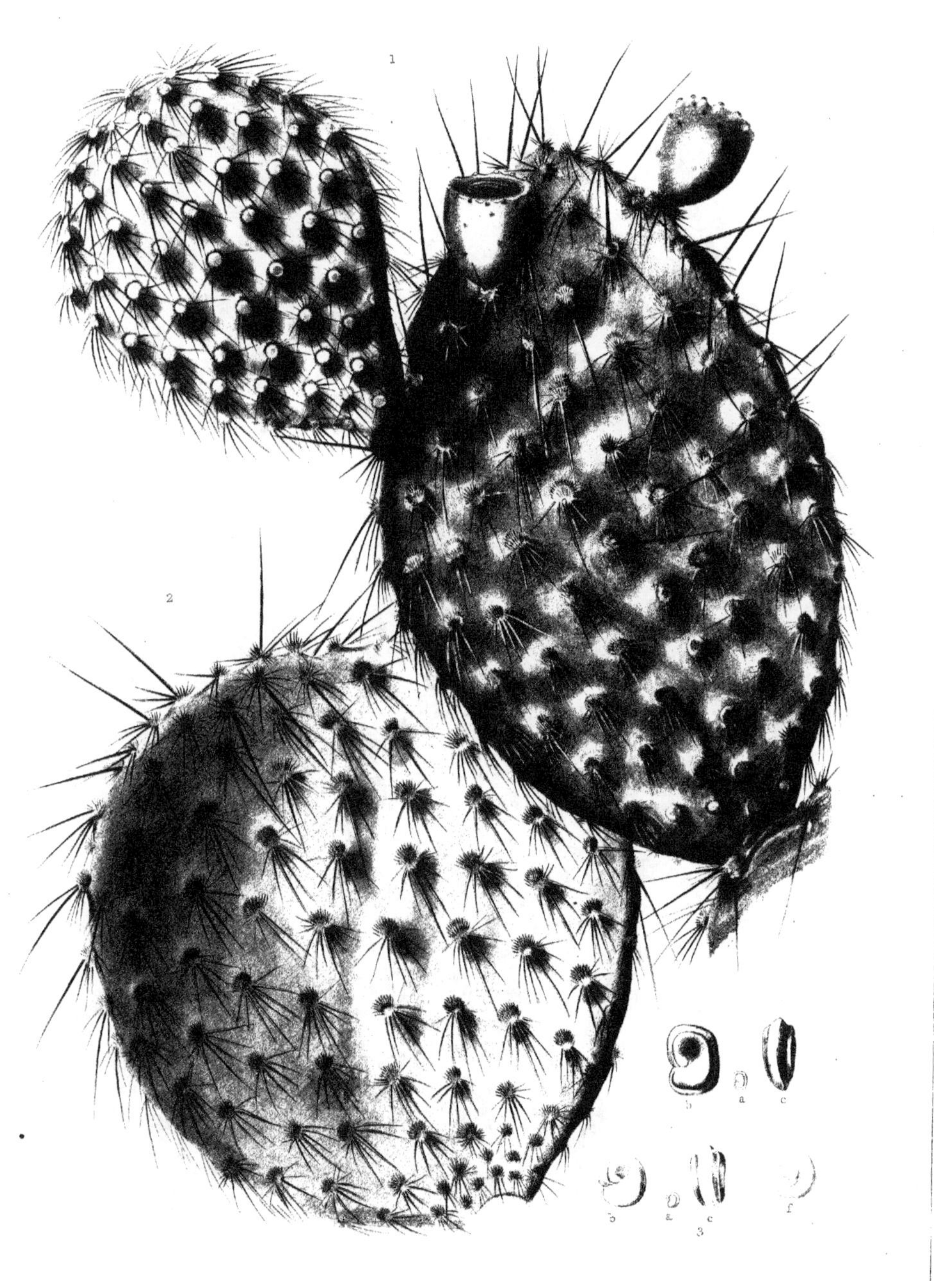


P. Roetter del.

Dougal sc.

OPUNTIA STRIGIL

P. Roetter del. Picart sc.

OPUNTIA FILIPENDULA

Roetter del. Rebuffet sc.

OPUNTIA MACRORHIZA

P. Roetter del. Picart sc.

OPUNTIA EMORYI

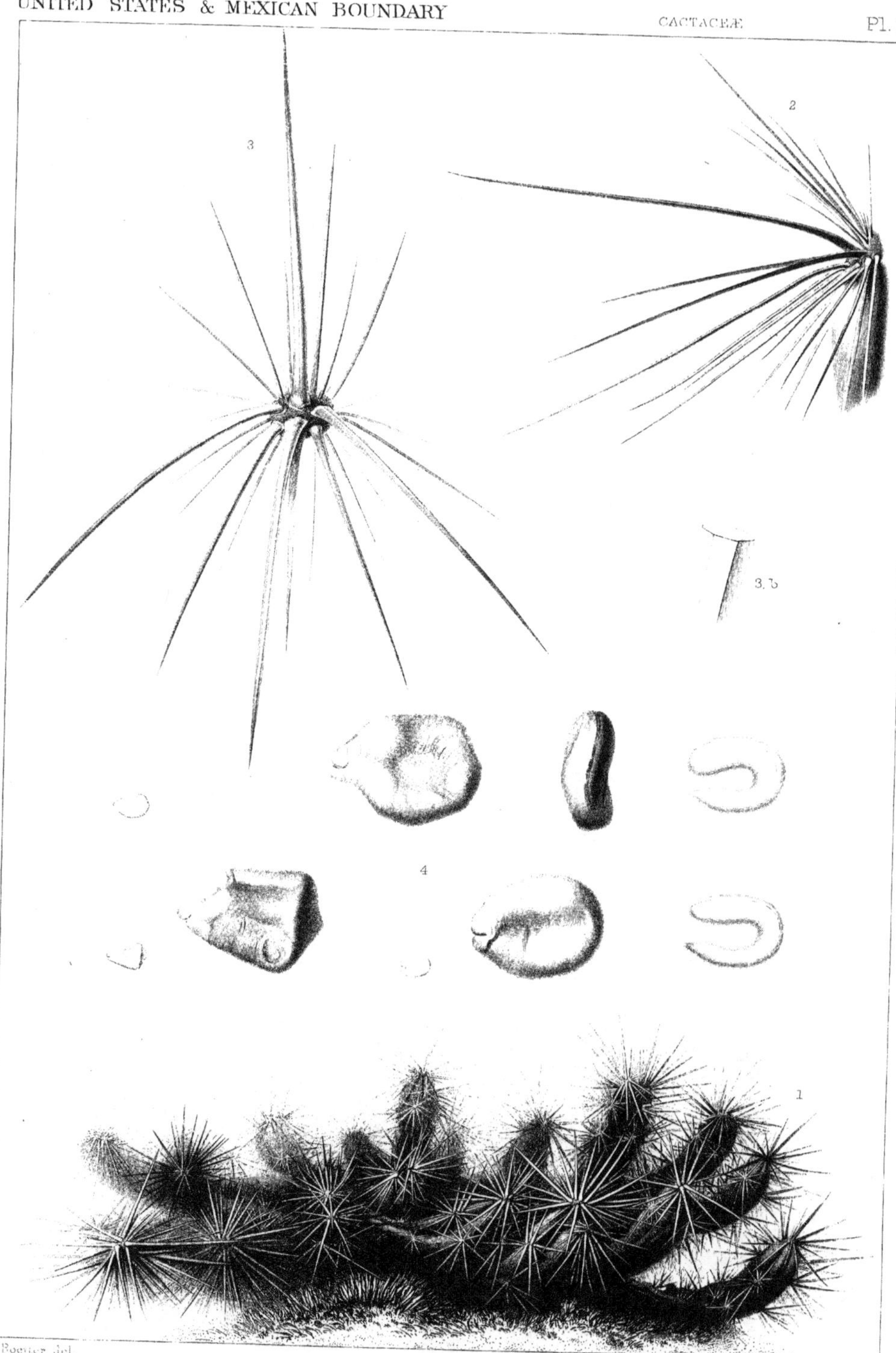


P. Roetter del. Picart sc.

OPUNTIA EMORYI

P. Roetter del.

Rebuffet sc.

OPUNTIA GRAHAMI

P. Roetter del. Rebuffet sc.

I-3. OPUNTIA SCHOTTII 4. VAR. GREGGII

5-6. O. BULBISPINA 7-8. O. IMBRICATA

1 2 3 4 5 6 7 8 9 10 11 12 13 14 15 16

P. Roetter, del. Picart sc.

SEEDS OF MAMILLARIAE, ECHINOCACTI AND CEREI

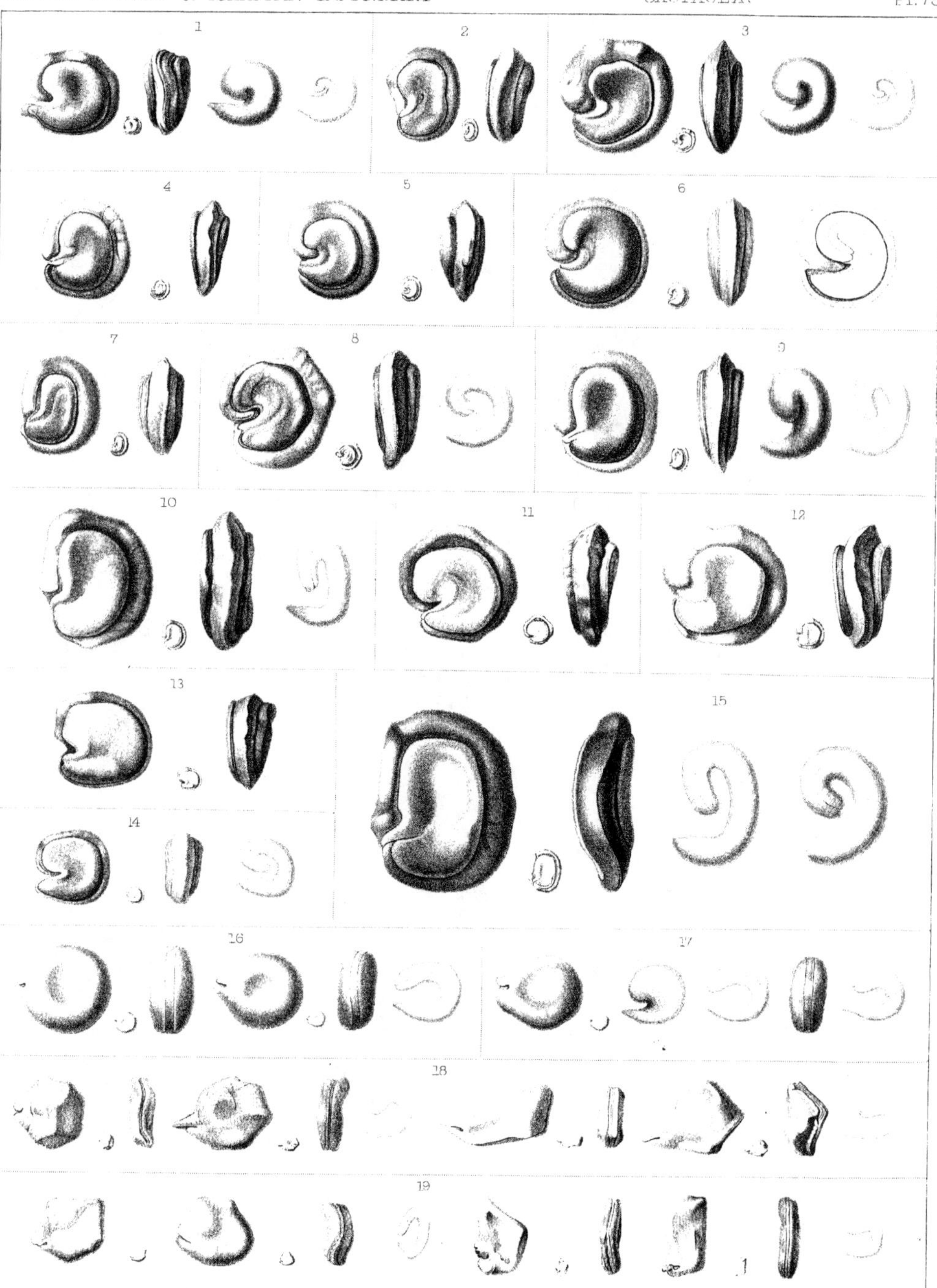


P. Roetter del. Picart sc.

SEEDS OF OPUNTIAE

www.ingramcontent.com/pod-product-compliance
Lightning Source LLC
LaVergne TN
LVHW050528100826
845148LV00002B/483

* 9 7 8 1 4 2 5 5 1 9 3 7 7 *